# Bureaucracy in the Modern State

*For Douglas E. Ashford (1928–1993)*

# Bureaucracy in the Modern State

An Introduction to Comparative
Public Administration

*Edited by*
Jon Pierre
*Associate Professor*
*School of Public Administration*
*University of Gothenburg*
*Sweden*

Edward Elgar

© Jon Pierre 1995

All rights reserved. No part of this publication may be reproduced, stored in a retrieval system, or transmitted in any form or by any means, electronic, mechanical, photocopying, recording, or otherwise without the prior permission of the publisher.

Published by
Edward Elgar Publishing Limited
Gower House
Croft Road
Aldershot
Hants GU11 3HR
England

Edward Elgar Publishing Company
Old Post Road
Brookfield
Vermont 05036
USA

**British Library Cataloguing in Publication Data**
Bureaucracy in the Modern State:
Introduction to Comparative Public
Administration
  I. Pierre, Jon
  350.001

**Library of Congress Cataloguing in Publication Data**
Bureaucracy in the modern state : an introduction to comparative
  public administration / Jon Pierre, ed.
     p.  cm.
    1. Public administration. 2. Comparative government. I. Pierre,
Jon.
  JF1351.B876  1994
650—dc20
                                    94–6261
                                        CIP

ISBN 1 85278 725 2
**Printed and bound in Great Britain by
Hartnolls Limited, Bodmin, Cornwall**

# Contents

| | |
|---|---|
| *List of figures* | vii |
| *List of tables* | ix |
| *List of contributors* | xi |
| *Acknowledgements* | xv |

| | | |
|---|---|---|
| 1 | Comparative public administration: the state of the art<br>*Jon Pierre* | 1 |
| 2 | Bureaucracy in a divided regime: the United States<br>*B. Guy Peters* | 18 |
| 3 | Public administration at the crossroads: the end of the French specificity?<br>*Luc Rouban* | 39 |
| 4 | Public administration in Germany: political and societal relations<br>*Hans-Ulrich Derlien* | 64 |
| 5 | 'Deprivileging' the UK civil service in the 1980s: dream or reality?<br>*Christopher Hood* | 92 |
| 6 | Japan: divided bureaucracy in a unified regime<br>*Ellis S. Krauss* | 118 |
| 7 | Governing the welfare state: public administration, the state and society in Sweden<br>*Jon Pierre* | 140 |
| 8 | Public administration in developing countries: Kenya and Tanzania in comparative perspective<br>*Goran Hyden* | 161 |
| 9 | The Europeanization of the national bureaucracies?<br>*Edward C. Page and Linda Wouters* | 185 |
| 10 | Conclusions: a framework of comparative public administration<br>*Jon Pierre* | 205 |

*Index*     219

# List of figures

| | | |
|---|---|---|
| 3.1 | The French administrative system | 44 |
| 5.1 | UK civil service staff numbers, 1974–92 | 97 |
| 5.2 | Cost of civil service pay and pensions as percentage of net total estimates, 1961–2 to 1984–5 | 99 |
| 5.3 | Civil service running costs as percentage of total supply estimates, 1985–6 to 1992–3 | 99 |
| 5.4 | Cost of civil service pay and pensions, 1966–7 to 1985–6 in constant 1985 prices | 100 |
| 5.5 | Civil service running costs, 1985–6 to 1992–3 in constant 1985 prices | 101 |
| 5.6 | Civil service and average pay trends, 1966–91 in constant 1985 prices | 104 |
| 5.7 | Grades 1–3 as percentage of total UK civil service staff, 1975–91 | 108 |
| 10.1 | Organizational structures and different types of political and administrative career patterns | 208 |

# List of tables

| | | |
|---|---|---|
| 2.1 | Employment of minorities in federal white-collar workforce | 23 |
| 2.2 | Levels of employment of women and minorities | 28 |
| 3.1 | Number and proportion of the civil service and the public sector among all wage-earners and the working population | 42 |
| 3.2 | Professional origins of members of cabinets | 51 |
| 3.3 | Social origins of senior-level competition candidates | 52 |
| 5.1 | Aspects of 'deprivileging': 13 tests | 93 |
| 5.2 | Types of departures from the UK civil service as percentage of total leavers, selected years 1977–92 | 106 |
| 5.3 | 13 tests of deprivileging: summary of assessment | 113 |
| 9.1 | Organizational divisions of the European Commission 1991 | 194 |
| 9.2 | Stated organizational divisions of permanent representations | 196 |
| 9.3 | Index of proportionality at different grades in the EC, 1989 | 198 |

# Contributors

**Hans-Ulrich Derlien** is Professor of Public Administration at the University of Bamberg, Germany. Before accepting the chair in Bamberg in 1978, he was Professor of Public Administration at the University of the Federal Army in Hamburg. He is author of numerous monographs, including *Die Erfolgskontrolle staatlicher Planung* (1976) and *Innere Struktur der Landesministerien in Baden-Württemberg* (1988). He has also published articles in *Governance, European Journal of Political Research* and *International Administrative Science Review*.

**Christopher Hood** has been Professor of Public Administration and Public Policy at the London School of Economic and Political Science since 1989. Before that he was Professor of Government and Public Administration at the University of Sydney, and has also worked at the Universities of Glasgow and York and the National University of Singapore. His publications include (with Andrew Dunsire) *Bureaumetrics* (1981) and (with Andrew Dunsire) *Cutback Management in Public Bureaucracies* (1989).

**Goran Hyden** is Professor of Political Science and an affiliate of the Center for African Studies at the University of Florida. He received his education at the University of Lund, Sweden. For twelve years he taught and did research in East Africa, being affiliated, in turn, with Makerere University, Kampala, Uganda, University of Nairobi, Kenya, and University of Dar es Salaam, Tanzania. From 1978–80 he served as Social Science Programme Officer for the Ford Foundation in Eastern and Southern Africa, then for another five years as the Foundation's representative in the region. He has published ten books in English and Swedish and edited another eight. Among these are *Beyond Ujamaa in Tanzania* (1980), *No Shortcuts to Progress* (1983), and *Governance and Politics in Africa* (co-editor Michael Bratton)(1992).

**Ellis S. Krauss** is Professor of Political Science at the University of Pittsburgh. He is the author or co-editor of several books on Japan, including *Democracy in Japan* (co-editor Takeshi Ishida), *Conflict in Japan* (co-editor Thomas P. Rohlen and Patricia G. Steinhoff), *Political Opposition and Local Politics in Japan* (co-editors Kurt Steiner and Scott C. Flanagan) and *Media and Politics in Japan* (co-editor Susan Pharr, forthcoming). He has also published several articles on Japan's political and administrative elites and the policy-making process in journals such as *The American Political Science Review* and *British Journal of*

*Political Science*. Among his other research themes has been industrial policy, including 'Targeting Resources for Industrial Change' (co-author: Jon Pierre) for *Do Institutions Matter?* (editors R. Kent Weaver and Bert Rockman, 1993).

**Edward C. Page** is a Reader in Political Science at the University of Hull. He has published numerous books and articles in the field of comparative public administration including *Political Authority and Bureaucratic Power* (2nd ed. 1992).

**B. Guy Peters** is Maurice Falk Professor of American Government and Chair of the Department of Political Science at the University of Pittsburgh. He previously taught at Emory University, Tulasne University and the University of Delaware. He has also had Fulbright Fellowships at the University of Strathclyde (Scotland) and at the Hochschule St. Gallen (Switzerland), a Hallsworth Fellowship at the University of Manchester, and has been a Fellow at the Canadian Centre for Management Development. Professor Peters has published a number of books including: *The Politics of Bureaucracy, The Politics of Taxation: A Comparative Perspective, Comparing Public Bureaucracies, Rethinking European Politics, Policy Dynamics* (with Brian Hogwood), *The Pathology of Public Policy* (with Brian Hogwood), and *Can Government Go Bankrupt* (with Richard Rose). He has also edited *Organizing Governance, Governing Organizations* (with Colin Campbell), and *Advising West European Governments* (with Anthony Barker). He is past editor of *Governance* and current editor of International Library of Comparative Public Policy.

**Jon Pierre** is Associate Professor of Political Science at the School of Public Administration, University of Gothenburg, Sweden and Adjunct Associate Professor at the Department of Political Science, University of Pittsburgh, US. He is currently Acting Professor at the Department of Political Science, University of Gothenburg. He has been Andrew Mellon Postdoctoral Research Fellow at the University of Pittsburgh (1991–92) and Academic Visitor at the London School of Economics and Political Science (March 1991). His publications include *Partikongresser och Regeringspolitik* (1986), *Challenges to Local Government* (1990, co-editor Desmond S. King), (ed.) *Självstyrelse och Omvärdsberoende* (1991), *Kommunerna, Näringslivet och Näringspolitiken* (1992), *Den Lokala Staten* (1994) and (ed.) *Urban and Regional Policy* (1994). He is past co-editor of *Scandinavian Political Studies*. He has also published a number of articles in journals such as *European Journal of Political Research, Policy and Politics* and *Urban Affairs Quarterly*.

**Luc Rouban** is Researcher at the National Center of Scientific Research (CNRS) at the Fondation Nationale des Sciences Politiques, Centre de Recherches Administratives. His most recent publications include *Le fonctionnaire détrôné? L'Etat au risque de la modernisation* (with Jean-Luc Bodiguel) (1991), *Les cadres* *supérieurs de la fonction publique et la politique de modernisation administrative* (1992) and *Le Pouvoir anonyme, Les Mutations de l'Etat à la française* (1994).

**Linda Wouters** holds degrees from the Universities of Leuven and Hull. She is currently research officer at the University of Hull working on a project on the European Community civil service.

# Acknowledgements

This volume grew out of a frustration with the current state of comparative public administration. The contributors to this volume agree that this is a scholarly field with a tremendous potential but where scholars so far have only made few and not very systematic attempts to generate comparative observations. However, we have reason to believe that the next few years will see comparative public administration present itself as a dynamic and promising research area.

The purpose of this volume is to present an overview of current public administration in an era of retrenchment, fiscal austerity and challenges from civil society. The volume also aims at discussing a 'middle-range' theoretical model of public administration that might help structure comparative studies in this field.

Edward Elgar at Edward Elgar Publishing Ltd has been consistently encouraging and supportive of this project. Among his staff, Julie Leppard has been immensely helpful in turning a manuscript into a coherent volume. I am most grateful for their support and help. Needless to say, this also applies to the contributors to the volume. Among these, I would like to mention particularly B. Guy Peters whose ideas and enthusiasm helped advance the project from its initial stage to its completion.

The volume is dedicated to the memory of Douglas E. Ashford, former Andrew Mellon Professor of Political Science at the University of Pittsburgh. In his scholarly work he was consistently able to combine an insightful comparative analysis with immense sensitivity for the many contextual factors of the individual cases he was observing. His work sets an example for all social science comparativists.

# 1. Comparative public administration: the state of the art

**Jon Pierre**

*There were theories, theories about theories, analysis of other's theories ... we find each other more interesting than our subject matter.*
(Ilchman 1971, pp. 44–5)

*One thing certain about the future of comparative public administration is that it has one.*
(Caiden and Caiden 1990, p. 384)

## INTRODUCTION

It is probably no exaggeration to argue that the public administration of most Western democracies experienced greater pressure for change during the 1980s and early 1990s than during their entire previous existence. While much of the post-war period witnessed a steady expansion of public bureaucracies, the past ten years or so have seen a profound reassessment of the role of public administration in modern society.

These pressures have taken many different forms of expression. Citizens have to an increasing extent come to question the legitimacy of bureaucratic decisions and actions; policy-makers have forced public administration to implement extensive cutback programmes dismantling core segments of the bureaucracy in order to ameliorate the fiscal crisis of the state; private businesses have proved that public services can be delivered more efficiently and less expensively under private auspices than under public; local governments have pushed for decentralization and greater autonomy from state control; citizens are becoming perceived as 'consumers' (Daneke and Lemak 1985; Osborne and Gaebler 1993) and expect the public sector to offer a variety of different types of public services; and as a result of the overall internationalization of society, transnational bureaucracies have rapidly expanded and confronted national bureaucracies with a whole new set of demands and adaptive measures (Jacobsson

1993; Sbragia 1992). A case in point is the public bureaucracies in Western Europe that are facing the challenge of becoming what Jacobsson (1993, p. 114) calls 'euro-compatible'.[1] We can see similar trends towards bureaucratic internationalization between the public administrations of the developing countries and transnational organizations such as the World Bank and the International Monetary Fund.

The list of challenges and catalysts of change could be much longer, but these examples will suffice to illustrate the changing environment for the public bureaucracies. What appears to be clear is that the public bureaucracies of most Western democracies today face a new type of demand, qualitatively speaking, from both policy-makers and citizens.

The common denominator of most of these challenges is that they are directly or indirectly derived from the rapid emergence of market-based ideologies which have gained a firm ground both in civil society and among policy-makers. Public administration – and indeed the public sector *tout court* – appears to be facing a legitimacy crisis.[2] Public institutions are believed to be incapable of offering customer-attuned services at low cost. In a more general sense, we can say that what appears to be happening is a major reassessment of public administration in most countries.

Particularly in Western Europe, where there is a more developed tradition of relatively extensive public sectors than in the United States, the shift has been from seeing public administration as a vehicle for social change towards perceiving it as a major obstacle to such change. The public bureaucracy has come to be perceived as essentially antithetical to the dynamics heralded by the *Zeitgeist* of the 1980s: strong anti-collectivist sentiments coupled with a belief in the market as the ultimate criterion of efficiency, skill and professionalism.

The joint effect of public policy change towards market solutions and of similar changes among the public – including not only the traditional critics of the public sector but also many of those who previously supported the notion of government's social responsibilities (Hula 1988, p. xiii) – has been the dismantling of public administration in many countries. There are several examples of this. In the US, the Reagan and also – albeit to a lesser extent – the Bush administrations portrayed the government not as the solution to societal problems but rather as the cause of most of those problems. Thus the 1980s witnessed the implementation of severe cutbacks within the federal administration and also of extensive deregulation and privatization of public services (Palmer and Sawhill 1984; Peters 1993).

Similarly, in Britain the Thatcher government immediately upon taking office, targeted the civil service as a major problem in itself. Subsequently, the government embarked on a wide range of projects that aimed to increase efficiency in public administration, to conduct major structural reform of the public sector and, in a more general sense, to instigate a 'managerial revolution' in public bureaucracy (Metcalfe 1993; Hood, Chapter 5 in this volume). We find similar examples of reassessment of the public sector in the Scandinavian countries, in France and in Germany, as subsequent chapters in this volume will show.

Coupled with these significant policy shifts we have also seen administrative reform becoming an increasingly important policy instrument. Most of these reforms have been implemented in part to improve the efficiency of the public sector and in part to make it more accessible to the public. However, there is also an additional reason for administrative reform. Such reforms, as Rouban (1993, p. 411) suggests, are 'a powerful instrument for separating political accountability from administrative accountability'. By giving public administration greater responsibilities and increased discretion, policy-makers may attempt to displace the responsibility for policy failures. In an era where the main catalysts for social change have moved from the sphere of politics to the sphere of the market, policy-making and implementation becomes surrounded by even more uncertainty than was previously the case; hence a need for elected officials to seek to displace the responsibilities for political error and failure.

At the same time, there is in many countries – as we shall see in subsequent chapters – a tendency among policy-makers to increase political control over the bureaucracy. Thus, on the one hand we see policy-makers using administrative reform to displace accountability for public policy; on the other hand, we see the very same policy-makers trying to increase their control over the bureaucracy. While this appears to be two inconsistent developments, they may in fact reflect a general desire among elected politicians to increase their influence over the bureaucracy while at the same time avoiding responsibility for the bureaucracy's actions. We shall return to this problem in the concluding chapter.

This book looks at how public administration in different countries has responded to these changes, and brings together these observations into a comparative framework. The framework, which will be presented later in this chapter, highlights three aspects of public bureaucracies: their relationships with policy-makers; their internal organizational dynamics; and their relationship with civil society. The contributors to the volume think that it is particularly important to study public administration in the present era when public institutions have come under unprecedented attack. How is the relationship between policy-makers and the civil service affected by these changes? What types of organizational challenges does market-based ideology pose to the public bureaucracy? To what extent and how has the interaction between public bureaucracy and civil society been affected by these new perspectives on the role of public institutions in modern society?

The contributors to this volume further argue that this analysis must be conducted in a comparative framework and, indeed, that social science to a very large extent is an inherently comparative process. Regardless of the type of method employed, comparison, as Gabriel Almond (1966, p. 878) argues in a frequently quoted phrase, is 'the very essence of the scientific method'. Without a comparative theory and framework we cannot ascertain the theoretical and empirical specificities of the individual cases. While studies of individual cases may generate findings which very well may be of interest in their own right, their theoretical significance and value can only be assessed in a comparative context. 'To neglect comparative analysis', argue the Caidens in harsh terms (Caiden and Caiden 1990, p. 377), 'is to be chained to amateur dilettantism.'

Given this comparative ambition, it might seem surprising that the volume is not structured thematically but mainly country-by-country. There are two reasons for this. First, the overall framework of the volume attempts to highlight and integrate features of public administrations which are currently undergoing rapid transformation in most countries. Prior to comparison we need to understand fully the political context and organizational dynamics of the individual cases (Heady 1990). Moreover, the design of the volume seeks to facilitate looking at the nature of the interfaces between public administration and policy-makers – a well-researched topic in most countries – and also that between public administration and civil society, of which we know much less (cf. Rockman 1992). The notion of perceiving the effective powers and autonomy of public administration as the joint outcome of these two relationships is more novel. This further increases the need for a deep understanding of individual cases prior to embarking on comparative assessments.

Secondly, while analyses of public administration in individual countries constitute the major part of the volume – as well as the study of public administration more generally – the concluding chapter presents thematic comparative analyses of the main themes of the volume. Furthermore, as the reader will soon discover, in most of the country chapters the authors make some comparative assessments of their respective cases.

The remainder of the present chapter presents a broad inventory of the study of comparative public administration. Using that discussion as a point of departure, it proceeds to outline the comparative framework of the volume.

## COMPARATIVE PUBLIC ADMINISTRATION: WHERE DO WE STAND?

At first glance, the state of comparative public administration as a scholarly field brings to mind Mark Twain's famous comment about the weather: everybody complains about it but very few seem to do anything about it. Many have bemoaned what is seen as the demise of the comparative study of public bureaucracies (Derlien 1992; Heady 1966; Hyden, Chapter 8 in this volume; Lundquist 1985; Page 1987; Peters 1988, 1992; Pierre 1994). At the same time, we have seen very few attempts to try and ameliorate this dismal state of affairs.

The comparative study of public administration is, as Heady (1990) argues, struggling to accommodate two seemingly inconsistent tendencies. One tendency is to try to 'generalize by making comparisons that are as inclusive as possible and by searching for administrative knowledge that transcends national and regional boundaries' (Heady 1990, p. 3). The other tendency is that towards case-specific or idiosyncratic analyses 'with only scant attention, or none at all, to foreign experience' (ibid.). Clearly, public administration has never experienced the same significant orientation towards comparative, cross-national analysis which characterizes most other fields of political science.[3] Therefore, in some ways the field of comparative public administration brings the study of public bureaucracies closer to political science and policy analysis (Peters 1992), a development which will probably infuse energy into this research (Peters 1988 p. 189).

The comparative study of public administration has developed in three phases. The first phase saw an institutional consolidation of the research field; for example, in the Comparative Administration Group (CAG) under the auspicies of the American Society for Public Administration (ASPA) and with significant financial support from the Ford Foundation (Caiden and Caiden 1990). The emphasis was on development administration (Dwivedi and Henderson 1990a; Hyden, Chapter 8 in this volume). These were the times of high-flying ambitions to create Grand Theory on public administration (Heady 1966; Riggs 1964). Public administration was cast in the functionalist theoretical approach which was the analytical fad and fancy of the time (cf. Mills 1959). However, while these models fulfilled every wish for high degrees of abstraction, they soon proved to be of little help in guiding empirical inquiry. The critique delivered in the early 1970s against comparative public administration as a scholarly discipline was nothing short of devastating (Ilchman 1971).

In the second phase, the behavioural revolution hit the comparative study of public administration. A number of cross-national studies using a quantitative methodological approach were conducted, the most widely cited being that by Aberbach, Putnam and Rockman in the early 1980s (Aberbach *et al.* 1981). During this phase, given the empirical emphasis of the projects, theory development was considered less important than producing a solid, data-based account of different aspects of public bureaucracies. Indeed, several of the studies conducted during this phase were not conceived of as engaging in comparative public administration research *strictu sensu*. Instead, what came out of this phase were comparative studies of sub-fields within the larger domain of comparative public administration. The Aberbach *et al.* study – a good case in point – was on comparative politico-administrative elites, not comparative administrative systems. While these studies helped us to understand the nature of the interface between elected officials and bureaucrats, they also disaggregated comparative public administration research and theory-building. Thus there was again a sense of frustration among scholars, albeit this time for the opposite reason compared to the initial phase.

Finally, in the third phase, theory and empirical studies have begun to connect more clearly than previously. The theoretical objective now is more at developing 'middle-range' theories on public administration and gathering data on carefully defined sub-fields within the larger discipline. Cases in point are Peters's study on comparative bureaucracies (Peters 1988) and the volumes by Rowat (1988), Dwivedi and Henderson (1990b) and Farazmand (1991). However, the legacy of development administration research is strong, as is the functionalist theoretical approach (see Heady 1984; Caiden and Caiden 1990, pp. 380–3).[4]

This body of literature – most of which is admittedly fairly descriptive, case-specific and fact-orientated – is of immense value as we try to develop a 'middle-range' theory. If the theorists of the 1960s began their work with abstract discussion, later to find this theory only vaguely reflecting the real world, we are now in the fortunate position of being able to draw on a very wide range of empirical data as we move towards theory. To the extent that Sherlock Holmes's classical comment to Watson in *A Study in Scarlet* – '[I]t is a capital mistake to theorize before you have all the evidence. It biases the judgement' – is relevant also in the present context, we should now be in a good position to begin to think about a theory of comparative public administration.

Thus, the task which scholars of comparative public administration are facing is by no means an easy one. The present volume can only make a very modest contribution to the field. There seems to be at least three sets of problems associated with comparative research on public administration. The *first* problem is that of conceptualization and definition. To be sure, we do not have any analytically useful definitions of some of the key phenomena in this field of research. As Peters (1988, 1992) notes, we need go no further than to try and define what a public organization is in order to encounter major conceptual problems: What is 'public'? What is an 'organization'?

This problem becomes all the more evident as we try to come up with definitions which allow us to conceive of similar phenomena across nations or even across time within the same nation. What, for instance, are the British, French and German functional equivalents of the Office of Management and Budget (OMB) in the United States, and what are the analytical consequences of conceiving of them as such? Or – to put it even more bluntly – can you compare public bureaucracies in states with Napoleonic legal systems with, for instance, that of the British common-law system? How important are national political and administrative cultures, and how important are contextual and sectorial properties? Clearly, these are very basic questions which must be addressed before we can embark on empirical research.

The second major problem is developing a framework for analysis which specifies the dependent and independent variables. Ideally, this should be a deductive process, starting from a series of theoretical assumptions from which we can derive which variables are relevant and in what context and what capacity they are worth investigating. However, we cannot embark on this deductive process unless we have at least some ideas on how the individual cases are organized and which mechanics they work according to. Thus, what is desirable is a research process where inductive studies form the basis for deductive theorizing that later will be empirically tested.

The literature is rich in suggestions about what should be the most important variables in comparative analyses of public bureaucracies. Heady (1966) saw the relationships between politicians and bureaucrats and the role of the public administration for national development as the most important aspects of public administration. Later, Peters (1988) suggested that public employees, organizational structure and bureaucratic behaviour are conceivable dependent variables in comparative public administration research. Arguing along a slightly different theoretical path, I have previously (Pierre 1994) advanced three dependent variables: the relationship between policy-makers and the bureaucracy; the internal organizational dynamics of the public administration; and the relationship between the public bureaucracy and civil society. These questions are derived from the framework of this volume and we shall therefore soon return to it.

The third problem is that of measurement and theory testing. Here we find – not surprisingly, perhaps – that much of the previously mentioned conceptual confusion causes tremendous problems. If we cannot agree on what constitutes a public organization, how are we supposed to be able to measure, let alone account for, changes in the structure of public bureaucracy?

This very brief discussion on some of the difficulties associated with comparative public administration research might suggest that the problems facing us are enormous. Fortunately, however, there are a couple of encouraging circumstances. First, as the reader may already have noticed, many of the problems mentioned here are not typical of comparative public administration but are in many ways endemic to all comparative social science research. If we glance for a second at the theoretical development of other areas in the social sciences, they certainly appear to have been more successful than have scholars of public bureaucracy in resolving many – although far from all – of these problems.

Secondly, while there are few systematic, cross-national analyses of public bureaucracies, there are a large number of studies whose results lend themselves easily to comparative assessments in secondary analyses (Derlien 1992; Pierre 1994). For instance, much of what has been reported from implementation research can be a very useful empirical foundation for comparative theory. Similarly, there are a large number of studies on public employees which also may play a similar role (Aberbach *et al.* 1981; Aberbach *et al.* 1990; Lundquist and Ståhlberg 1983). Finally, we also have a couple of comparative analyses on public administrations in different political systems (Page 1987; Peters 1988), a study of ombudsmen in six countries (Stacey 1978), and of the role of 'para-governmental organizations' in the delivery of public services (Hood and Schuppert 1988).

To sum up so far, we can return to Mark Twain: his comment on Wagner's music – that it is better than it sounds – seems to be a fairly good description of the state of the art of comparative, or at least comparable (Derlien 1992), public administration. There are a number of comparative analyses reported. We also have a number of edited volumes giving us the current situation for public bureaucracies in a large number of countries around the world. Therefore, the next logical question we have to ask ourselves is where we should go from here. Let us now turn to that discussion.

## COMPARATIVE PUBLIC ADMINISTRATION: WHERE SHOULD WE GO?

Before we begin to outline the framework of the volume, three general comments are in order. First, we need to be aware of the endemic differences between public administrations across the world. There are important features of these bureaucracies which will not lend themselves to analysis along continuous variables but are, rather, discrete phenomena. For instance, if it were the case that the public administrative systems of most countries were similar because they were all based on public law and a Weberian, *Rechtsstaat* model of bureaucratic structure and conduct, then comparing these systems might not be a very worthwhile project to embark upon. Most public administrative systems seem to be guided either by the *Rechtsstaat* model or by the Anglo-Saxon notion of the 'public interest'; very few systems fall between these two models which appear to be inherently inconsistent and irreconcilable.[5]

Secondly, we need to reaffirm the traditional notion of the concept of comparative research. In much of the US academic jargon, 'comparative' has become shorthand for any research which is not by design 'American'. Clearly, this is giving 'comparative' a connotation which is at best misleading and at worst completely confusing. The concept of comparative research, we suggest, should be reserved for studies which look at cross-national similarities and differences and where the research design, as Przeworski (1987, p. 32) suggests, enables the scholar 'to replace proper names of countries by explanatory variables'.

Finally, and derived from the previous comment, while development administration remains an important sub-field of comparative public administration, there appears to be no scholarly justification for making it *the* area of comparative public administration research, as was the case during the 1950s and 1960s. Apart from the quasi-normative nature of much of this research – the notion that the West should export their administrative systems to the third-world countries – it seems unreasonable that comparative public administration should not engage in, for instance, comparative analyses of West European administrative systems.

## Towards a Framework for Comparison

The framework of this volume relates to the state–society approach and discourse. This means that we are interested in how public administration relates to the policy-making process and its key institutions and actors as well as to civil society. This approach immediately raises a number of questions pertaining to the definition of the state, bureaucracy and civil society. Public administration is clearly a key element of the state (Rockman 1992). However, public administration has its own legal system, recruitment patterns, *esprit de corps*, organizational culture(s), and so on, which set it apart from policy-making institutions, local governments, state-owned companies and other sets of institutions which should also be seen as elements of 'the state'. Moreover, public administration is a key output linkage between policy-makers and civil society, and as such it is more likely to be influenced by non-public societal actors, compared to other elements of the state apparatus.

The concept of the state is notoriously difficult to define. Some approach the state from the vantage point of whose interests it supposedly promotes, domestically (Jessop 1990; Nordlinger 1981) or in the international arena (Krasner 1978). While this approach might help us solve some problems, at the same time it causes others, such as how to define 'interest', or to what extent state institutions can be attributed interests of their own.

Space will not allow us to embark on an in-depth discussion of different definitions of 'the state', nor of its 'interests' or its societal roles.[6] Instead, by 'state' we shall simply mean the public organizations constituting the system of governmental institutions. This, of course, includes public administration. We conceive of public administration as the key output linkage of the state towards civil society. However, the interface between public administration and civil society is a two-way street, including public policy implementation as well as policy demands from private actors towards policy-makers. We do not know very much about the complex nature of the role of public administration in these exchange processes between the state at large and civil society; nor do we have

> How can all this be treated while neglecting the ec. theory of bureaucracy?

any broader understanding of how this role has altered during the dramatic changes in state–society relations during the 1980s.

Let us now elaborate further on the three dimensions of public administration which the volume will address.

## The Relationship Between Policy-makers and the Bureaucracy

The public bureaucracy's relationship to elected officials and policy-making institutions is a core theme of any study of public administration. This relationship effectively determines the discretion of the public bureaucracy on matters of budgets and policy implementation.

While there is a clear functional divide between policy deliberation and policy implementation, few, if any, will today argue that politics and administration constitute two separate spheres of government. The bureaucracy's influence on policy matters is significant, as is the politicization of public administration – broadly defined – which has been a prominent theme in the post-war development of most Western countries. Both policy-makers and bureaucrats have a strong interest in influencing each other's domains. Indeed, as Rockman argues (1992, p. 160),

> the politicization of bureaucracy is testimony to the growing importance that the governors attach to the administrative aspects of policy making and the need to ensure that its direction is in safe hands.

That said, it would be misleading to think that politicians and bureaucrats invariably share an adversarial relationship. On the contrary: policy-makers and bureaucrats frequently develop networks promoting common, for example, sectorial, interests. There are various models to describe these different types of relationship between politicians and bureaucrats. Aberbach *et al.* (1981) suggest that there exist four basic models of the relationship, ranging from the ideal model of highly distinctive politician and bureaucrat roles to the model where the roles almost converge. This latter outcome is what they call the 'Pure Hybrid' model. In a similar vein, Peters (1987) outlines five different models. One difference between his taxonomy and that advanced by Aberbach *et al.* is that Peters's model takes into account more explicitly the close coalitions which may occur between politicians and bureaucrats within a certain policy sector.

The nature of the interaction between politicians and civil servants depends not only on systemic factors; it is also contingent on contextual factors: it varies between different policy sectors, over time, and under political regimes of different ideological orientations. Thus we would expect the nature of the politics–bureaucracy relationship to be influenced by a wide range of variables, ranging from national political-administrative culture to sector-specific properties.

Given the dramatic changes in the politics of most advanced states discussed in the introduction to this chapter, we expect to find processes of adaptive change in the public administration of most countries. The types of changes we would expect to find are manifold. One type relates to the bureaucracy's relationship with policy-making institutions. Here, we expect to find one of two different types of changes: either increasing political control over public administration to ensure that the bureaucracy adapts to new political signals, or a relaxation of political control in order to enable public administration to adapt to external changes by virtue of its organizational capacities. However, given the fact that most of the changes mentioned earlier are coming to a greater extent from civil society than from the political echelons of government, the latter type of change appears to be more likely. Phrased differently, we would assume that the challenges generated by the market caused – or at least appeared simultaneously with – a relaxation of the political steering and control of public administration.

In this section, we are interested both in the formal aspects of this politico-administrative relationship, that is, how (and to what extent) the legal framework regulates the relationship between elected politicians and administrative officials, as well as the actual working nature of this relationship.

## The Internal Working Forms and Organizational Dynamics of Public Administration

Organizational structure remains a key variable in any analysis of public administration. In some studies, the organizational setting can be seen as a cluster of independent variables, explaining for instance bureaucratic behaviour, administrative efficiency, intra-organizational power relations (Pfeffer 1978), or communication flows within the public administration. In other studies the organizational structure is perceived as the dependent variable, to be explained for example, by extraorganizational power relations (such as between the legislative and executive branches of government, or between these branches and organized interest groups; Moe 1989). Regardless of which research design we choose we shall always have to take organizational factors into serious consideration.

In the present study we see organizational characteristics as important in explaining the changing nature of the public administration's relationship both to civil society and to policy-makers. The ways in which the bureaucracy conducts these relationships are to a significant extent contingent on its organizational structure as well as the legal framework pertaining to public administration. Thus, organizational design is essentially a political matter, both with respect to the organization of government and the ways in which public organizations relate to their environment (Moe 1989; Rothstein 1991) and with regard to the intra-organizational distribution of power. Put differently, the organizational structure and discretion of a public bureaucracy reflects at any given time the existing power relationships between policy-makers, bureaucrats and civil society.

Public bureaucracies are often assumed to be fairly rigid structures. They were designed primarily to ensure hierarchical communication, legal security and routinization. While most public bureaucracies over time have been decentralized, much of the original system of rules and organizational culture remains unchanged. This has become evident since the efficiency of public organizations has begun to be measured less according to the structure and rules system characterizing the organization and to an increasing extent according to market-based criteria of organizational efficiency. Thus, public organizations have had to try to respond to efficiency criteria which are different from those which guided the initial process of organizational design. Today, public administrative organizations must be cost-efficient; previously they were designed in such a way as to make them efficient with regard to their capacity to enforce rules and legislation. In budgetary terms, there has been a shift from input control to output control; previously, agencies were in part controlled through the economic resources they were given, but today they are increasingly controlled through careful evaluation of their efficiency.

Given these and other changes in organizations' environments, we are interested in what processes of organizational adaptation have taken place in different countries. In this section, the country chapters report the most important and recent organizational changes in public administration and what were the chief aims behind these changes. Public administration can be said to be squeezed between policy-makers' demands for increasing efficiency on the one hand and challenges from market-based actors on the other. Together, these two forces induce public administration to develop new routines and new organizational concepts which make them efficient enough to compete with private actors in the sphere of service delivery. These changes, we suggest, may have had a significant impact on the organizational culture of public administration.

**The Relationship Between Public Administration and Civil Society**

We noted earlier that while the *Rechtsstaat* model still characterizes the public bureaucracies of the Western democracies, there has lately been a powerful drive towards increasing the efficiency of public administration and sometimes also towards enabling private actors to deliver public services. Associated with that process is what appears to be a global development towards opening up public administration towards civil society at large. In a number of countries the 1980s and 1990s have seen strong political efforts to reaffirm the position of the citizen in relationship to public administration. Cases in point include the 'Citizens' Charter' in Britain, the 'Charter of Rights and Freedoms' in Canada, and a new chapter in the Constitution on Human Rights and the new Public Administration Act in Sweden.

Moreover, in many countries there have been attempts to make the delivery of public services a customer-driven process. The basic concept is that citizens are to act as consumers in a market and to choose between different types of services provided under different auspicies. By empowering the citizens in this way, the idea is that there will be a strong incentive for public-service providers to improve the quality of their product (Osborne and Gaebler 1993). Also, customer choice and customer satisfaction will be key variables for resource allocation and the most reliable indicator of public-service quality and competitiveness. Needless to say, this model introduces a significant element of uncertainty in public-service planning and causes tremendous problems for public-sector management (Lundquist 1993; Ranson and Stewart 1989).

Finally, in several countries we have seen increasing co-operation between public administration and private actors in the process of public-service delivery. Here, the idea has been to allow for the users of public services to engage in the delivery of those services; in this way, services have become both less expensive to deliver and more responsive to the needs of its clients. At the same time this strategy raises questions about how to delineate the exercise of public authority from the civic functions of voluntary associations and about the final accountability for these services.

In sum, we see a number of important changes over the last decade or so with respect to public administration's relationship to civil society. We need to know more about the nature of these changes, how they impact on public administration, and also how the changes relate to the relationship between public administration and policy-makers. We also want to know more about organized interests' influence on public administration, as well as their influence on policy-makers *through* the public bureaucracy. Equally important are citizens' rights to appeal against public administration's decisions and rulings and the role of ombudsmen (where these exist). Finally, since we are interested in exchange processes across the boundary between the public and private spheres of society, we need to know something about tendencies towards privatization of public services. In some countries, public services are either 'contracted out' or completely privatized; in other countries, measures are taken in order to encourage individuals and voluntary associations to engage in the process of policy implementation. These examples suggest that the boundary between the political system and civil society – where public administration relates intimately to both spheres – is highly dynamic and flexible.

## A NOTE ON THE CHAPTERS IN THE VOLUME

In order to facilitate a truly comparative analysis, it has been deemed important that the country chapters have a similar approach and structure. At the same time, it is important that the authors of the individual accounts are given a certain amount of discretion so that they can describe and explain the specificities of the particular cases. Thus, the countries selected for the study are to be seen as cases of different political and public administrative systems. The chapters are ordered according to the nature of the cases they present. Thus, following the introductory chapter are chapters on presidential systems, parliamentary systems and, finally, those which cover more than one country.

Within the overall framework of the volume, the contributors have been given substantial discretion to decide to which aspects of public administration they wish to give special attention. In some countries, for instance the United Kingdom, the past ten years have witnessed considerable friction emerging between the civil service and policy-makers. Consequently, Christopher Hood centres his chapter around these issues. Similarly, in the United States, the institutional fragmentation and alleged inefficiences of the federal bureaucracy have been seen as a growing problem, hence the emphasis in Guy Peters's chapter on administrative reform and institutional change in the American administrative system.

## NOTES

1. Ed Page and Linda Wouters (Chapter 9 in this volume) presents a detailed analysis of this process of adaptation.
2. For a further discussion on this problem, see the theme issue of *International Political Science Review*, 14 (4), (1993) on 'Public Administration and Political Change'.
3. I realize that perceiving public administration as a sub-discipline of political science may appear to be controversial, not least in the United States where public administration has a long tradition as an independent academic discipline (cf. Stillman 1991). In Europe, public administration has for a very long period of time been an integrated part of political science. These differences in the relationship between public administration and political science have probably been very important for the development of the study of public administration; whereas scholars in the US were more aware of the special features of their scholarly field, most Europeans developed their research design by applying theories and methods from other sub-fields to the study of public bureaucracies.
4. This strong sentiment to remain focused on development administration is very clear in a recent volume, *Public Administration in World Perspective*. 'Ultimately', say the editors (Dwivedi and Henderson 1990a, p. 18), 'the test of comparative public administration is its usefulness in development administration'. However, as Heady's comments in his introduction to the volume indicates (Heady 1990, pp. 6–7), there does not seem to exist a consensus on the significance of this criterion alone.
5. I am grateful to Guy Peters for drawing my attention to this meaning of the 'public interest'.

6. For conceptual analyses of the state, see, for example, Hall and Ikenberry 1989; Jessop 1990; Krasner 1984; Lane 1993; Skocpol 1985. For clarifying discussions on the issues of state interests and its societal roles, see Rockman 1989, 1992.

# REFERENCES

Aberbach, J. D. and B. A. Rockman (1985), *The Administrative State in Industrialized Democracies* (Washington, D.C.: American Political Science Association).

Aberbach, J. D., R. D. Putnam and B. A. Rockman (1981), *Bureaucrats and Politicians in Western Democracies* (Cambridge, Mass: Harvard University Press).

Aberbach, J. D., E. S. Krauss, M. Muramatsu and B. A. Rockman (1990), 'Comparing Japanese and American Administrative Elites', *British Journal of Political Science*, 20, 461–88.

Almond, G. (1966), 'Political Theory and Political Science', *American Political Science Review*, 60, 869–79.

Anton, T. J. (1980), *Administered Politics: Elite Political Culture in Sweden* (Boston, Mass.: Martinus Nijhoff).

Caiden, G. and N. Caiden (1990), 'Towards the Future of Comparative Public Administration', in O. P. Dwivedi and K. M. Henderson (eds), *Public Administration in World Perspective* (Ames, Iowa: Iowa State University Press), pp. 363–99.

Daneke, G. A. and D. J. Lemak (1985), *Regulatory Reform Reconsidered* (Boulder, Col.: Westview Press).

Derlien, H.-U. (1992), 'Observations on the State of Comparative Administration Research in Europe – Rather Comparable than Comparative', *Governance*, 5, 279–311.

Dwivedi, O. P. and K. M. Henderson (1990a), 'State of the Art: Comparative Public Administration and Development Administration', in O. P. Dwivedi and K. M. Henderson (eds), *Public Administration in World Perspective* (Ames, Iowa: Iowa State University Press), pp. 9–20.

Dwivedi, O. P. and K. M. Henderson (eds) (1990b), *Public Administration in World Perspective* (Ames, Iowa: Iowa State University Press).

Farazmand, A. (ed.) (1991), *Handbook of Comparative and Development Public Administration* (New York and Basel: Marcel Dekker).

Hall, J. A. and G. J. Ikenberry (1989), *The State* (Minneapolis, Minn.: University of Minnesota Press).

Heady, F. (1966), *Public Administration: A Comparative Perspective* (Englewood Cliffs, N.J.: Prentice-Hall).

Heady, F. (1984), *Public Administration: A Comparative Perspective,* 3rd edn (New York and Basel: Marcel Dekker).

Heady, F. (1990), 'Introduction', in O. P. Dwivedi and K. M. Henderson (eds), *Public Administration in World Perspective* (Ames, Iowa: Iowa State University Press), pp. 3–8.

Hood, C. and G. F. Shuppert (eds) (1988), *Delivering Public Services in Western Europe* (Beverly Hills, Cal., and London: Sage Publications).

Hula, R. C. (1988), 'Preface', in R. C. Hula (ed.), *Market-based Public Policy* (New York: St Martin's Press and the Policy Studies Organization), pp. xiii–xiv.

Ilchman, W. (1971), *Comparative Public Administration and 'Conventional Wisdom'* (Beverly Hills, Cal., and London: Sage Publications).

Jacobsson, B. (1993), 'Europeiseringen av statsförvaltningen', *Statsvetenskaplig Tidskrift*, 96, 113–37.
Jessop, B. (1990), *State Theory* (University Park, Pa: Pennsylvania State University Press).
Kooiman, J. (ed.) (1993), *Modern Governance* (Newbury Park, Cal., and London: Sage Publications).
Krasner, S. D. (1978), *Defending the National Interest* (Princeton, N.J.: Princeton University Press).
Krasner, S. D. (1984), 'Approaches to the State: Alternative Conceptions and Historical Dynamics', *Comparative Politics*, 16, 223–47.
Lane, J.-E. (1987), 'Introduction: the Concept of Bureaucracy', in J.-E. Lane (ed.), *Bureaucracy and Public Choice,* Sage Modern Politics Series, vol. 15 (Beverly Hills, Cal., and London: Sage Publications) pp. 1–32.
Lane, J.-E. (1993), *The Public Sector* (Newbury Park, Cal., and London: Sage Publications).
Lundquist, L. (1985), 'From Order to Chaos: Recent Trends in the Study of Public Administration', in J.-E. Lane (ed.), *State and Market: The Politics of Public and Private* (Beverly Hills, Cal., and London: Sage Publications), pp. 201–30.
Lundquist, L. (1993), *Ämbetsman eller direktör?* (Stockholm: Norstedts Juridik).
Lundquist, L. and K. Ståhlberg (1983), *Byråkrater i Norden* (Åbo: Stiftelsens för Åbo Akademi Forskningsinstitut).
Metcalfe, L. (1993), 'Conviction Policies and Dynamic Conservatism: Mrs Thatcher's Managerial Revolution', *International Political Science Review*, 14, 351–71.
Mills, C. W. (1959), *The Sociological Imagination* (New York: Oxford University Press).
Moe, T. M. (1989), 'The Politics of Bureaucratic Structure', in J. E. Chubb and P. E. Peterson (eds), *Can the Government Govern?* (Washington, D.C.: Brookings Institution), pp. 267-329.
Nordlinger, E. (1981), *On the Autonomy of the Democratic State* (Cambridge, Mass: Harvard University Press).
Osborne, D. and T. Gaebler (1993), *Reinventing Government* (New York: Plume Books Penguin).
Page, E. C. (1987), 'Comparing Bureaucracies', in J.-E. Lane (ed.), *Bureaucracy and Public Choice,* Sage Modern Politics Series, vol. 15 (Beverly Hills, Cal., and London: Sage Publications), pp. 230–54.
Palmer, J. L. and I. V. Sawhill (eds) (1984), *The Reagan Record* (Cambridge, Mass.: Ballinger).
Peters, B. G. (1987), 'Politicians and Bureaucrats in the Politics of Policy-making', in J.-E. Lane (ed.), *Bureaucracy and Public Choice,* (Sage Modern Politics Series, vol. 15 (Beverly Hills, Cal., and London: Sage Publications), pp. 256–82).
Peters, B. G. (1988), *Comparing Public Bureaucracies* (Tuscaloosa, Ala.: University of Alabama Press).
Peters, B. G. (1992), 'Comparative Perspectives on Bureaucracy in the Policy Process', in Larry B. Hill (ed.), *The State of Public Bureaucracy* (Armonk, N.Y. and London: M. E. Sharpe), pp. 87–110.
Peters, B. G. (1993), 'Searching for a Role: the Civil Service in American Democracy', *International Political Science Review*, 14, 352–86.
Pfeffer, J. (1978), 'The Micro-politics of Organizations', in M. W. Meyer *et al.* (eds), *Environments and Organizations* (San Francisco, Cal.: Jossey-Bass Publishers), pp. 29–50.

Pierre, J. (1994), 'Public Administration, the State and Society: Towards a Comparative Framework', *International Journal of Public Administration*, forthcoming.

Przeworski, A. (1987), 'Methods of Cross-national Research, 1970–83: an Overview', in M. Dierkes *et al.* (eds), *Comparative Policy Research: Learning from Experience* (Aldershot: Gower), pp. 31–49.

Ranson, S. and J. Stewart (1989), 'Citizenship and Government: the Challenge for Management in the Public Domain', *Political Studies*, 37, 5–24.

Riggs, F. (1964), *Administration in Developing Countries: The Theory of Prismatic Society* (Boston, Mass.: Houghton Miffin).

Rockman, B. A. (1989), 'Minding the State - or a State of Mind?', in J. A. Caporaso (ed.), *The Elusive State* (Beverly Hills, Cal., and London: Sage Publications), pp. 173–203.

Rockman, B. A. (1992), 'Bureaucracy, Power, Policy, and the State', in L. B. Hill (ed.), *The State of Public Bureaucracy* (Armonk, N.Y., and London: M. E. Sharpe), pp. 141–70.

Rothstein, B. (ed.) (1991), *Politik som Organisation* (Stockholm: SNS Förlag).

Rouban, L. (1993), 'France in Search of a New Administrative Order', *International Political Science Review*, 14, 403–18.

Rowat, D. C. (ed.) (1988), *Public Administration in Developed Democracies* (New York and Basel: Marcel Dekker).

Sbragia, A. (ed.) (1992), *Europolitics* (Washington, D.C.: Brookings Institution).

Skocpol, T. (1985), 'Bringing the State Back In: Strategies for Analysis in Current Research', in P. B. Evans, D. Rueschmeyer and T. Skocpol (eds), *Bringing the State Back In* (Cambridge and New York: Cambridge University Press), pp. 3–37.

Stacey, F. (1978), *Ombudsmen Compared* (Oxford: Clarendon Press).

Stillman, R. J. II (1991), *Preface to Public Administration* (New York: St Martin's Press).

# 2. Bureaucracy in a divided regime: the United States

## B. Guy Peters

## INTRODUCTION

The government of the United States is deeply divided, so much so that at times it is difficult to speak of the existence of a single government. The division that derives from the constitutional separation of powers and federalism has been exaggerated by the control of the executive and legislative branches of government by different political parties for 20 of the past 32 years (Fiorina 1991; Kernell and Cox 1991). Even within the executive branch there is a great deal of fragmentation. The executive departments are nominally under presidential control but have traditions and policy stances of their own that any cabinet secretary must attempt to bridle if he or she wants to achieve different policy goals. Further, sub-departmental agencies possess considerable latitude to engage in political activities on behalf of their own budgets and policy initiatives. The divisions within the executive branch are mirrored in the numerous committees and subcommittees in Congress. The constitution was written to attempt to prevent a unified and monolithic government from running rough-shod over its citizens (Gormley 1991). That design has been fulfilled, and has been enhanced by the politics of the late twentieth century, to the point that it makes little sense to speak of the government of the United States and it is seemingly more appropriate to speak of the governments of the United States. In Richard Rose's (1980) phrase, institutional politics in the United States is 'government against subgovernments'.

Despite the numerous divisions that exist within American government, there are also some unifying forces. One such force has been the constitutionalism and legalism of the governing system (Hodder-Williams 1992). Another unifying factor has been a relatively homogeneous (if decreasingly so) political culture. Still another important unifying force has been the civil service. Although the United States has not had the tradition of a strong and autonomous civil service such as those that exist in most European states (Aberbach and Rockman 1988), still it has had a well-qualified civil service that staffs almost all positions across almost all organizations within the federal government. The members of that civil service have been recruited centrally, have similar pay regardless of where they work, and are subject to the same set of personnel regulations across almost the entire federal government. At least for the upper echelons of the civil service there has also been an *esprit de corps* concerning their importance for the management of the state, and their effectiveness in reaching their goals.

That positive self-image of many employees of the civil service is not shared by the public. Although it is a unifying force for the governing system, the civil service is far from a popular institution with the average American. The traditional disdain for 'bureaucracy' in the United States has been reinforced politically over the past several decades as a string of successful candidates for President have campaigned against Washington and its bureaucracy. With those Presidents have come a variety of reforms of the civil service (Gormley 1991). Some of those have improved the lives and the professional capacity of the civil service, while many have been directed toward reducing its pay, perquisites and power (Peters 1992). Taken together, these 'reforms' have had the impact of reducing the constructive capacity of the civil service and making it an even less desirable employer of scarce talent in the society. The negative popular image of the civil service, in turn, may become a self-fulfilling prophecy and further threaten the capacity of the federal government to make and implement programmes in a timely and appropriate manner. There is a quiet, and continuing, crisis of the civil service (Levine and Kleeman 1992) in American democracy.

## BASIC CHARACTERISTICS OF AMERICAN PUBLIC ADMINISTRATION

This section will outline some of the basic facts about public administration in the United States. First, we shall discuss the nature of the organizations in the federal government and the importance of structures for determining performance. We have a tendency to think of the large, cabinet-level departments, but the federal government is much more complex organizationally than that. Then we shall discuss the people employed by in those organizations, their numbers, their characteristics and the manner in which public personnel issues are managed. Finally, we shall discuss some of the major political issues about government employment.

### Organizations

The approximately 3.1 million civil federal employees of the federal government work for a large variety of public organizations. While most Americans think about the federal government as composed of the fourteen cabinet departments, there are in fact a number of organizational formats used in the federal government. Further, there is a great deal of variation within each of those categories. Those cabinet departments, for example, vary substantially in size, from the over 1 million civilian employees in the Department of Defense to the roughly 5000 who work for the Department of Education. In addition to their size, the cabinet departments differ in their internal structures. The Department of Agriculture, for example, is organized around over 50 relatively autonomous agencies (examples are the Animal and Plant Health Inspection Service, the Commodity Stabilization Service, and the Forest Service). Housing and Urban Development (HUD), on the other hand, is organized more around the assistant secretaries and appears to have closer administrative linkage from top to bottom than does Agriculture. In addition, some departments such as Justice have extensive field staffs (the Federal Bureau of Investigation, the Immigration and Naturalization Service), while others such as Energy have a very small field staff structure. These are all cabinet departments, but they vary rather dramatically, and each has a personality and an administrative style of its own.

In addition to the cabinet departments, there are at least eight other types of organizations in the federal government. The group with the largest organizations, after the cabinet departments, is composed of independent executive organizations. Again, these range from large organizations such as the Environmental Protection Agency and the National Aeronautics and Space Administration to smaller organizations such as the Federal Labor Relations Authority. In every case, however, these organizations are responsible for executing some policy but exist outside the cabinet departments to ensure greater flexibility and autonomy, so that they can provide services across the rest of government (General Service Administration) or so that more talented executives can be recruited to lead them (Seidman and Gilmour 1986).

There are also at least ten independent regulatory commissions. These organizations are a historical legacy of the reform movement in American government that sought to depoliticize many important aspects of decision-making. The first of the independent regulatory bodies was the Interstate Commerce Commission (1887) charged with fixing rates for common carriers such as (originally) railroads and (later) trucks. This was followed by organizations such as the Federal Trade Commission (1914), the Federal Communications Commission (1934), and the Securities and Exchange Commission (1934). These commissions are composed of commissioners appointed for long terms by the President, and have staffs to aid the commissioners in making and implementing appropriate regulations in their policy area. The underlying political theory that by depoliticizing a function it can be made to work 'in the public interest' has largely been disproved by the histories of these commissions (Lowi 1979), but they continue to provide economic regulation in a number of vital sectors of the economy.[1]

As well as regulating the economy the federal government also engages directly in some economic activities through public corporations. The United States is usually described as a free market economy, and that description is largely accurate. However, the federal government does engage in a number of economic activities that could in principal be performed privately. For example, the largest single electrical utility in the United States is a federal corporation – the Tennessee Valley Authority – and the federal government also generates electrical power through other hydroelectric projects. The federal government also engages in loan guarantee and insurance activities through public and quasi-public corporations such as the Federal Deposit Insurance Corporation. The public sector in the United States is smaller than in most democracies, but it is larger than most American citizens usually realize, in part because of the use of a variety of indirect means of influencing the economy and society.

There are also a number of presidential organizations that are crucial for understanding how policy is made and implemented in American government. The most important of these is the Office of Management and Budget (OMB), which serves as the major source of advice for the President on the annual budget, and does most of the work of preparing that budget and monitoring its execution. In addition, the President is advised by the National Security Council, the Council of Economic Advisers, and a host of other domestic policy organizations within the Executive Office of the President. Finally, there is the White House Office that organizes the political and policy-making life of the President.

Although not a part of the executive bureaucracy *per se*, several legislative organizations have a great deal of importance for the life of that bureaucracy. The most important are the Congressional Budget Office (CBO) and the General Accounting Office (GAO). The CBO is the legislative equivalent of OMB. It is responsible for setting budgeting guidelines within the Congress and for providing the relevant committees of Congress with needed information about public spending and fiscal policy. The GAO is also concerned with public spending, although primarily with what happens to money as it is being spent. This organization originally performed just the post-audit function for Congress, and monitored spending by the executive branch. The GAO has, however, evolved into an effective policy analytical and advice organization for Congress (Mosher 1979; Rist 1990).

Finally, there is a catch-all category of 'other' organizations that exist in the federal government; this has been referred to as the 'twilight zone'. These are primarily quasi-public organizations that are engaged in public activities through rather indirect means. AMTRAK, the long-haul passenger railroad system, is an example. It has partial public ownership and receives public funds, but often operates as if it were private. Although more directly public, and highly politicized under the Bush administration, the several foundations established to support science (National Science Foundation) and the arts (National Endowment for the Arts) were devised to permit government to enter these policy areas at arm's length. To some extent, because of its separation from direct political control and its self-financing, the Federal Reserve Board, which sets American monetary policy, also falls into this category.

## People

The federal government is a major employer in the American economy, despite its small size relative to the public sector in most industrialized democracies. There are over 3 million federal civilian employees, with almost another 2 million uniformed employees in the armed forces.[2] The combined civilian and military employment constitutes approximately 4 per cent of total employment in the American economy; federal civilian employment alone is approximately 2.4 per cent. This is, however, a relatively small part of the total public sector in the United States. The federal government depends upon state and local governments for the implementation of many of its programmes, especially social programmes (Stoker 1991). Therefore, while the federal government makes almost two-thirds of all public expenditures, it employs only about 15 per cent of all civilian public employees.

Taken together, governments employ over 20 million people, or over 16 per cent of the total employed labour force. The majority of these employees work for the 84,000 local governments, with almost 8 million of those local government employees being in education. Historically, Americans have sought to get by with a small public sector, but largely by incrementalism have managed to produce a large and extremely complex public sector that contemporary politicians seek to bring under tighter control. Most of the public sector, however, is located outside Washington, although the part that is in Washington receives the most attention and the most criticism.

## The merit system

The idea of a career civil service at the federal level is just over 100 years old in the United States. Prior to the passage of the Pendleton Act in 1883, federal government positions were filled through patronage and the 'spoils system'. Even after the passage of the Pendleton Act a large proportion of the civil service remained appointive; at first the competitive service covered only 10 per cent of federal jobs. Compared to most other industrialized democracies, the United States continues to employ a large number of political appointees in the executive branch. Of the over 3 million civilian federal employees, somewhat more than 4000 are appointed by the President or by his appointees. This does not seem many, but it is more than in other countries, and these appointees occupy most of the important positions in government. The number of political appointees has actually increased since the late 1970s, as the Civil Service Reform Act of 1978 permitted additional political appointments in what had been career reserved positions in the Senior Executive Service (SES).

The merit system in the United States is managed by two organizations, both independent executive agencies. These were created by splitting the former Civil Service Commission in the Civil Service Reform Act of 1978.[3] One is the Office of Personnel Management (OPM) which is responsible for the implementation of personnel laws, including testing, grading, recruiting and placement of personnel. The OPM is also responsible for keeping personnel management in the federal government in line with national and international developments in the field, and therefore for proposing reforms of the system. During the 1980s 'reform' meant particularly attempting to transplant private-sector management practices such as merit pay into government (Perry et al. 1989). The second organization involved with federal personnel is the Merit System Protection Board (MSPB), responsible for resolving conflicts between individual employees and the government over the administration of the laws. The MSPB handles several thousand personnel grievances each year, and also houses a Special Counsel responsible for actively investigating personnel problems in the federal government.

Table 2.1  Employment of minorities in federal white-collar workforce (%)

|  | Federal civilian workforce | Civilian labour force |
|---|---|---|
| Black | 16.6 | 10.3 |
| Hispanic | 5.4 | 8.5 |
| Asian | 3.5 | 2.3 |
| Native American | 1.8 | 0.7 |
| Total minority | 27.3 | 21.8 |
| White | 72.7 | 78.2 |
| Total | 100.0 | 100.0 |

Source: Office of Personnel Management, *Federal Civilian Workforce Statistics: Affirmative Action Statistics* (Washington, D.C.: Government Printing Office, September 1990).

The non-appointive components of federal public employment are divided into five large groups. The largest single component is the General Schedule (GS) appointments, comprised of most white-collar employees (see Table 2.1). This system involves personnel performing a huge variety of jobs, including messengers, secretaries, meteorologists, computer technicians, middle managers, and any number of other white-collar occupations. Prior to 1982 recruitment for most entry-level General Schedule positions was done using a common test called PACE.[4] In a consent decree in 1982 the OPM agreed that PACE may have discriminated against minorities and promised to replace it (Horner 1989). The difficulties in designing a general test that could cover the range of jobs in the federal government in an unbiased manner has led to a more decentralized pattern of recruitment, with many organizations devising their own tests and placement procedures.

The top positions of the white-collar civil service are in a separate personnel system – the Senior Executive Service. Entry to these positions is based primarily on academic achievement and interview. Prior to the 1978 Act the employees in the equivalent positions were part of the General Schedule system, but the reformers wanted to create a cadre of senior administrators similar to those in European democracies. These administrators would hold their rank in their person rather than in the position they filled, would move relatively easily among appointments, and would receive bonuses for outstanding performance. They could also be dismissed for substandard performance without the usual civil service protections. As we shall point out below, all the expectations of this reform have not been fulfilled, but the SES must be seen as a significant attempt to change the American civil service (Ingraham and Ban 1984).

The majority of blue-collar workers in the federal government are employed under the several Wage Schedule (WS) systems. These systems, with over 400,000 employees, employ a variety of different manual skills and again provide personnel of this type for almost the entire federal government; most work for the Department of Defense. The fourth major personnel system in the federal government is the Postal System, with approximately 820,000 employees. This personnel system was traditionally distinct from other personnel groups in the federal government, and has become even more distinctive since the former Post Office Department became a public corporation in 1971. Personnel management in the postal system is also heavily influenced by unions, so that there are two levels of protection against unfair dismissal or other disciplinary actions for postal employees.

The final category of personnel systems in the federal government is a catch-all, 'other' category containing about ten small personnel groups. Several organizations in government have their own autonomous personnel systems. This autonomy from the General Schedule may have been accepted because of the distinctive nature of the work involved (the Central Intelligence Agency), their being a public corporation (the Tennessee Valley Authority), or their independence from the executive branch (Congressional organizations such as the General Accounting Office and the Library of Congress). These autonomous personnel systems follow most of the same procedures as the General Schedule system, but also can maintain their independence in some practices.

## Pay and perquisites

Working for the federal government is not a good way to become wealthy. In general, the rewards of public office have been better (relative to those of the private sector) at the bottom of the hierarchy, and have tended to diminish relative to responsibilities, and relative to private sector counterparts, the higher one climbed up the organizational ladder (Peters and King 1992). These pay policies reflect a historical lack of commitment to public-sector employees, as well as short-term political events. As noted, the citizens of the United States have never had a great deal of respect for civil servants and have assumed that they need not be paid well. This is true even though the civil service employs a large and increasing number of highly skilled professionals, as well as a number of administrators responsible for organizations as large or larger than most businesses. Further, those administrators must manage those organizations under a larger set of restraints – personnel laws, freedom of information and the like – than they would encounter in the private sector.

The short-term events that tended to depress public-sector pay even more were found in the Reagan administration and its strong ideological commitment to 'deprivilege' civil servants, and in the problems surrounding Congress's attempts to increase its own salaries. The Pay Act of 1970 had enshrined the principle of comparability between public- and private-sector wages, and had also enshrined the principle that civil servants should not be paid more than members of Congress. A number of research and advisory bodies were mandated to help Congress and the President determine how civil servants should be paid (Hartman 1983). The decision of what actually to pay the civil service remained, however, a political decision. For much of the 1980s the President and Congress did not provide the type of pay increases that they were advised were needed to maintain comparability with the private sector. Also, they only provided enough money to pay for a small percentage of the number of bonuses that had been envisaged in the reform act. Likewise, the amount that might be paid reached a ceiling as Congress found it politically unpopular (to say the least) to raise their own salaries. By the late 1980s it was estimated that senior managers in government were underpaid by 30 to 40 per cent, and the top several grades were all being paid the same amount because of the cap placed by Congressional salaries, combined with negotiated increases for the lower ranks. Many of the best federal managers reacted to low pay and pay compression by leaving for better-paid jobs in the private sector.[5]

After Congress had been able to pass a pay increase for itself in the 'pay for ethics' deal in 1990, there was greater latitude for pay increases for the civil service. Further, the Pay Act of 1990 loosened the connection between Congressional salaries and civil service salaries, so that managers could be paid something closer to what they could earn in the private sector. Provisions for special-rate pay had allowed professionals such as doctors and lawyers to earn salaries comparable to what they would get in the private sector, but after 1990 that higher level of pay became more possible for general managers.

In addition to general levels of pay that would apply to all employees within a grade, there has been increasing concern about merit pay in the federal government. As noted, the Senior Executive Service had a system of bonuses mandated for its members. The same act also mandated the extension of merit pay throughout the middle-management echelons (GS13 and above). Initial problems led to the introduction of a revised programme – the Performance Management and Recognition System – in 1984. This managerialist idea of merit pay coming from the private sector appears to be an admirable means of encouraging greater productivity and better performance from civil servants. This idea has proved difficult to implement in the public sector, however, without a clear 'bottom line' against which to measure performance. Political considerations also may intrude in merit compensation decisions, especially those made about senior managers. Personnel experts in the Office of Personnel Management continue to discuss decentralizing pay decisions and implementing both merit pay and site-base pay, but those reforms appear as yet to be a long way from full operation.

The perquisites associated with working for the federal government traditionally have been very competitive, but they also declined somewhat during the 1980s. Federal employees began (after 1984) to pay social security taxes and had some of their pension benefits eroded because of their new membership in social security. One positive change was that federal pension rights became vested more quickly so that employees could move in and out of government more readily. Also, other employee benefits such as health insurance became less competitive than in the past. Even before the 1980s the value of federal employee benefits were probably overestimated,[6] but after the 1980s they were even less generous and could keep even fewer people with real employment options in the civil service.

**Political Issues**

Although public employment and the civil service are rarely front-page news, even in Washington where government is the principal 'industry', there are still several important political issues about the civil service. These issues reflect both the peculiar role that Americans expect their civil service to play in government and the issues of whether government should be a 'model employer' and use its personnel policies as a means of producing social and economic change.

A primary political question is just how political should the civil service be. We have already pointed out that positions that would be within a career path in other countries are filled by political appointees in the United States. Even though the careerists elsewhere may have declared some political allegiance, there is a marked difference in the level of political involvement of the civil service. On the other hand, however, members of the civil service in the United States are forbidden to engage in most overt political acts beyond voting. The Hatch Act, passed in 1939, was designed to ensure that neither citizens nor politicians would be faced with civil servants whose politicization might inhibit an open exchange of views. Congress has passed legislation twice that would permit members of the civil service to participate in campaigns more actively, and each time the President has vetoed the legislation. The movement among civil servants and civil libertarians to have some of the restrictions on civil servants removed continues. Although civil servants themselves cannot be political, their organizations can be to a degree, and the question of unionization is another issue that has arisen often in discussions of personnel management in the federal government (Freeman and Ichniowski 1988). At present approximately 74 per cent of the federal workforce belongs to, or is represented by, unions, the largest proportion being in the Postal Service. The unsuccessful strike by PATCO, the union of air traffic controllers, at the beginning of the Reagan administration, has been taken as a signal that the federal government is not particularly receptive to unionization of its labor force (Shostak 1986). Even if the government is not, in principle, opposed to union membership for its employees, the use of many of the weapons associated with collective bargaining is severely curtailed by federal law. Again, there is a question of how free federal employees are to exercise their normal rights as citizens by virtue of working for a government that is supposed to protect those rights.

The final political and social question affecting employment in the federal government is equal opportunity. The issue of representative bureaucracy, or the extent to which public employment reflects the social composition of society, is a long-standing concern in the study of public administration. Representativeness is of particular importance in a country such as the United States with an ethnically diverse population and a history of discrimination against at least some of its ethnic and racial minorities (Krislov and Rosenbloom 1981). This importance has been increased by the growing awareness of the rights of women for more equitable treatment in the work place.

The record of accomplishment of the federal government in equal employment has some positive aspects, but also a number of negative features. On the positive side, total minority and female employment in the federal government is better than in the economy as a whole (Table 2.1). For example, black employment in the federal government is 16.6 per cent of the total, while it is 10.3 per cent in the total labour force, and Native American employment is almost three times higher than in the labour force (Office of Personnel Management 1990). Likewise, almost exactly half federal employees are now female.

*Table 2.2  Levels of employment of women and minorities*

| | |
|---|---|
| Average General Schedule grade | |
| Minorities | 7.5 |
| Whites | 9.3 |
| Women | 7.3 |
| Men | 10.3 |
| Executive employment (%)[a] | |
| Black | 4.7 |
| Hispanic | 1.5 |
| Asian | 0.9 |
| Native American | 0.6 |
| Total Minority | 7.7 |
| White | 92.3 |
| Women | 11.1 |
| Men | 88.9 |

[a] This category includes both career and appointed executives.

*Source*:  As Table 2.1.

On the negative side, the employment of minorities and women tends to be concentrated in the lower echelons of the civil service. For example, although approximately half of total federal employment is female, only about 11 per cent of executive positions are filled by women (Table 2.2). Also, a very small fraction of SES and other highly compensated executive positions are filled by blacks (4.7 per cent) and hispanics (1.5 per cent). Those proportions have been increasing over the past several decades, but there is still a long way to go before reaching anything like equality of outcomes in recruitment for the best federal jobs.[7]

## RELATIONSHIPS WITH POLITICAL AUTHORITIES

One of the principal questions for public administration in any regime is the relationship between the permanent parts of the public service and the more transient political forces. This relationship is made especially difficult in the United States because of some aspects of political culture in the US, as well as because of the divisive institutional factors mentioned above. First, the tradition of a marked differentiation between the political and the 'neutrally competent' civil service (Sayre and Kaufman 1960), going back at least to Woodrow Wilson, remains enshrined in the minds of many practitioners, even if academics long ago dismissed this concept (Appleby 1949). Thus, politicians elected to office believe that they should have control over the civil service and become very upset when they find that their civil servants have ideas of their own about what constitutes good policy, and often have the capacity to have those ideas enacted into law and regulations. In part because of the separation of the two groups, the civil service is placed in the position of having to defend what in most political systems would be their natural role in policy-making.

This tendency of the civil service to engage in its own political and policy 'games' is exacerbated by the decentralized agency structure within the executive branch. Cabinet secretaries find it more difficult to gain control over their departments because of the numerous component organizations within those departments that have ties of their own with clientele groups, and with Congressional committees and subcommittees. The former 'iron triangles' in the federal government are now considerably more penetrable than they were (Heclo 1978; Walker 1991). Jones (1982) refers to them as 'big sloppy hexagons', but still the game of politics in Washington tends to be played at an agency and committee level with Presidents and even cabinet secretaries as outsiders.

Finally, the constitutional separation of powers in and of itself makes the relationship between civil servants and their nominal political masters within the executive branch more tenuous than it might otherwise be. The civil service must serve three different masters who may want three different and probably incompatible types of behaviour from that service (Rosenbloom 1983). The political executive tends to want efficient management and obedience, the Congress wants programme commitment and social justice, and the courts want administrative legality and civil rights. Those differences in expectations are particularly important when there are partisan differences between the legislative and executive institutions, as has been true for much of the last several decades.

Agencies in the public bureaucracy have reason to feel that they must serve at least two masters. On the one hand, they are in the executive branch and subject to the President and his appointees such as cabinet secretaries, under-secretaries and assistant secretaries. Civil service laws may present a political executive from dismissing most civil servants (note the exception of the SES), but they can make the life of an agency or of the individuals within it rather miserable. The department secretary, the Office of Management and Budget and the President also have strong roles in the budget process, and often are able to reduce appropriations for an agency that does not co-operate with their programme. At the individual level a recalcitrant civil servant need not be dismissed in order to feel unwanted. He or she can be transferred to a remote part of the country,[8] or to an undesirable job within Washington. With the introduction of merit pay for many grades, a disfavoured civil servant can be punished financially even while retaining the same position. The political executive may not exercise total control over the civil service, but neither is it impotent.

The control exercised by executive branch officials over the civil service extends beyond politics and matters of policy. There are also questions of managing incompetence and malfeasance within government. The number of protections coming from the civil service system and from unions makes disciplining workers somewhat more difficult than it might be in the private sector, but it is far from impossible. The federal government has been attempting to strengthen controls over the bureaucracy within the executive branch. For example, Inspectors General now review internal management and search for 'fraud, waste and abuse' within the bureaucracy (Moore and Gates 1986). The Freedom of Information Act, 'sunshine laws' and protection for whistleblowers make administrative secrecy more difficult to maintain. While far from perfect, the executive branch has been making efforts to police itself for greater accountability.

The agency and the individual administrator must also maintain a good relationship with Congress. Just as the President and his people have a decided impact on the budget an agency receives, so too does Congress, or more specifically the relevant appropriations subcommittees, in both houses. An agency that does not maintain good working relationships with those subcommittees is likely to see its budget reduced until it sees the correctness of Congress's (particularly the committee's) position. In addition to the appropriations subcommittees, an agency also must stay in the good graces of their relevant functional committee and subcommittee. These committees review legislation in the policy area, and can help or hurt an agency's efforts to have new laws passed. Also, the committees are responsible for oversight, and if they want to avoid too many potentially damaging investigations (Aberbach 1990) an agency must be co-operative with its committees. An agency in the bureaucracy may be a part of the executive branch, but it can not survive well without the co-operation of Congress.

Another manner in which Congress becomes involved in administration is through constituency service. If the arguments of Fiorina (1989) and others are correct, then Congress has relatively little to gain by being activist legislators, but rather can enhance their chances of re-election through helping out their constituents when those voters encounter difficulties with the Social Security Administration, the Department of Veterans Affairs, or any of the other federal agencies with whom citizens interact (Johannes 1984). Casework leads to a great deal of Congressional involvement with the bureaucracy, and both uses up a great deal of administrative time and helps to redress some cases of maladministration. The reported balance of those two outcomes may depend upon whether one talks to Congressmen or to the civil servants.

Although less visible in day-to-day administration, American civil servants must also be cognizant of the courts and of legal restraints on their actions (Robinson 1991). These restrictions are especially important as agencies make regulations in pursuance of the laws of Congress (Bryner 1987). Again, the average American citizen would not realize that the bureaucracy makes many more rules than does Congress. These rules are made through the procedures specified in the Administrative Procedures Act of 1946 (Freedman 1980), and involve mechanisms for public involvement in the decisions.[9] Although they are given wide latitude to make rules following from statutes, the courts can review those rules to determine if the procedures followed to make them were correct, and to determine that they are not 'arbitrary and capricious' uses of power. There are also legal checks on the implementation of policies, with most agencies having some internal review procedures followed by appeals to the regular federal court system.

From their point of view the civil service has valid and important reasons for engaging in their own pursuit of policy. They consider themselves to be the experts in the policy area, while the political appointees have often been relatively unskilled and untrained. That characterization of political appointees is decreasingly true, as the issue networks that surround almost all policy areas now serve as the incubators for new political executives with real knowledge about policy. Even if the political executives do know the policy area, however, they are less likely to know how Washington works in the detailed way that a career civil servant will, or to have the continuing contacts with Congress or the clientele groups that are necessary for playing an effective game of politics. Civil servants believe that they know what is needed for their agency, and how to get it through the policy process.

In addition to their knowledge, civil servants in an agency also often have commitment to certain goals for their policy area. The senior civil service is not necessarily, or even usually, composed of the dull, anonymous bureaucrats of the popular image. Rather, many of the civil service are themselves policy entrepreneurs (Doig and Hargrove 1987) with ideas about change and the ability to craft legislation and regulations to achieve their goals. The pattern of recruitment and of careers tends to reinforce the policy thinking and entrepreneurship of civil servants. Many have specialized education before they come to work for government, and then they tend to spend an entire career within a single policy area or even a single agency. This specialized, if narrow, background provides them with knowledge, experience and commitment to the policy they are administering.

The structure of American government, divided into numerous agencies and the separate 'fiefdoms' associated with them, makes the entrepreneurship of the civil servant all the more feasible. They are not trained or socialized to consider the 'big picture' in government, but rather are successful primarily when they concentrate on their own organization and its priorities and programmes. This career pattern may produce huge problems of incoherence and lack of co-ordination – even within a single department such as the Department of Defense (Allard 1990) – but the individual civil servant need not be particularly concerned about that. Rather, he or she can concentrate on doing the best possible job for his or her clientele and let the President and Congress worry about co-ordination and setting priorities for government as a whole.

## RELATIONSHIP TO THE CIVIL SOCIETY

In addition to a number of complex relationships to political actors, public administration in the United States also has a number of important linkages to the society. Almost by definition bureaucracies (whether public or private) tend to be directed by their internal sets of rules and procedures, but still public organizations do have some legal and moral responsibility to the public, and a need to respond to claims from the public. Just as the bureaucracy must be accountable to Congress and to the courts, so too must it be responsive to the general public and its clients. That responsiveness, however, can only go so far and the first responsibility of the bureaucracy must be to uphold the laws that it administers.

The multiple claims on the public bureaucracy place it in a very difficult position. On the one hand it is expected to be responsible to laws and to its political masters. On the other, it is in daily contact with a set of clients who deserve, or at least believe that they deserve, some response from government. The types of contacts with client groups that members of the bureaucracy experience differ according to their level within the organizations. Those at the bottom of organizations tend to have daily contact with clients and often take the side of their clients in any dispute with the bureaucracy. The federal government implements almost no social programmes directly, so that many of the problems associated with 'street-level bureaucrats' (Lipsky 1980) are eliminated. However, analogous problems may arise in regulatory agencies (whether independent or a part of larger departments), so that regulators become 'captured' by the interests they were meant to control.[10]

The upper echelons of an agency are more likely to encounter societal interests in the form of lobbying and political pressure. That lobbying may be direct, or it may come to the agency through Congress. As noted, the conventional idea of the 'iron triangle' in American government is now somewhat outmoded, but still there are close connections remaining among interest groups, individual congressmen and the public bureaucracy. The agencies also must be receptive to the interventions of congressional committees, given the importance of that institution for the continued financial well-being of any organization in the federal government.

Also, in its rule-making activities administrative agencies are required to be open to the demands and ideas of interest groups. Whether through formal hearings or through informal, 'notice and comment', rule-making agencies are required to notify the public of their intentions to make new rules and to listen to the public. This requirement for participation does not eliminate the discretionary powers of the agencies, but it does at least open their proceedings. Further, if rules that are made are at wide variance from the representations received, there is a chance of their being challenged in court as a violation of due process.

The difference between the contemporary 'issue network' view (and reality) of lobbying and the older 'iron triangle' view is that there is now only rarely a single interest with exclusive ties to the agency. Rather, there will be a number of different interests, all with some legitimate claim on the ear of the agency leadership. In particular, consumer groups have become more active and successful in influencing agencies, whereas producer groups had tended to dominate. Likewise, Congress has become more decentralized so that no single leadership group and no single committee can completely control the future of an agency. The game of influence in Washington is now more open, but also more indeterminate.

## BUREAUCRATIC CHANGE

The rather low regard in which the American bureaucracy is held by most of its fellow citizens has made it a ready target of reform efforts. This has been true of much of American history but has been even more true during the 1980s and the 1990s than in the past. In particular, the changes occuring in the 1980s were less analytical and more rather simple attempts to produce the change that political leaders (thought they) wanted. Thus, we have gone from (relatively) sophisticated efforts such as the Brownlow and Hoover Commissions to very simple efforts such as the Grace Commission and 'Reform 88'. These latter reforms have provided relatively simple answers to the complex problems facing government. The Grace Commission and its private sector executives, for example, tended to assume that private-sector managerial methods would solve any problems in government. In general, these reforms have sought to reduce the apparent power of the bureaucracy and to reduce the size of government.

The Grace Commission was an aggregation of over 2000 private-sector executives brought to Washington under the direction of businessman J. Peter Grace to make suggestions for cost savings in federal programmes. These businessmen produced some 2500 recommendations that they argued would save

$424 billion over the next three years (PPSSCC 1983). Subsequent analyses have argued that the prospective savings were overstated (GAO/CBO 1984) and that they emerged from a very fundamental misunderstanding of the political process (Kelman 1985; Goodsell 1986). In the end, relatively few of these proposals have ever been implemented, despite their rhetorical appeal.

Many of the other reforms adopted in the 1980s were more management-orientated and sought to improve the way in which government conducted its day-to-day business (Caiden 1991, pp. 213–20). These have been less dramatic than the sweeping changes proposed in the Grace Commission report, but have perhaps produced more real change. They have included factors such as regulatory review, increased auditing, the founding of a 'Quality Institute', and a host of other changes intended to make public managers more efficient and accountable. All these changes had in common the assumption that the public bureaucracy, left to itself, would be inefficient and probably corrupt.

The Bush administration was less concerned with large-scale administrative reform than the Reagan administration. Much of the same pro-market rhetoric persisted during this administration but there was less creative reform activity. At one level what happened was the continued attempt to fine-tune the free market approach to governance, and to some extent also an attempt to revitalize the civil service after at least two decades of persistent political attacks. As a long-time political insider in Washington, President Bush was somewhat more sensitive to the value and the needs of the civil service. Further, there were several counterattacks by the civil service and other groups concerned with the possible deterioration of the quality of government in the United States. For example, the Volcker Commission (National Commission on the Public Service 1990) was a large-scale research and political effort to attempt to revitalize the civil service. Several professional organizations concerned with the public sector also mounted major efforts at reasserting the role of the public bureaucracy in American government, especially at the senior, policy-making level. It should be noted, however, that despite those more positive approaches to the civil service, the Bush administration did attack 'The Bureaucracy' vigorously during the 1992 election campaign when it appeared politically expedient to do so.

One of the relatively few important changes in the role of the bureaucracy to occur under the Bush administration was the emphasis on regulatory review. As noted, the public bureaucracy in the United States (and elsewhere) must achieve most of its policy-making goals through secondary legislation, or regulations as they are called in the United States. Agencies in the federal government make literally thousands of such regulations each year, many of which the Bush administration considered detrimental to economic productivity and competitiveness. First the Office of Regulatory Review in OMB and later the 'Quayle Commission' were established to review regulations and to weed out those that might harm the competitive position of American industry. These organizations became what one commentator called a 'regulatory KGB' (Kritz 1987) that has limited the activity of agencies such as the Environmental Protection Agency (EPA) and the Occupational Safety and Health Administration (OSHA).

The reforms proposed by the Gore Commission conform to the managerialist model so common in administrative reforms during the 1980s and 1990s. The general emphasis is on streamlining government by reducing middle management, empowering lower-echelon personnel and clients, and making government orientated more towards service to clients than towards procedures. These reforms have gained the commitment of President Clinton and Vice-President Gore, and the Commission has paid a great deal of attention to the possible barriers to the future implementation of its proposals. The implementation ideas include creating an electronic network of federal, state and local advocates of 'reinventing government'; but even the advocates of the Gore Commission proposals believe successful implementation will require at least ten years. While few of its recommendations are highly innovative, they do illustrate the extent to which bureaucratic reform is a part of the agenda for both Democratic and Republican administrations.

In summary, the public bureaucracy has been undergoing a variety of pressures for change. Most of these have come from their political masters, who want a more responsive, more accountable and more efficient civil service. To some extent the means used to achieve these goals have been contradictory and the tools used to achieve greater accountability may actually reduce the efficiency of administration.

## SUMMARY AND CONCLUSIONS

American bureaucracy is large and complex, despite the tradition of limited government and the recent political pressures to further reduce the size and impact of the public sector. The numerous pressures for reform and change have, to some extent, altered behaviour within government, but many long-term patterns persist. In particular, the fragmentation of American government and the fragmentation of the bureaucracy itself makes it more complex and perhaps less controllable than other more integrated administrative systems.

The exercise of control is one of the major political issues in the American bureaucracy. The use of numerous political appointees in decision-making positions, the need of the executive agencies to serve Congress as well as the President, and the openness of the system to a variety of societal pressures point to the importance of control, and the number of actors involved in the struggle over who really runs government. In that struggle the bureaucracy itself is not a passive actor. It, or more precisely its components, have ideas about policy, and have the political skills and the persistence to press for the adoption of those ideas. It is indeed this struggle between the permanent repositories of ideas, influence and interest and the short-term political actors that defines much of the politics of bureaucracy within the United States.

## NOTES

1. Some of the newer independent commissions, such as the Consumer Products Safety Commission, have cross-cutting jurisdictions that make them less prone to capture by the affected interests than were the earlier, limited-function commissions.
2. This number continues to decline after the end of the Cold War, although not as rapidly as assumed by most citizens.
3. The logic of the split was that the Civil Service Commission was responsible both for making and implementing personnel regulations and for judging the fairness of those regulations. The Carter administration used the same logic to break up the Atomic Energy Commission into the Energy Research and Development Agency and the Nuclear Regulatory Commission.
4. Professional, Administrative and Clerical Examination.
5. This did not displease many members of the Reagan administration, however, who argued that excellence was not the goal for the civil service. What was needed was a civil service that was 'good enough'. Further, civil servants were told that if they were really talented they *should* work for the private sector (Levine and Kleeman 1992).
6. For example, the Grace Commission argued that federal benefits were excessively generous, but a subsequent study showed that they were less generous than those for employees in Mr Grace's own company.
7. It must be remembered, however, that recruitment to these positions is dependent upon having a qualified pool from which to choose (Peters 1989), and there is still a relative shortage of minorities and even women with the appropriate qualifications for these top positions.
8. J. Edgar Hoover, for example, tended to exile FBI agents he did not favour to Cut Bank, Montana.
9. Other laws controlling rule-making, such as the Freedom of Information Act, are technically amendments to the Administrative Procedures Act.
10. The simple capture notions, such as that of Huntington (1952), have been replaced by more complex versions in which legislators attempt to design tamperproof controls over the behaviour of the regulatory agencies.

## REFERENCES

Aberbach, J. D. (1990), *Keeping a Watchful Eye* (Washington, D.C.: Brookings Institution).
Aberbach, J. D. and B. A. Rockman (1988), 'Mandates or Mandarins?: Control and Discretion in the Modern Administrative State', *Public Administration Review*, 48, 602–12.
Allard, C. K. (1990), *Command, Control and the Common Defense* (New Haven, Conn.: Yale University Press).
Appleby, P. H. (1949), *Policy and Administration* (Tuscaloosa, Ala.: University of Alabama Press).
Bryner, G. C. (1987), *Bureaucratic Discretion: Law and Policy in Federal Regulatory Agencies* (New York: Pergamon).
Caiden, G. E. (1991), *Administrative Reform Comes of Age* (Berlin: de Gruyter).

Doig, J. W. and E. C. Hargrove (1987), *Leadership and Innovation: A Biographical Perspective on Entrepreneurs in Government* (Baltimore, Md.: Johns Hopkins University Press).
Fiorina, M. P. (1989), *Congress: The Keystone of the Washington Establishment* (New Haven, Conn.: Yale University Press).
Fiorina, M. P. (1991), 'Coalition Governments, Divided Governments, and Electoral Theory', *Governance*, 4, 236–49.
Freedman, J. O. (1980), *Crisis and Legitimacy* (Cambridge: Cambridge University Press).
Freeman, R. B. and C. Ichniowski (1988), *When Public Sector Workers Organize* (Chicago, Ill.: University of Chicago Press)
General Accounting Office/Congressional Budget Office (1984), *Analysis of the Grace Commission's Major Proposals for Cost Control* (Washington, D.C.: Government Printing Office).
Goodsell, C. T. (1986), 'The Grace Commission: Seeking Efficiency for the Whole People', *Public Administration Review*, 46, 196–204.
Gormley, W. T. (1989), *Taming the Bureaucracy* (Princeton, N.J.: Princeton University Press).
Gormley, W. T. (1991), 'The Bureaucracy and its Masters: the New Madisonian System in the US', *Governance*, 4, 1–18.
Hartman, R. W. (1983), *Pay and Pensions for Federal Workers* (Washington, D.C.: Brookings Institution).
Heclo, H. (1978), 'Issue Networks and the Executive Establishment', in A. King (ed.), *The New American Political System* (Washington, D.C.: American Enterprise Institute), pp. 87–124.
Hodder-Williams, R. (1992), 'Constitutional Legitimacy and the Supreme Court', in G. Peele, C. J. Bailey and B. Cain (eds), *Developments in American Politics* (London: Macmillan), pp. 138–64.
Horner, C. (1989), 'Securing Competence and Character in the Public Service', *Governance*, 2, 115–24.
Huntington, S. P. (1952), 'The Marasmus of the ICC', *Yale Law Review* (April), 467–509.
Ingraham, P. W. and C. Ban (1984), *Legislating Bureaucratic Change: The Civil Service Reform Act of 1978* (Albany, N.Y.: SUNY Press).
Johannes, J. (1984), *To Serve the People* (Lincoln, Neb.: University of Nebraska Press).
Jones, C.O. (1982), *The United States Congress* (Homewood, Ill.: Dorsey).
Kelman, S. (1985), 'The Grace Commission: How Much Waste?', *Public Interest*, 78, 62–82.
Kernell, S. and G. W. Cox (1991), *The Politics of Divided Government* (Boulder, Col.: Westview Press).
Krislov, A. and D. H. Rosenbloom (1981), *Representative Bureaucracy and the American Political System* (New York: Praeger).
Kritz, M. (1987), 'Kibitzer with Clout', *National Journal*, 30, 1404–8.
Levine, C. H. and R. S. Kleeman (1992), 'The Quiet Crisis in the American Public Service', in P. W. Ingraham and D. F. Kettl (eds), *Agenda for Excellence* (Chatham, N.J.: Chatham House), pp. 208–73.
Lipsky, M. (1980), *Street-level Bureaucracy: The Dilemmas of the Individual in Public Service* (New York: Russell Sage).
Lowi, T. J. (1979), *The End of Liberalism: The Second Republic of the United States*, 2nd edn (New York: W.W. Norton).

Moore, M. H. and M. J. Gates (1986), *Inspectors-General: Junkyard Dogs or Man's Best Friend?* (New York: Russell Sage).
Mosher, F. (1979), *The GAO: The Quest for Accountability in American Government* (Boulder, Col.: Westview Press).
National Commission on the Public Service (1990), *Leadership for America: Rebuilding the Public Service* (Lexington, Mass.: Lexington Books).
Office of Personnel Management (1990), *Federal Civilian Workforce Statistics* (Washington, D.C.: Office of Personnel Management).
Perry, J. L., B. A. Petrakis and T. K. Miller (1989), 'Federal Merit Pay, Round II: an Analysis of the Performance Management and Recognition System', *Public Administration Review*, 89, 29–36.
Peters, B. G. (1989), *The Politics of Bureaucracy*, 3rd edn (New York: Longman).
Peters, B. G. (1992), 'Searching for a Role: the Public Bureaucracy in the United States', paper presented at a conference on Structure and Organization of Government Research, Committee of the International Political Science Association, Stockholm, Sweden.
Peters, B. G. and D. S. King (1992), 'Rewards of Higher Public Office in the United States', paper presented at a meeting of the European Consortium for Political Research, Limerick, Ireland.
President's Private Sector Survey of Cost Control (1983), *Report to the President* (Washington, D.C.: PPSSCC).
Rist, R. (1990), *Program Evaluation and the Management of Government* (New Brunswick, N.J.: Transaction).
Robinson, G. O. (1991), *American Bureaucracy: Public Choice and Public Law* (Ann Arbor, Mich.: University of Michigan Press).
Rose, R. (1980), 'Government against Sub-governments: a European Perspective on Washington', in R. Rose and E. N. Suleiman (eds), *Presidents and Prime Ministers* (Washington, D.C.: American Enterprise Institute), pp. 47–82.
Rosenbloom, D. (1983), 'Public Administration Theory and the Separation of Powers', *Public Administration Review*, 43, 219–27.
Sayre, W. and H. Kaufman (1960), *Governing New York City* (New York: Russell Sage).
Seidman, H. and R. Gilmour (1986), *Politics, Power and Position,* 4th edn (New York: Oxford University Press).
Shostak, A. B. (1986), *The Air Controller's Strike: Lessons from the PATCO Strike* (New York: Human Sciences Press).
Stoker, R. P. (1991), *Reluctant Partners: Implementing Federal Policy* (Pittsburgh, Pa.: University of Pittsburgh Press).
Walker, J. L. (1991), *Mobilizing Interest Groups in America* (Ann Arbor, Mich.: University of Michigan Press).

# 3. Public administration at the crossroads: the end of the French specificity?
## Luc Rouban

### INTRODUCTION: FRENCH PUBLIC ADMINISTRATION AS A DIVERSIFIED AND FRAGMENTED TOOL

The politics of public administration is one of the major and most salient issues of the French political debate. Since the 1789 Revolution, and even earlier, the role and weight of the state apparatus were always subjects of public concern and controversy. In recent years, political confrontations have largely been fed by passionate debates about the necessity for nationalization or privatization, civil servants' rights and duties, the costs of regulation and deregulation. However, unlike most Western countries, public bureaucracy does not immediately raise questions of accountability nor is it considered, along the lines of Weberian assumption, as a threat to democratic government. The concept of the state is embedded in the national political culture, and public administration is expected to achieve effectiveness as well as democratic values through social modernization and organizational experiments. This republican consensus has not been affected by recent political changes. But, because it proved to be a fragmented machine whose efficiency at a time of budget austerity was questionable, the organizational rationale of public administration was confronted with the new managerialist quest in the 1980s.

**Public Administration and Social Modernization**

Public administration is at the heart of the French political system. This privileged situation is due to its economic weight as well as to its crucial role in national polity-building since the Third Republic. As an agent of state power in a long-divided nation, public administration has always been endowed with high legitimacy. Civil servants have been likely to defend an impartial and legalistic conception of state intervention against particular and conflictual interests. Closely linked with a specific 'republican' policy style, both functional and territorial, the national administrative system was intended to articulate local leaders' demands with state regulatory power. Backed up by a strong historical tradition, public administration has always been characterized by two main features.

First, there is the emphasis on the basic role of the *grands corps* in concentrating technical expertise, through which the higher civil service was closely involved with top-level policy-making, social reforms and economic development. Highly mobile members of the *grands corps* (such as the *Conseil d'Etat*, the *Cour des Comptes*, the *Inspection Générale des Finances*) have controlled the strengthening and uniformity of administrative law in public services administration. Moreover, their role proved to be crucial in modernizing economic structures after the Second World War. As members of governmental thinktanks or public entreprise directors, they served as a social surrogate for political elites whose inefficiency had been severely criticized. This trend was dramatically reinforced during most of the Fifth Republic, at least until the 1980s, to such a point that many observers concluded that political and administrative elites had become indistinguishable (Birnbaum 1977; De Baecque 1981; Suleiman 1974).

Secondly, the key role assumed by public administration in upward social mobility should be stressed. From the time of the Third Republic, public administration was looked upon as a good social investment for poor but hardworking young people. The introduction of a civil service career system in the late nineteenth century allowed professional merit to gain official recognition. It can be seen that social changes which transformed France from a rural into an urban country largely operated through the social integration process at work in specific public-service sectors, such as the police, army and railways. Public administration soon became a major component of middle-class socialization mechanisms. This explains why the public sector always provided an example of social advancement to private sector wage-earners.

The Fifth Republic was built upon these basic strategic and social features. As Quermonne (1987) puts it, high civil service became at this time a real political force that provided a counterweight to deficient political parties. It was from the state that a solution was expected by the modernist elites who rallied around De Gaulle. However, this strong movement for across-the-board modernization did not follow a legalistic administrative design. Rather than being a mythical 'Napoleonic' system, characterized by its rigidity, public administration was viewed as a flexible tool for the implementation of welfare state programmes and as a major source of organizational innovations. Fifth Republic administrative specificity was based on the fact that institutional modernity could not be found in private firms nor in the legalistic tradition of previous Republics. National planning, economic forecasting procedures and large-scale science programmes called for imaginative administrative structures and networks.

## Public Administration as a Political Problem

This overwhelming presence of administrative apparatus at the centre of the polity as well as the policy structure is compounded by its outstanding economic weight. About 40 per cent of yearly current public expenditures are devoted to civil service salaries. There is a steady increase in the number employed by the state civil service and the territorial authorities. During the decade 1970–80, the number employed rose by about 1 million, reaching about 4 million in 1981. At this time, the newly elected Socialist government implemented a structural reinforcement of the civil service to combat unemployment and to improve the functioning of priority sectors (education, cultural and social services, post and telecommunications). Until the austerity plan of 1983 and the government's conversion to market economics, the public sector as a whole was put at the centre of Keynesian state intervention. Between 1981 and 1983, more than 170,000 jobs were created (although the original budget for 1981 provided for the creation of only 1889 jobs) (Bodiguel and Rouban 1988). This rise was brought to a halt in 1983–4 when the emphasis was put on the need to modernize the administration. But, as a consequence of the previous bureaucratization of local authorities in the aftermath of decentralization laws, the percentage of the public sector among the total working population kept rising, as is shown in Table 3.1. The new era that began in 1981 with the Socialist government and its ambitious projects, and which was then followed by two other major political changes (in 1986 and 1988 when the Right and the Left alternately returned to power), put the administrative question at the centre of dramatic political controversies for the first time in the history of the Fifth Republic. Drastic proposals to cut back management were announced by the Right leaders before they took office, but things remained largely unchanged. However, public administration was transformed into a political problem. As ideological mobilization declined (as was clearly shown during the low-key 1988 presidential election) and the Left–Right dichotomy vanished on many issues, management and public administration gained a new interest. Yet though the managerial revolution in France is connected with a degree of rejection of the state-centred social model, the enhancement of managerial solutions under different Socialist governments had no links with global cost-cutting objectives. Emphasis shifted from social modernization to the effective implementation of government decisions when strategic initiatives of 1980s reformers (especially programmes to fight unemployment) were jeopardized by organizational pitfalls. Public administration proved to be a more complex and fragmented tool than it appeared to be at first sight.

Table 3.1  Number (millions) and proportion of the civil service and the public sector among all wage-earners and the working population

|  | 1969 | 1980 | 1985 | 1989 |
|---|---|---|---|---|
| State[a] | 2.068 | 2.719 | 2.855 | 2.847 |
| Local authorities | 0.618 | 1.021 | 1.185 | 1.254 |
| Total civil service[b] | 3.046 | 4.442 | 4.827 | 4.891 |
| Public services[c] | 0.667 | 0.578 | 0.586 | 0.527 |
| Total public sector | 3.713 | 5.020 | 5.413 | 5.418 |
| Percentage of public sector among wage-earners | 23.1 | 27.8 | 30.2 | 29.4 |
| Percentage of public sector among the total working population | 17.8 | 21.4 | 22.4 | 22.5 |
| Percentage state + local authorities among total working population | 12.8 | 15.9 | 16.7 | 17.0 |

*Notes*
[a] Including civil and defence departments.
[b] Including state, local authorities and hospital civil servants.
[c] Does not include companies newly nationalized in 1982.

*Source*: Based on INSEE, *Annales statistiques de la fonction publique* (Paris: INSEE, 1992); and INSEE, *Population active, emploi et chômage depuis 30 ans*, (Paris: INSEE, Division Emploi, 1987).

## A Fragmented Machine

Although French public administration is currently characterized as a highly centralized system, the central agencies in Paris employ less than 30 per cent of the total civil service work-force. At the departmental or regional level, field services account for a huge part of human resources. The 'statist' explanation, which puts emphasis on the French state's centrality, pays insufficient attention to the fact that the actual policy network brings together field services and local authorities. Local autonomy is widespread. As the 1982 decentralization process, which empowered local administrations to implement social welfare and urban planning programmes, grows stronger, field institutional arrangements prove to be more crucial for policy implementation than central regulations. The 'pyramidal' representation of French public administration is as far from accuracy as it has ever been (Wright 1990).

For political scientists, the administrative system deviates strongly from what it used to be for law scholars. From a legalistic or formal perspective, hierarchical lines are few. Article 20 of the Fifth Republic Constitution clearly states that public administration is at the disposal of government for policy implementation under the supervision of the prime minister. Executive power is shared between the prime minister and the President of the Republic but executive authority is concentrated in the hands of the latter. Public administration matters generally do not have to be debated in a Parliament whose constitutional power was severely limited by the 1958 Constitution. Outside the budget cycle, Members of Parliament cannot exert substantial control over administrative operations. Administrative discretion is supposed to be constrained by a comprehensive system of administrative law courts, whose efficiency in a democratic oversight process remains a subject of controversy (D'Arcy and Dreyfus 1989). In brief, as shown in Figure 3.1, such a highly integrated administrative apparatus seems to offer a case study of administrative presidency.

In fact, functional and hierarchical lines cross each other. Because administrative organization is much more nebulous than a pyramid (Sadran 1992), administrative integration is highly problematic.

In the 1991 Edith Cresson government there were 46 ministries and state secretaries as compared with 28 during the Pompidou government in 1967. It is worth noting that, during the Fifth Republic, the mean number of ministries is about 20, while this number was between 15 and 20 during the Fourth Republic. The factors explaining such ministerial proliferation are twofold. Not surprisingly, the first is a political will to demonstrate that the government is managing some key issues of the moment through institutionalization. For instance, the Mauroy government created a Ministry for the Expansion of the Public Sector, while the 1986 conservative government created a Ministry for Privatizations. Another factor is the need to deal with new issues that create co-ordination problems without modifying the existing institutional structure. It was noticeably the case for the Environment Ministry or the European Affairs Ministry. Changing official attributions from one ministry to another is a very common but also confusing game. For instance, industrial policy issues were handled in the late 1960s by an independent state secretary. They were then associated with the Trade Ministry in the early 1970s. In the 1980s these issues were alternatively devoted to a big Ministry of Research and Industry, built on the Japanese MITI model, and to a Ministry of Industry and Research (!), and were finally handled by a Ministry of Industry and Foreign Trade, while technological innovation issues were given to a new Ministry of Research and Technology. All these changes reflect political compromises, territorial battles and, corporate self-interest as well as systematic research for the best organizational formula. They generally imply personnel transfers and internal reorganizations which compromise any attempt to draw a clear sketch of internal structures.

*Figure 3.1   The French administrative system*

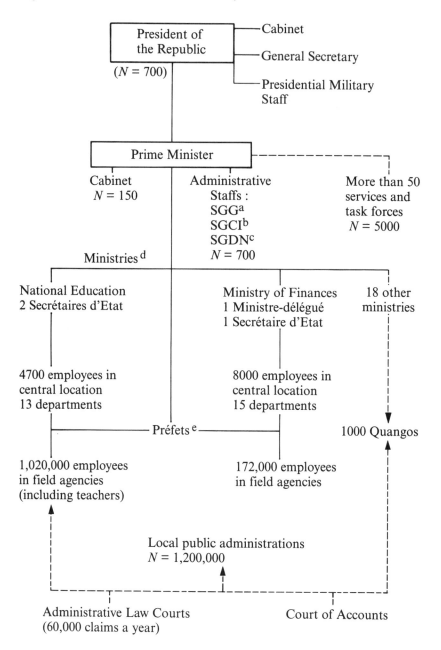

*Notes*
a  Secrétariat Général du Gouvernement
b  Secrétariat Général du Comité interministériel pour la coopération économique internationale
c  Secrétariat Général de la Défense Nationale
d  We detail here the two largest ministries. Of course, as is the case for other ministries, they exert oversight but not hierarchical power on many Quangos
e  As representatives of the different ministers and the prime minister at the regional and departmental levels, *préfets* have hierarchical power over field offices' heads.

Dotted lines indicate an oversight relationship while continuous lines indicate a hierarchical relationship.

Ministerial structures are always in turmoil and constitute a bewildering world for any observer. Each year, managers have to scrutinize new directories to discover where some of their former colleagues have gone. Moreover, organization charts, which officially distinguish clearly between *directions* (departments), *sous-directions* (divisions) and *bureaux* (offices) have been blurred by the proliferation of task-forces and 'micro-cabinets' at the department- or division-head level which are supposed to compensate for overlap among administrative jurisdictions.

Decision-making channels do not obey any rationalistic or legalistic logic but favour a degree of duplication between administrative structures defending their own traditions, culture and autonomy. Watertight compartments between services is an old French malaise. For instance, it is easy to find central departments opposing each other within the same ministry, whether it is to stir up conflictual issues (as was the case in the Education Ministry over university research programmes budgeting) or because they do not share a common purpose (as has always been the case between the Budget and the Treasury) or because each has been, at least partially, invaded by various corporatist interests (in the Industry Ministry one can distinguish 'departments' headed by technical *corps* – such as Polytechnique or Mines – and 'departments' headed by generalist *corps* – for example, *administrateurs civils* who have been trained by the *Ecole Nationale d'Administration*).

Another factor for disintegration can be found in the density of territorial administrative coverage. As a matter of fact, field services have close relationships at local levels. The Ministry of Infrastructures' departmental offices (*directions départementales de l'équipement*) or Industry and Research regional offices offer good examples of functional autonomy. Because they rely upon their specific professional know-how, institutional arrangements with local authorities and political bargaining with local leaders, they are well-protected from any central intrusion (Thoenig 1987). At the local level, public administration is a game for four or five players, a complex arena featuring the prefect (the prime minister's representative with theoretical control over each ministerial field service), field offices and their well-trained experts, central-department inspectors and regulations, local leaders and their own administrative staffs (whose members are generally former state civil servants who changed post for pecuniary reasons). With the decentralization process granting local authorities more power for social and economic intervention, new impetus was given for the consolidation of sub-departmental structures through an administrative devolution process. Devolution of administrative authority to field agencies is intended to smooth the regulatory flood of instructions from central departments, reducing their status to 'holding companies', and offering users better and adequate services. This is a major component of the public-sector 'modernization' policy initiated in 1986. Current expenditures and up to 30 per cent of investment expenditures are now likely to be decided by field managers. Moreover, a 1992 law relating to local authorities and territorial administration clearly lays down administrative devolution as a general principle.

Nevertheless, it would be unrealistic to imagine that a perfect link between functions and organizations is possible or even desirable. Rationalistic structural reforms regularly proved to be ineffective. The creation of 'super-ministries' integrating several areas of ministerial responsibility (as was the case in 1992 at the Ministry of Finance, which supervises the activities of the Ministry of Budget and those of the Industry Ministry) is an old idea that various governments have tried to implement for 50 years. Unfortunately, this solution has demonstrated nothing but new co-ordination difficulties, as the minister becomes more isolated from line departments. On the contrary, one may contend that the French ministerial system suffers from the internal fragmentation of giant machines, as in the case of the National Education Ministry which tries to manage nearly 1 million employees scattered all over the country. A possible theoretical solution could be to separate central agencies from line departments, a recently conducted experiment in Great Britain. Of course, this would imply a bridling of cabinets' power.

Last, but not least, another cause of instability is the proliferation of administrative hybrids which do not fit classical legal criteria.

The *établissements publics* category constitutes a very common legal structure (there are more than 1000 at the national level alone!) because it allows for financial autonomy and flexible tools well fitted to problem-solving in the scientific, industrial and professional sectors. Unfortunately, the official categorization indicates nothing about their spending power or their regulatory authority. Each gets its own chart that results from its historical background and negotiated compromises. Some are exclusively administrative organizations (such as the *Chambres de Commerce*) while others are devoted to business activity (such as the *Aéroports de Paris*). The use and abuse of this unspecified legal category of public organization has raised many questions about the extent to which administrative law rules should be applied (Conseil d'Etat 1985).

To this first group, must be added the 60 public entreprises that carry on business activities (bank, insurance) or public services duties (urban transportation, gas and electricity supply), whose number increased dramatically in 1982 with the newly nationalized companies. Since their partial privatization in 1986, the new direction given to national industrial policy in 1988, and concern about the 1993 European market, public corporations were given a large degree of functional autonomy from direct political control (as demonstrated by the low turnover rate of their managers) in order to compete or to co-operate with private business.

# RELATIONSHIPS BETWEEN POLICY-MAKERS AND THE BUREAUCRACY

As Peters (1988) points out, the relationship between political executives and career civil servants in France is at one extreme of a continuum, implying a blending of the two into a single career, while the United States is at the other extreme, with truncated hierarchies. As a matter of fact, most ministers and national politicians come from civil service ranks. Political careers are all the more attractive for civil servants since they can return to bureaucratic occupations after an electoral defeat.

Paradoxically, executive control over interdepartmental aspects of policy always required strong central staff agencies able to overcome the formalism of line administration. A common misconception about French public administration is to suppose that all civil servants share the same values and positive perceptions about government programmes just because long-term structural mechanisms allow exchanges between politics and administration (Suleiman 1974). The statist modernization movement of the 1960s was largely based upon a delicate alliance between modernist elites who tried to short-circuit conservative or leftist colleagues. Political changes and state retreat made this problem more acute.

**Staff Administration Dominance**

Administrative integration has been pursued by various routes. A main trend is the reinforcement of staff administration in charge of the control of national policies (Quermonne 1991). The prime minister's office is a 5000-official complex bureaucratic tool consisting of the Cabinet, which deals with political co-ordination, the *Secrétariat Général du Gouvernement* whose staff and functions have grown since 1946, the *Secrétariat Général du Comité Interministériel pour la coopération économique internationale* (SGCI), co-ordinating ministerial action and permanent representatives' initiatives relating to EC authorities, the *Secrétariat Général de la Défense Nationale*, the general military headquarters, and many other task-forces. As a transmission-belt between the prime minister, Parliament and the President of the Republic, the *Secrétariat*

*Général* assumes the monitoring of decisions taken during meetings of the Council of Ministers. By way of comparison, the presidential staff is surprisingly tiny, with about 50 members. Most of them come from elite *corps* even though their proportion has slightly declined since François Mitterrand's presidency (40 per cent are civil servants as compared with 90 per cent during Valéry Giscard d'Estaing's presidency). As the real power centre of national political life, the presidency's influence on major policy issues is considerable. However, the staff characteristics at the Elysée are dissimilar from those at the White House. Even though the President's inner circle is made up of personal friends or long-time political associates, its initiatives are strictly controlled. Special advisers are assigned to specific fields and act as the President's eyes and ears.

These institutions are in permanent contact with the staff of individual ministries through institutionalized relations. Permanent or *ad hoc* meetings take place at the Elysée (*conseils restreints*) or at the prime minister's office (*comités interministériels*). It can be seen that at the prime minister's office the number of formal meetings, attended by minister and civil servants, and chaired by the prime minister himself, has slightly decreased in recent years (116 in 1965 compared with 72 in 1978 and 25 in 1989) in favour of informal meetings (356 in 1965 compared with 778 in 1975 and 1066 in 1989), which are attended only by high civil servants.

Integration is also attained between *grands corps* members through informal contacts based on long-term acquaintance and networks. These networks, linking governmental or presidential staffs, ministries and public corporations, have been accurately described as assuming 'institutional memory' at a time of greater political instability (Hayward 1982). This integration framework came to maturity during the De Gaulle years.

## Towards a Policy-centred System

After 1974 new phenomena emerged which contributed to altering the underlying logic of public administration. To sum up this change, one could say that the state-centred system, dominated by civil service professional interests, became a policy-centred system. The core of this new administrative deal can be found in the more systematic involvement of policy-makers in policy implementation.

As domestic politics became increasingly similar to those of other European countries (Wright 1990), public administration 'neutrality' and social power were challenged by pluralist conceptions of State action. Civil servants, accustomed to some kind of functional autonomy, were put under pressure to be more accountable as policy-makers became more concerned with the results of administrative action. This basic trend involved two administrative changes : ministerial cabinets received more power as the politicization of high civil service ranks severely modified the equilibrium between administration and politics.

## Ministerial cabinets

Ministerial cabinets are made up of ministers' personal collaborators, special advisers as well as technical staffs. Most cabinets vary from ten to thirty political appointee members. Because of their knowledge of internal communication channels and processes, an increasing number of civil servants have entered the cabinets. Before 1981, this proportion was about 90 per cent. In fact, their role has changed dramatically. During the Third and Fourth Republics, as well as at the start of the Fifth, cabinets were likely to master routines which left the minister isolated from outside environment or line services. Of course, cabinet members developed political sensitivity but their activity remained on the technical border of administrative action as long as the parliamentiary majority was stable. In 1981, when the Socialists took power, cabinets were called upon to enforce drastic changes in close liaison with the President's own cabinet and centres of decision-making. The new administration relied heavily on their support to prevent possible hostility from line administration. Since the end of the 1970s, cabinets had been closely connected with presidential politics and shared the charismatic power of the presidency. In the 1980s, however, because policy choices required more political resources they acted as real centres of agenda-setting. Cabinets' interference with department heads and even middle managers became more and more frequent. This trend was further amplified by two other factors. First, as well as official members, 'unofficial' advisers were hired to cope with particular questions on a one-off basis. For professional civil servants, this meant that a shadow hierarchy was being created. Secondly, though cabinets have always offered a means of faster promotion to the better administrative posts, this social function was enhanced, because cabinets proved to be very useful in giving rewards to political friends.

## Administrative integration

Administrative integration was also achieved in reinforcing subordination by politicizing the senior civil service. This politicization was not born in 1981 or in 1986, but one can observe the ever-growing extension of a French-style 'spoils system' (Bodiguel and Rouban 1991). Until the second half of the 1970s this phenomenon was not very obvious. In the long term, public administration is characterized by some kind of functional interweaving of political and administrative elites. According to Jean-Louis Quermonne (1987), around 40 per cent of Parliament's members and 55 per cent of ministers are former civil servants. Between 1959 and 1991, ten out of eleven prime ministers were recruited from civil service ranks. This confusion between the political and the administrative world strengthened the stability of the Fifth Republic and favoured administrative initiatives in launching social or scientific programmes. A specific equilibrium appeared during the first years of the Fifth Republic that overrode the political market as regards any serious attempt to set some pluralistic policy evaluation process. For twenty years, technocratic politics and majoritarian party rule dominated the policy-making process.

Those days are now gone. Governments, even Socialist ones, no longer claim to have all the answers to economic problems. In fact, though the Socialists stopped the privatization process initiated between 1986 and 1988, they continued to deregulate the public sector and strongly encouraged public corporations to work according to business rules. New guidelines of action were established in order to satisfy sectorial or intersectorial demands, heavily supported by newborn public interest groups (environmental protection, urban planning, industrial local development). In other words, highly politicized new arenas called for a new deal between public administration and politics. Public administration was suddenly confronted with political pluralism and diversified policy communities. Emphasis was put on political responsiveness. Of course, staff administrations were particularly concerned. In 1967, one scholar observed that most cabinet members did not belong to any political party. When asked, only 44 per cent stated that they shared some political conviction (Kesler 1985). As for the department heads, 90 per cent stated that they did not belong to any political party and only 15 per cent stated some political attraction. By way of comparison, in 1981 up to 69 per cent of cabinet members belonged to major parties.

This politicization process found expression in a higher rate of turnover in the 500 posts 'at the government's discretion'. The turnover rate of department heads, which was about 14 per cent between 1958 and 1974, rose to 25 per cent between 1974 and 1976, then climbed up to 31.4 per cent between 1981 and 1984 and peaked at 40.5 per cent between 1986 and 1987. Furthermore, the rate and direction of these changes have been rather selective. For instance, between 10 April and 26 June 1986, almost all department heads in the Ministry of the Interior were changed. The trend was particularly noticeable in those sectors where newly elected governments wanted to change policy quickly (Cultural Affairs, Justice, Education in 1981; Interior and public corporation heads in 1986). It should be noted that most of the newcomers in the administrative or commercial public sector have come from civil service ranks. French-style politicization is much more an internal dynamic moving civil servants within the state apparatus than a true 'spoils system' opening offices to outsiders. As shown in Table 3.2, statistical data on cabinet members, the prime minister's office and Elysée advisers clearly demonstrate that the proportion of civil servants remained largely unchanged.

Nevertheless, politicization is increasingly significant below high civil service ranks, disturbing middle-level managers and clerical staff who find themselves suddenly confronted with a new rule of the game where seniority is challenged by revolving-door politics. The public administration politicization has contributed to blurring the professional lines traditionally drawn between politicians and civil servants and has fostered a new separation between those politicians or civil servants who base their decisions on political criteria, on the one hand, and civil servants in charge of their implementation, on the other. Such a role division is particularly clear at the local level where one can distinguish between local leaders who act as real policy managers with their own staffs through a 'boss system', and more traditional elites who devote their time to political bargaining or administrative routine.

Table 3.2  Professional origins of members of cabinets (%)

| Administrations: | Mauroy 1981 | Chirac 1986 | Rocard 1988 |
|---|---|---|---|
| High civil servants | 65 | 66 | 70 |
| Teachers | 10 | 4 | 7 |
| Political militants | 15 | 14 | 9 |
| Private sector | 8 | 14 | 7 |

($N = 618$)

This task redefinition, causing a new kind of subordination for career civil servants, was all the more sensitive because the public-sector modernization policy was likely to increase the organizational dynamics of the bureaucracy.

## ORGANIZATIONAL DYNAMICS

Administrative modernization policy has been a priority item on the government's agenda since 1986. It is strongly propounded and advanced as a necessarily far-reaching change in administrative culture by socialists and conservative governments alike. In many respects, modernization policy is an unusual administrative reform. It aims at articulating the efficiency/effectiveness imperative and civil service management. Comprehensive structural reforms have been discarded in favour of measures adapted to the administrative field, along the lines of a bottom-up reform. It is argued by its originators that service quality depends upon an improved socio-professional status for civil servants. Over the last ten years it has been evident that human and organizational conditioning factors have prevented management requirements being unconditionally accepted.

### Factors Causing Tension

First, higher civil servants have suffered a severe loss in their average purchasing power. For instance, calculated in real income terms, their purchasing power decreased at 1.5 per cent per annum between 1984 and 1987, whilst those of private-sector managers climbed 0.5 per cent per annum. Of course, some categories suffered much more than others. For instance, it was estimated that high civil servants at pay grades B, C and E lost 20 per cent of their purchasing power between 1980 and 1988 (Denoueix 1990). Higher civil servants have felt their social status declining particularly because their working conditions suffered from management cut-backs and increasing pressures for personal productivity. It is worth noting that this period of decline followed another, beginning in the 1950s and ending in the late 1970s, during which public-sector wage increases were largely comparable with those in the private sector. As a major consequence of such a decline, public services could not afford to hire the best and the brightest, as could the private sector, or to retain experienced senior civil servants. Today, the public personnel deficit is worsening specifically in the technical and scientific sectors (telecommunications engineers, arms system specialists) where private salaries are currently between 50 and 100 per cent higher than those offered in the civil service.

Secondly, the civil service no longer offers upward social mobility. On the one hand, the higher civil service is becoming elitist, as compared to the socioprofessional composition of society as a whole. The upper classes are increasingly over-represented, as can be demonstrated by a systematic analysis of social recruitment (see Table 3.3). Posts open in the higher *corps* are increasingly elitist whilst the positions of middle managers (category A outside the higher *corps* and category B) suffer from chronic instability and social tension as promotion via internal competition becomes harder.

*Table 3.3 Social origins of senior-level competition candidates (%)*

|  | ENA | | Polytechnic | |
| --- | --- | --- | --- | --- |
|  | 1955–62 | 1981–5 | 1953 | 1979 |
| Higher officials, managers | 38.7 | 65 | 57.8 | 65.5 |
| Clerical and manual workers | 11.1 | 7.2 | 7.5 | 4.4 |
| N = | 400 | 738 | 233 | 308 |

On the other hand, applicants entering the competition in the 1980s were overqualified. From 40 per cent to 50 per cent of B category competition applicants had higher education diplomas. In all competitions, the average job to applicant ratio was 1:11 in 1987 compared to 1:6 in 1978 (Ministère de la fonction publique 1991). Posts in the middle or low civil service are now frequently sought, sometimes in absurd numbers. For instance, in 1979, 5235 applicants entered the competition for *préfecture* clerks; there were only 40 positions available. For all category C and D competitions, the job to applicant ratio was 1:5 in 1974 and 1:17.2 in 1987. By way of comparison, senior civil service competitions attract fewer applicants. In category A competitions, the job to applicant ratio has remained stable at around 1:7 since 1980.

This situation produces three effects (Bodiguel and Rouban 1988). First, young middle-level managers are increasingly competent and better trained whilst the positions at the top of the hierarchy are occupied by those who were recruited in the 1950s, in times of weaker competition. Secondly, and as a result of this, the huge difference between actual advancement opportunities and the qualifications of civil servants entails both disintegration of the hierarchy and demoralization. The rush towards higher *corps* through internal competitions favours the disorganization of personnel management. Thirdly, as the senior civil service is becoming a place of 'heirs' where mobilization of social capital is more noticeable than ever, the intermediate civil service is gradually becoming the last resort of the middle classes in holding on to their social gains of the 1960s in a time of proletarianization and a dualistic society. This social and organizational pressure was at the heart of conflicts and strikes between 1986 and 1988.

A third factor of crisis can be found in the evolving understanding that civil servants have of their role. At the very time when right-wing politicians were developing the thesis about welfare state crisis and ideological opposition between the public and private sector, careful social analysis demonstrated that, to the contrary, civil servants and private wage-earners shared increasingly common organizational situations (Bodiguel and Rouban 1991). If civil servants seem to be more involved in public life and to trust public institutions more than private sector workers do, both groups share a common trust in private firms for economic development (68 per cent in the two groups); they do not trust political parties or labour unions (only 38.6 per cent of public workers trust labour unions as opposed to 33.8 per cent of private-sector wage-earners); and they are more attracted to EC or regional programmes than to those elaborated through the state channel. When asked 'What kind of institution is best suited for preparing the future?', only 9 per cent of public-sector workers answer 'the state' (as opposed to 10.2 per cent of private-sector workers), 19 per cent answer 'the European Community' (as opposed to 19.2 per cent in the private sector), and 44.5 per cent 'the regions' (as opposed to 36.8 per cent in the private sector).

As a result, public-sector employees are going through a critical time. Legal structures or traditional civil service frameworks can no longer offer civil servants the social means to support their occupational specificity. Day-to-day professional requirements no longer fit organizational systems which delineate a career and professional future. As proclaimed during the 1988 strikes, three problems seem to be crucial for civil servants: the disassociation of organizational recompense and individual results; a more pressing demand for greater account to be taken of their special responsibilities; and a relative lack of identification within the organization that leads to both dissatisfaction and demotivation (Bodiguel and Rouban 1991).

## Administrative Modernization Policy

In this context, modernization policy was intended to improve public management while giving the civil service new impetus and maintaining social peace. Through pragmatic considerations more than legalistic ambitions, the modernization process is founded on a twofold systematization (Rouban 1989):

- public officials are becoming more closely linked with service delivery. The idea of 'user' seems to be taking over from that of 'subject'. At the same time, emphasis is put on the idea of 'profession' by paying greater attention to individual responsibilities;
- administrative productivity can only be improved if civil servants are mobilized around it. Modernization is primarily geared towards the implementation stage.

Since the first initiatives in 1983–6, administrative modernization has taken the form of a quality and innovation strategy based on employee participation in defining administrative duties and operational targets. Using quality task forces, ministerial 'administrative statements' that clearly specify tasks and objectives and performance indicators, the modernization policy aims at stimulating behavioural change on a case-by-case basis. In some ministries (notably the Ministry of Infrastructures and Facilities), and other public services (La Poste, France-Télécom), experiments are carried out in order to emphasize human resources management programmes. Personnel evaluation procedures have multiplied, connected with more coherent professional training sessions. Emphasis has been placed on improving internal communications: think-tank sessions for bureau chiefs, the circulation of house newsletters, and the introduction of computerized papers. Budget appropriations for administrative modernization have increased from Fr. 10 millions in 1987 to Fr. 13.6 millions in 1988 when prime minister Michel Rocard gave modernization a high priority on the government agenda. Regular meetings have been organized at regional and national levels to mobilize administrative executives with strong support from the Ministry for the Civil Service. Pilot schemes are under way in most field services. At the central department level, many initiatives have been taken for training staff in management and communication techniques.

Largely implemented by departments themselves, this strategy has had a real impact on administrative management. In many respects, modernization has improved user services and internal management. Delays have been shortened, costs brought down, and professional relations eased. Indeed, modernization appears to be a substitute for – or a transition towards – more radical solutions. The setting up of quality circles or internal strategic planning may be seen as an alternative to contracting out (this is especially true at the local level).

Modernization policy offers a good example of a political and organizational compromise. When resources get scarce and promotion opportunities restricted, public administration cannot continue with incremental reforms that generally imply cost externalization. On the other hand, it has been all the more difficult to change the administrative rationale without launching a step-by-step learning process of new duty requirements. In many respects, the modernization strategy has been considered a means of articulating traditional career system with the new geographical and functional mobility that a policy-centred administrative model would require. Fortunately, the modernization process has benefited from improvements in pay bargaining with labour unions after years of stalemate. The 'Durafour agreement' reached in 1990 between government and union representatives sets out a complex system of professional measures in order to facilitate upward professional mobility and a reorganization of the position system. In 1991 another agreement was reached on a general 6.5 per cent pay increase for the following two years. In 1992, more than 400 strategic plans had been adopted in most ministries, and 85 quasi-contractual agreements had been settled between the Civil Ministry, the Ministry of Finance and the minister in order to set up independent management units that enjoy financial and staff autonomy. The successful implementation of the modernization process is mainly due to the fact that this bottom-up reform did not raise ideological and legalistic questions about the general status of the civil service. Dogmatism in previous reform attempts, in the aftermath of the 1981 Socialist victory as well as in 1986 during the Conservative government of Jacques Chirac, impeded any real improvement.

A recent study (Rouban 1992) shows that most administrative executives feel satisfied with this reform. Up to 84.4 per cent of these executives are currently engaged in modernization procedures.[1] More than 70 per cent of them think that the modernization process has had a positive impact on administrative management (17.8 per cent think that this impact was 'very sensitive' while 53.1 per cent think that this impact was only 'moderate'). Up to 61 per cent of the sample state that agency productivity increased, and 63.6 per cent think that user service quality was improved. Public administration is undergoing a cultural change as managers spontaneously ask for more power in policy implementation. Personnel management control is their main concern (for instance, up to 65.7 per cent of them ask for further improvements in personal performance appraisal systems). Nevertheless, for the time being, legal barriers and financial constraints (rigorously imposed by the Finance Ministry in a time of competitive disinflation) still prevent them from engaging freely in a managerial revolution.

## PUBLIC ADMINISTRATION AND CIVIL SOCIETY RELATIONSHIPS

In recent years the classic relationship between public administration and civil society, which implied some monarchical flavour, has been profoundly altered in France. As a political change occurred that shifted interest from decision-making to policy implementation, new structures of interaction had to be created. On the one hand, administrative law protection seems unsatisfactory because users were viewed – and viewed themselves – as real customers. On the other hand, public action became more complex with a growing number of policy actors and stronger demands for policy evaluation. As a main consequence, new regulatory agencies appeared, constituting a fourth branch of government.

### When Users Become Consumers

Until recently in France, users' involvement in public services was considered as just raising legal questions. In the 1970s, many important official reports were devoted to such questions as individual access to official computer files, quasi-judicial conflict-settlement procedures, detailed explanation of administrative regulations, and so on. The aim of this policy was to enhance some kind of 'administrative citizenship' in order to legitimize the central state apparatus.

During the 1980s a new interest concerning quality questions became evident as public administration faced new political controversies about its costs and duties. The *'alternance'* process speeded up the introduction of management tools which were praised by conservative governments (looking for efficiency) as well as by socialist governments (looking for effectiveness).

The administrative modernization process favoured new considerations for quality procedures, especially at the local level. Dramatic institutional changes, such as the decentralization process initiated in 1982, called for new strategies. State field agencies were confronted with complex strategic environments as local political leaders looked for cheaper services and relied more frequently on their own sources of expertise, hiring consultants and setting up advisory boards. Public services as a whole adopted businesslike strategies in order to challenge private-sector initiatives: the Directions Départementales de l'Equipement, which carry out urban engineering and public real-estate projects, designed a set of new 'commercial' products in order to counter the growing power of private firms; La Poste, the national mail service, was recently transformed into a commercial quango in order to develop financial services (savings, loans); more than 65 per cent of its resources are now from financial activities.[2] SNCF, the French national railroad company, inaugurated new services that pay due attention to the costs of road delivery services.

Paradoxically, the introduction of quality considerations, closely associated with management technology, favoured the transformation of users into customers who expect satisfaction for the money they spend. This shift in the user–administration relationship implies some kind of distinction between 'big' customers (private firms and local political leaders), on the one hand, and 'common' users (laymen) who generally cannot afford to deal with public services, on the other. Users' associations were recently infuriated by the new rail transport policy when they discovered that it implied the termination of non-profitable services in many local stations. EC regulation, or more exactly EC deregulation, of public services is likely to benefit significantly the 'big' customers who can choose their service providers, as can be observed in the deregulation process in the United States (Daneke and Lemak 1985).

Users' involvement in quality definition depends on whether public services are incorporated into the framework of national policies. If they are (as is the case in secondary education) any debate on quality standards (degrees, programmes) becomes a political debate because users (the parents and sometimes the pupils) are confronted with a professional structure whose power is somewhat limited ('we apply the official programme'). In such cases, users' information about national regulations is at the heart of their involvement.

In other circumstances, national policies are now implemented through a relatively free process. This is the case in the eradication of unemployment: officials have to meet their users and establish personal contact in order to find the best solution. In such an example, user involvement, that is, public service co-production, is necessary for policy fine-tuning and operational definition (Jeannot and Gillio 1992).

If there are no national policy requirements, and this is increasingly common within the decentralization process, quality standards are defined locally through comparisons with other cities' services (especially through the local tax effort). The point here is not quality *per se* but the range of services which can be offered, the acceptable 'quality threshold'. Users now decide upon a local service 'package' and are involved in the service definition to the extent that they may 'vote with their feet'. As a result, local elites are strongly encouraged to put emphasis on management procedures.

The relationship between big public services and users is channelled through users' associations whose existence and activities are generally poorly known. Citizen participation on advisory boards of major public services, which has been institutionalized since the 1945 nationalizations, has not succeeded in improving the policy process or avoiding strikes and social conflicts. Scholars have observed that in many cases such participation transformed the so-called people's representatives from users' associations into real professionals dealing with their bureaucratic counterparts (Chevallier and Lochak 1978). Spontaneous public participation is generally reactive and appears only in order to prevent the setting up of some undesirable facilities such as nuclear plants or chemical waste disposal. In France, the 'communality' tradition is underdeveloped and citizens prefer to protest through political pressure (as exemplified by personal contacts with the mayor or their parliamentiary representative). One can generally observe a triangular relationship between users, (local) political leaders and public services managers. Fees for major public services are never set through direct bargaining between users' associations and service managers. Local service priorities are generally debated during local elections and are highly politicized.

## Opening Up Policy Communities

Is there a French national style of corporatism ? The Fifth Republic was largely dominated by executive action and parliamentary weakness. This does not mean, as is usually contended, that pressure groups were non-existent. They were merely discrete. The fragmentary nature of pressure groups and ideological divisions have enabled governments to divide and rule. Though some occupational groups, such as farmers, have succeeded in infiltrating their ministry (Keeler 1987) or in influencing national issues, one can observe only few elements of neo-corporatism. In practice, such processes of incorporation did not amount to much because major decisions tended to be made in the inner circles of power. Labour unions have generally exercised some kind of veto power in policy-making (this is noticeably the case with education issues) but their conflictual relationship with successive governments did not result in institutionalization. Far from being a social democratic system, political-administrative interaction with interest groups generally favoured the *ad hoc* or sectorial treatment of professional demands. The Planning Commission or the regional planning bodies were designed in such a way that they could incorporate demands from representatives of social elites but not from public interest groups. As a matter of fact, these bodies acted as socialization tools working for the benefit of the centralized decision-making process.

This social and strategic environment was recently upset. Over the last ten years, the European integration policy as well as the decentralization process have fragmented the national policy arena in such a way that pressure group action is more sensitive than ever. The policy process became more complex and was open to a growing number of actors. Emerging local policies have given more political power to public interest groups who received official recognition. The 1992 regional elections demonstrated that environmental protection groups could get substantial results and act as a real political force (they scored 13.9 per cent at the regional level). This upheaval of pluralistic corporatism is particularly remarkable at the local level where business or industrial stakes are getting higher. This change resulted in a radical questioning of the internal functioning and professional roles of civil servants. They were called upon to act more frequently as negotiators and translators in multilevel strategies, and were compelled to co-ordinate complex mechanisms and disparate initiatives. This is especially the case of *préfets*, who discovered that they could compensate for their recent loss of power by becoming institutional mediators between the Brussels bureaucracy and local authorities as direct regional intervention from the EC grew stronger.

**The Quest for New Regulation Systems**

These changes in the policy-making process have led to some institutional innovations. First, one can observe a proliferation of *ad hoc* administrative bodies based on the special task force model born in the 1960s. Intersectorial issues (urban planning, energy policy, rural renewal, industrial modernization) have been committed to task forces, variously designated *commissariats, délégations, missions,* that enjoy significant decision-making powers in order to insulate issues from sectorial demands. As another proof of a changing public administration model, the recent development of independent regulatory agencies received attention from both scholars and politicians. With no hierarchical power in the mainstream administration and endowed with collegial management, independent regulatory agencies were set up wherever private (or public) interests were likely to generate high political pressures, for the sake of public ethics or individual protection (Media Superior Council, Polls National Central Commission, National Committee for University Assessment, Freedom of Information Act Committee).

A final factor is the emphasis on policy evaluation. This new trend appeared in the early 1980s. Since then, evaluation committees have been created in the Research and Technology Ministry, the Education Ministry, and within the parliamentiary committees which developed a growing interest in new ways of auditing government action. In 1990, in the aftermath of several official reports, evaluation was institutionalized at the prime ministerial level. A new institutional set was elaborated (including an Interministerial Committee of Evaluation, a National Fund for the Development of Evaluations and the Scientific Council of Evaluation) in order to encourage and supervise the evaluation process at work in different ministries. The Interministerial Committee, chaired by the prime minister, receives and selects evaluation proposals from ministries and other government agencies. The Scientific Council, whose members are appointed by the President of the Republic for their expertise, gives recommendations before and after the evaluation process on its quality and methodology. As pointed out by Jean-Pierre Nioche (1991), this is a centralized organization, under executive branch control, which does not really meet the requirements of a pluralistic evaluation process. Parliament is largely absent from this mechanism, even though it was given lip service in the 1990 decree. Moreover, the first issues to have been selected (social housing projects, social aid, child-care programmes, and so on) do not deal with hotly disputed programmes. Anyway, policy evaluation systems are now largely proved, challenging the traditional executive monopoly on expertise.

## CONCLUSION

French public administration has recently been called to account in the name of efficiency, user involvement, accountability, speed of decisions, competitive responsiveness and so on. Locked into a number of conflicting requirements, civil servants feel uneasy. How can better quality be achieved when scarce human resources or political pressures prevent the hiring of qualified people? How can workplace relationships be improved when legal rules or the traditional veto from labour unions prevent the giving of rewards to outstanding employees? In many respects, civil servants are now paying the price of a more general change affecting the relationship between state and civil society in France. Politicization has created a new kind of subordination. Sectorial and local demands are invading field services whose technical expertise is now challenged by private sector firms or by local authority staffs. Traditional sources of administrative legitimacy, such as public service or general interest, are still strong, but civil servants have lost their privileged social status. For the first time in French history they feel like bureaucrats and no longer like decision-makers.

What does this mean for the future? Of course, in the realm of developmental analysis, this trend could be analysed as a democratization process, a standardization mechanism adjusting French public administration to EC integration and the pluralistic political market. From a different perspective, one may observe that social structures in the higher civil service ranks remain untouched and that elites' networks are more closely linked than ever. For the time being, it is hard to predict whether the traditional separation–confusion cycle between politics and public administration will give way to another statist interpretation of political life (implying some kind of overlap between elites' circles and common managers) or to a real policy-centred model which largely implies some kind of politicized managerialism.

What can be learned from a comparative public administration perspective from the French situation? It seems that one should depart from traditional 'blackbox' theories that generally produce two symetrical, and unconvincing, ways of reasoning. On the one hand, public administration is supposed to suffer from some kind of dysfunctional self-development, the so-called 'bureaucratization process'. On the other hand, public administration is no more than a political product, largely dependent upon policy-makers' control or citizens' will. In the first case, one may wonder, however, why there is a limit to the bureaucratization process. Why are not all Western countries over-bureaucratized? There is strong evidence that many sectors (education, health care) are under-staffed. The first explanation, political intervention, is not very convincing. In general, politicians are not very aware nor very interested in organizational matters (with the noticeable exception of those policy-makers who are daily confronted with field implementation). Political action is scarcely efficient in promoting better management. Far from being a miracle solution, privatization is just a way of avoiding public management and of separating politics from managerial considerations. The other explanation, bureaucratic crisis and general stalemate, as evoked by Crozier in the 1960s (Crozier 1964), has never been matched by field observations. Administrative systems demonstrated that they could be imaginative when involved in internal or external disputes and when allowed to investigate solutions of their own (as was the case with French public administration in the 1960s). In fact, the exchange process between public administration and civil society plays a crucial role in drawing limits beyond which public administration becomes a bureaucracy. There is no automatic or rationalistic warning signal that says 'Now we are under Soviet rule'.

In the second case (bureaucracy as a political instrument), recent experiments in drastic reform in industrialized countries clearly show that administrative change is unattainable without the consent of civil servants. For instance, politicization is unthinkable in those systems where tradition and internal professional rules prevent any 'external' intrusion (as was demonstrated by the British civil service of the 1970s).

Change dynamics can be found in the building of administrative rationales that articulate professional perspectives and social understanding of what a good civil service is supposed to be. This means, first, that public administration change is triggered simultaneously by combined external and internal pressures, producing role understanding as well as new expectations from civil society. In France, the administrative modernization policy was triggered by a clear political will from 1988. Nevertheless, this reform would be quite inoperative without structural changes that allowed civil servants to change their career strategies and professional values. Secondly, micro changes (sectorial), such as those produced by pressures from private business, politicians or voluntary associations, cannot automatically involve macro structural changes without translation features. This translation process is generally operated through channels allowing specific information to circulate between policy-makers and civil servants. For instance, policy evaluation is supposed to rationalize the bottom-up decision-making process (that is, to make it understandable through common knowledge) in the same way as the national planning system was supposed to channel the 1960s top-down policy-implementation rationale (Rouban 1990).

Finally, we must pay attention to two major dimensions of public administration. First, it is important to highlight the implicit functions of public administration in the social and political realms. For instance, as long as French public administration offered a promotional way for the middle class and a counterweight to political instability, civil servants were highly motivated to protect themselves against competing social groups and demands through administrative law and professional rules. When there was political and governmental stability during the first twenty years of the Fifth Republic, they could enforce their expertise in policy-making, devoting less attention to legal safeguards. When political stability and social consideration vanished in the 1980s, they found that they were required to act as common wage-earners do.

Secondly, administrative change is likely to occur when, and only when, theoretical frameworks are available. External pressures or political decisions are ineffective as long as 'administrative action' theories are not set up. In many respects, administrative reform is a conceptual question.

## NOTES

1. These numbers are calculated on the basis of a 501 administrative executives sample (over a total population of about 5000). This sample has been defined with geographical, gender, sectorial and administrative spatial density quotas in order to certify its representativeness.
2. In 1990 the national mail service was given a new legal structure transforming this former ministerial department into a quasi-autonomous non-governmental organization (a 'quango' in the British meaning) that enjoys great financial autonomy. As a matter of consequence, the career system of Postal Service employees was designed around the lines of functional positions, softening the traditional bureaucratic categorization in ranks and levels.

## REFERENCES

Birnbaum, P. (1977), *Les Sommets de l'Etat* (Paris: Seuil).
Bodiguel, J.-L. and L. Rouban (1988), 'Civil Service Policies since 1981: Crisis in the Administrative Model or Inertia in Policies?', *International Review of Administrative Sciences*, 54, 179–99.
Bodiguel, J.-L. and L. Rouban (1991), *Le Fonctionnaire détrôné?: L'Etat au risque de la modernisation* (Paris: Presses de la Fondation Nationale des Sciences Politiques).
Chevallier, J. and D. Lochak (1978), *La Science administrative* (Paris: LGDJ).
Conseil d'Etat (1985), *Les Établissements publics nationaux* (Paris: La Documentation Française).
Crozier, M. (1964), *Le Phénomène bureaucratique* (Paris: Seuil).
Daneke, G. A. and D. J. Lemak (eds) (1985), *Regulatory Reform Reconsidered* (Boulder, Col.: Westview Press).
D'Arcy, F. and F. Dreyfus (1989), *Les Institutions politiques et économiques de la France* (Paris: Economica).
De Baecque, F. (1981), 'L'Interpénétration des personnels administratifs et politiques', in F. De Baecque and J.-L. Quermonne (eds), *Administration et politique sous la*

*Cinquième République* (Paris: Presses de la Fondation Nationale des Sciences Politiques), pp. 19–61.

Denoueix, J.-M. (1990), 'Haute fonction publique où vas-tu?', *ENA mensuel*, 202, 12–14.

Hayward, J. E. S. (1982), 'Mobilizing Private Interests in the Service of Public Ambitions: the Salient Elements in the Dual French Policy Style', in J. J. Richardson (ed.), *Policy Styles in Western Europe* (London: George Allen and Unwin), pp. 111–40.

Jeannot, G. and C. Gillio (eds) (1992), *Droit des usagers et co-production des services publics* (Paris: Plan Urbain/RATP/DRI).

Keeler, J. T. (1987), *The Politics of Neocorporatism in France: Farmers, the State, and Agricultural Policy-making in the Fifth Republic* (London: Oxford University Press).

Kesler, J.-F. (1985), *L'ENA, la société, l'Etat* (Paris: Berger-Levrault).

Ministère de la Fonction Publique et de la Modernisation de l'Administration (1991), *La Fonction publique de l'Etat 1991* (Paris: La Documentation Française).

Nioche, J.-P. (1991), *Institutionalizing Policy Evaluation in France: Skating on Thin Ice* (Jouy-en-Josas: Cahiers de recherche HEC).

Peters, B. G. (1988), 'The Machinery of Government', in C. Campbell and B. G. Peters (eds), *Organizing Governance, Governing Organizations* (Pittsburgh, Pa.: University of Pittsburgh Press), pp. 19–53.

Quermonne, J.-L. (1987), *Le Gouvernement de la France sous la Cinquième République* (Paris: Dalloz).

Quermonne, J.-L. (1991), *L'Appareil administratif de l'Etat* (Paris: Seuil).

Rouban, L. (1989), 'The Civil Service and the Policy of Administrative Modernization in France', *International Review of Administrative Sciences*, 55, 445–65.

Rouban, L. (1990), 'La modernisation de l'Etat et la fin de la spécificité française', *Revue française de science politique*, 40, 521–45.

Rouban, L. (1991), 'Le client, l'usager et le fonctionnaire: quelle politique de modernisation pour l'administration française?', *Revue française d'administration publique*, 59, 435–44.

Rouban, L. (1992), 'Les cadres supérieurs de la fonction publique et la politique de modernisation administrative – premier bilan', rapport pour le Commissariat Général du Plan et la Direction Générale de la Fonction Publique (Paris: Fondation Nationale des Sciences Politiques).

Sadran, P. (1992), *L'Appareil administratif de l'Etat* (Paris: Montchrestien).

Suleiman, E. N. (1974), *Politics, Power and Bureaucracy in France* (Princeton, N.J.: Princeton University Press).

Thoenig, J.-C. (1987), *L'Ére des technocrates* (Paris: L'Harmattan).

Wright, V. (1990), 'The Administrative Machine: Old Problems and New Dilemmas', in P. Hall, J. Hayward and H. Machin (eds), *Developments in French Politics* (London: Macmillan), pp. 114–32.

# 4. Public administration in Germany: political and societal relations
## Hans-Ulrich Derlien

### INTRODUCTION

The reunification of the Germanys in 1990 and the subsequent integration problems facing the country underlined the importance of public administration in restructuring the ramshackle former GDR command economy, its functional importance for the working of a market economy and its indispensability for citizens in adapting to post-totalitarian economic and societal conditions. The role that government bureaucracy played in the unification process as well as the transfer of Western administrative and political structures and the peculiar environmental conditions under which these are starting to operate highlight important features of the German administrative system. At the same time, current reform issues in other Western countries are confronting the country on a much larger scale; for instance, privatization of state enterprises and establishing satisfactory bureau–client relationships.

Dealing comprehensively with public administration's political and societal relationships in a federal system, with a high degree of local government autonomy in addition, is impossible in a short article such as this. While the following section tries to give a picture of the system and its formal characteristics, the subsequent sections will be more selective in concentrating on central government bureaucracy and its political aspects and relations, as well as its internal operations. When treating public administration's societal relations the focus will be shifted from Bonn to the *Länder* (state governments) and local levels.

The analytical model implied in this procedure derives from the phases of the policy-making and implementation process. While the former is exposed to political inputs from parliament, parties, interest groups – to mention just the most important – on the national level, service delivery and rule enforcement necessarily takes place at the local level aiming at the economy and society. This model, though, is unsatisfactory, for it leaves out of consideration the fact that political inputs in the three-tiered German state structure occur also on the level of the *Länder* and local government where policy development takes place, too. Also, implementation of federal programmes is overwhelmingly a matter for the *Länder*. Furthermore, the socio-economic environment of the administrative system does not merely enter during the policy cycle, but might well be justified to account for these relationships in a non-interactionist, more analytical perspective by focusing on the resource flow on which the administrative system depends on all levels: revenues, people and legitimating beliefs. These aspects, however, will only guide the treatise in secondary perspective, in particular when we are dealing with the civil service and its recruitment and role understanding.

## GENERAL OVERVIEW

### Macro-structure

The Federal Republic of Germany is not a unitary state but a system with vertical separation of powers between federal and *Länder* governments; local governments are part of the *Länder* and their constitutions and formal structures are devised by the individual *Länder*. Thus, there is a high degree of variation of formal structures between units on the lower levels of government, but since the foundation of the second German republic in 1949 there has also developed a trend towards harmonizing not merely special substantive *Länder* policies but also the structural multiplicity to achieve a core model of organizing subsystems, notwithstanding special ramifications.

### Federal Administration

The federal level consists of the federal government and its 15 to 18 ministries and 25,000 civil servants and public employees in Bonn, who are expected to move to Berlin by the year 2000. This dislocation, together with the federal parliament (662 MPs and a staff of 3000), is bound to cause some friction. On the other hand, federal non-governmental institutions, some 50 quasi-autonomous governmental and 250 quasi-autonomous non-governmental organizations (predominantly social insurance systems), as well as the five federal courts of justice, the army, and the federal rail and postal services have traditionally been distributed throughout the country. Nevertheless, reallocation of these offices is due to occur in the course of moving some of these institutions to East Germany and to compensate the city of Bonn for the losses it is bound to encounter. Typical of German federalism is a functional division of labour that delegates the implementation of federal laws and programmes to the *Länder*; with a few exceptions, the federal government does not control field offices, but has to rely on the *Länder* (and local governments) for the execution of policy.

## *Länder* Administration

The eleven western and five new eastern *Länder* are of different sizes, ranging from the city states of Berlin, Hamburg and Bremen to larger territorial units such as Bavaria, Baden-Württemberg, Lower Saxony and Brandenburg. Consideration was already being given in 1969 to merging some of the Western *Länder* to make them economically and fiscally more powerful and less dependent on grants from the federal government or horizontal revenue-sharing between the *Länder*. These arguments have recently been raised again, because they apply even more strongly to the Eastern territories that, because of the soaring economy, depend greatly on fiscal transfers from the West. The argument for restructuring the *Länder* has also gained importance in view of European unification and the need for a strong regional level in the EC, which in the German case would be the *Länder*. However, once the new East German *Länder* have become institutionalized with their own constitutional bodies, there will be little chance to change matters in the foreseeable future, despite fears that 'poor' *Länder* could well gain a majority in the Federal Chamber (*Bundesrat*), which has to approve most federal legislation, and that they could start to exploit federal government and rich *Länder,* or block policies (Scharpf 1991). At the moment, each *Land* constitutes too important a political reference point to East Germans for them to be abolished in the near future.

## Vertical Division of Powers and Functional Interdependence

In principle, federal government and *Länder* are independent of one another. Jurisdictions are neatly separated, leaving the *Länder* basically cultural affairs (universities and schools, which are almost entirely public), the police, the judicial system (with the exception of the five federal courts) and administrative organization. The federal government, with a few exceptions (foreign service, military, customs, rail, mail and waterways), has no field offices of its own but relies completely on the *Länder* (and local governments) for the execution of federal policies. The *Länder* governments (and not elected senators, as in the US) have a say in the Federal Chamber when it comes to legislation involving regulations extending to administrative affairs; the federal government is entitled to supervise the implementation of certain laws by the *Länder*. However, this pattern of confederate federalism has not prevented over time more and more policy areas becoming regulated by federal legislation. Owing to the so-called 'competing legislation' that, after 1949, left rule-making to the *Länder* where Bonn could not take the initiative, federal legislation has now superseded *Länder* competences in many policy areas, in particular that of taxation.

Further, constitutional reforms between 1967 and 1969 entitled Bonn to 'frame-legislation' (for example, in university matters and in civil service pay) and the so-called joint tasks of federal and *Länder* governments were institutionalized. This occurred in the areas of basic research, educational planning, university construction, regional economic policy and agricultural and coastal infrastructure, with the federal government paying 50 per cent of the costs. This blurring of formerly clear jurisdictions has attracted criticism, either that there is a lack of central control due to 'decision-making traps' (Scharpf *et al.* 1976), or that this development is assessed as a 'unitary state in disguise' (Abromeit 1992).

## Reconstructing Public Administration in the New *Länder*

The sixteen *Länder* governments are composed of from six to eight ministries each under a prime minister (or *Bürgermeister* in the case of the city states) and his office. *Länder* government personnel vary in number according to size of the territory, as do state legislatures.

In East Germany, the ministries as well as the *Länder* administration in general are shaped after Western models. Not only was capital and manpower massively exported to East Germany after unification but also institutions. The most important mechanism through which this transfer of institutions took place was partnerships between the Western *Länder* and those newly established in the East. Even where two of the old *Länder* helped the same *Land* in the East, the influence of particular West German advisers is visible in the way individual ministries are internally structured and regional authorities and field offices are organized.

## Regional Authorities

This influence can be traced in the decisions on institutionalizing regional administrative bodies, of which 26 exist in the Western territorial states except in the Saarland and Schleswig-Holstein. Owing to the latter's influence, Mecklenburg-Western Pomerania has not established this decentralized institution of state government (neither did Brandenburg and Thuringia). Thus, by 1993 there are six additional *Regierungsbezirke* (regional districts) in East Germany, increasing the total number to 30. According to the German principle of structuring the macro-system, this gives territorial specialization superiority over functional specialization. These regional authorities have the function of co-ordinating sectorial ministerial policies in their respective areas; they are to compensate for departmental selective policy-making. Apart from comprehensively implementing government policy in the specific region, their task is to supervise counties and cities as to the legal aspects of their autonomous operations and to substantive aspects where local authorities carry through programmes 'on behalf of the *Land*'.

## Local Governments

Below the regional authorities, which belong to what Germans conceive of as 'unmediated' state administration, local government is situated in the administrative hierarchy – juridically conceived of as 'mediated' state administration subject merely to reviews of legality in genuinely local government affairs (and substantive supervision in implementing state and federal legislation).

Besides the 117 cities, there are 426 counties to which 15,952 communes belong. Of these, 27 cities and 7563 communes are grouped in 191 counties in the considerably smaller Eastern part of the country. This means that they are territorially, in terms of population as well as in terms of financial capacities, considerably smaller than the Western communes. These, however, had gone through a process of territorial amalgamation between 1964 and 1978, in a politically painful process that had reduced the number of local units from 24,000 and brought about the present structure. Not surprisingly, the same local government concentration is to be achieved in the new *Länder* by 1994, the year of the next local elections. The new *Länder* will, however, rely more strongly on the voluntary formation of associations of rural local governments, according to the South German example. Thus, to complete the structural picture, it should be mentioned that there are 1037 of these associations in existence in the West that basically carry through administrative affairs requiring professional staff, whereas policy matters continue being decided in the individual local councils, thus preserving some kind of political local identity in the countryside.

Beside the hierarchy of general (*Länder* and local government) administrative offices, there are special *Länder* authorities down to county level. These are predominantly concerned with the implementation of tasks involving scientific analysis (for example, in environmental affairs, mining, forestry and health). Also, there are the only federal field offices in the areas of employment and, as mentioned above, customs, army, post and railways.

It deserves mention that a number of *Länder* allowed for the formation of higher-level local self-governing bodies on the regional level to deal with cultural affairs, area planning (for example, in the Rhine–Ruhr area) or running special hospitals. These associations are sometimes considered a functional equivalent of regional state authorities, although their tasks are genuinely communal.

Thus, the administrative structure is characterized by a high degree of geographical, vertical and horizontal differentiation requiring co-ordination activities or integrative mechanisms to prevent fragmentation. Traditionally, these are seen in formal institutions such as the administrative hierarchy, conferences of

*Länder* ministers, and the Federal Chamber. Federal and state parliaments as well as local councils and the respective political party organizations complement the system by providing a parallel political structure. In fact, the major political parties, which since 1989 have expanded into East Germany or merged with their extant nominal 'sister parties', are one of the informal basic integrating forces across this vertical and territorial differentiation.

## THE CIVIL SERVICE

Another integrating force is the professional civil service, in particular the predominantly juridically trained higher civil service. Although there is no centre in Germany for educating the administrative elite comparable to the Ecole Nationale d'Administration (ENA) in France or the University of Oxford in Britain, law training in the universities is regulated by federal legislation standardizing training. The curriculum for judges, state attorneys, barristers and solicitors, as well as for the higher civil service, is the same throughout the entire university system, thus providing a high degree of uniformity of content and, it might be assumed, a common basic understanding of the role of all law professions and higher officials in all branches of government and on all levels of the administrative system. Other professional groups besides the jurists: engineers, physicians, scientists, or economists, are a minority in the general administration and instead cluster in special authorities. Combined they comprise not more than 20–30 per cent of the higher civil service in the federal and *Länder* ministries. Despite a gradual expansion of the number of economists in the federal ministries since the mid-1960s to roughly 15 per cent in the two top positions and an increase in mixed external and internal career elements (Derlien 1990b), there may still be justification in speaking of a monopoly of jurists and the predominance of closed internal careers when looking at the total administrative system.

The traditional concept of a professional career civil service was revived by Article 33, Section 5, of the 1949 federal constitution, which declared that the civil service should be ruled by its 'traditional principles'. This, according to the reaffirmed jurisdiction of the constitutional court, implies the principles that were valid in 1919 and even in 1873. After 1949, during the second republic, there was only one attempt, between 1969 and 1973, to reform the structure of the civil service.

**Career and Status Groups**

There are four categories of civil servants corresponding to the hierarchy of educational institutions and certificates attained. The university-trained higher civil service (400,000) amounts to 18 per cent and is the most characteristic of the personnel structure of federal (34 per cent) and *Länder* administrations (55 per cent) – in the latter case because of their control of cultural affairs, and thus the (university) teachers constitute an important share of *Länder* administration.

One of the aims of the 1969 civil service reform commission was to abolish the distinction between civil servants proper, whose privilege is the production and execution of authoritative state acts and who must not go on strike, and the other so-called status groups of public employees and labourers. Their terms of employment are regulated not by (federal) law, as is the case for civil servants on all levels of government, but are negotiated through normal labour relations. Public service strikes, though, are extremely rare (1973, 1992). To abolish the distinction between these three status groups and the resulting duality of the public service, the constitution would have to be changed, but the required two-thirds majority is unlikely to be available, for the Christian Democrat opposition in the *Bundestag* and the Federal Chamber in 1973 supported objections from the German civil service association (*Deutscher Beamtenbund*). Therefore, the roughly 1.8 million civil servants of federal, *Länder* and local governments enjoy a status different from the 1.7 million public employees predominantly engaged in clerical jobs and the health service, and the 1 million labourers most frequently found in local administration and federal railways.

In addition to the structural differentiation depicted above, there is, thus, a high degree of social differentiation in the administrative system. University training in law received by the higher civil service and the law-focused administrative college training received by the career stratum below produce generalist civil servants with common professional values and skills. It might, however, be questioned whether the public service in its entirety is still held together by a strong *esprit de corps* as it allegedly was in pre-democratic times; nor is it any longer an estate (*Berufsstand*) as it was perceived in Max Weber's days.

## Integrating the East German State Functionaries

Unlike this persistence of the traditional civil service in the West after the catastrophe of the Nazi regime, in East Germany the institution of the civil service was abandoned after 1945 in a revolutionary move and was replaced by a uniform system of labour relations, which no longer differentiated between public functionaries, including cadres of the communist party, and 'peasants and labourers'. The notion of the impartial execution of office, like the overarching concept of *Rechtsstaat*, was alien to the communist system, while loyalty to the party and explicit partisanship for the cause of 'the masses' was the ultimate imperative. Thus, the problems of re-educating and incorporating some of those 1.8 million state functionaries into the Western system are tremendous.

In East Germany, knowledge of public law was of no importance, since there existed neither administrative courts nor a constitutional court. Blatant ideology and legal opportunism came to replace professional knowledge of law. Management skills were taught that helped to fit future functionaries into the existing authoritative state and party machinery which permeated economy and society. Thus, for the first time after a regime change in German history, professional competence turns out to be a core civil service problem, whereas in 1918 and 1945 political loyalty constituted the crucial weakness of the system.

Borrowing a category from Colin Campbell (1986) I have elsewhere (Derlien 1991b) described the situation in the GDR public service as 'politicized incompetence'. After undertaking further education courses, those parts of the East German public service whose jobs have not become superfluous will ultimately be transferred to civil service status. Although due to the changed character of public tasks functionaries in certain fields such as economic planning have been dismissed, the majority of the public service – as is the rule after regime changes in industrial societies – is functionally indispensable. However, the former *nomenklatura*, collaborators with the security police STASI, and those who have committed crimes against humanity were dismissed too. Vacancies in top positions resulting from this purge and positions newly created in the *Länder* administration are being filled by importing the administrative elite (and judges) from the Western part of the country.

## SIZE OF THE PUBLIC SECTOR

To continue this discussion to West Germany, as few figures are available for the East and the centrally controlled economy and society of the communist system is still in the process of transformation, there are two aggregate indicators of the size of the public sector.

First, there is the size of the public service. In 1986 16 per cent of the labour force were engaged in the public sector, not counting the armed forces. Of the roughly 4.7 million public servants 800,000 were part-time employees. In addition there are some 270,000 employed in corporations and enterprises that are under private law but publicly financed. According to this indicator the German public sector is comparable in size to that of the United States and Italy and considerably smaller than the 20 per cent or more in the Scandinavian countries, France and the United Kingdom (Hauschild 1991, p. 86).

Secondly, the public sector's share of GNP used to be about 45 per cent, but was increased to 49 per cent if unemployment subsidies (from a compulsory public insurance fund) are taken into account. However, since unification, the massive transfers into East Germany of DM 180 billion annually since 1991 have resulted in dramatically increasing public debts which at present would disqualify Germany from membership of the European Monetary Union.

**De-bureaucratization and Privatization**

Since Wagner's law of ever-expanding public budgets and Brecht's law of civil service growth in response to population density, the quantitative and qualitative development of public tasks and the costs incurred have been a political issue. The recent international neo-conservative trend to withdraw the state from society has been less spectacular in West Germany (König 1989) than in other countries. While deregulation basically consisted of a strategy to cancel a couple of thousand (outdated) administrative regulations (Ellwein 1989), attempts to curb public spending were less successful and tended to concentrate on the spiralling costs of the public health system and on certain social subsidies. The privatization policy that transferred entire agencies to private law status and sold them to the public, hoping that public goods would be provided by the market, was not a concerted effort of federal and state governments. Nevertheless, changing public agencies to private law status without giving up financial control was, or is being, undertaken with the federal postal service by splitting it into the profitable Telecom and Postbank services and running its traditional mail service at a deficit. Also, the federal railways, which are being merged with the ramshackle East German *Reichsbahn*, will be divided into a branch for operating the train service and one for providing the costly tracks; and the federal air control authority is to be put under private law status thus enabling the government to pay officials more generously than under the civil service pay scheme. Like contracting-out in local government, these measures are primarily, though not exclusively, taken for financial rather than ideological reasons. What tends to be completely overlooked is the effect on public control where mere mutations to private law corporations exempt business operations from (local) parliamentary scrutiny.

The basic reasons why deregulation and privatization policies, compared to other countries, are less than major issues on the political agenda are to be found in the constitutional principle of *Sozialstaat* that obliges the state to engage in (re)distributive policies and social regulations, or at least limits the possibilities of redrawing the boundaries of the state *vis à vis* civil society. Also, there is a broad consensus and a hidden grand coalition between the major parties, the Social Democrats and the Christian Democrats, with their strong labour wings (Lehmbruch 1992). Secondly, whenever the term 'privatization' has been used since 1990, everybody thinks of a completely different scale of privatization, unprecedented in the Western world: the dissolution and transformation of the East German state economy into private enterprises by the *Treuhand-Anstalt*. At the same time, any attempt to 'withdraw the state from society' in other policy areas is shattered by the requirements to intervene in East Germany with the entire arsenal of public policy instruments and resources.

## POLITICO-ADMINISTRATIVE RELATIONSHIPS

When dealing with the relationship between politics and administration one is immediately caught by the intricacies of political theory, constitutional traditions and orthodox administrative science views, which customarily treat the problem under consideration in the framework of the institutional politics–administration dichotomy.

In functional perspective, one faces the problems of political control over bureaucracy, of matching legitimate power with expertise, linking civil service neutrality to parochial politics, or ultimately relating efficiency to democracy.

The analysis of this relationship in the German case could, in principle, extend to the political environment of bureaucracy on federal as well as on state and local levels, for in an institutional sense the politics–administration relationship can be found on each of these tiers of the state. We shall, however, confine this description to the level of federal, i.e. national, government. After a brief outline of the formal constitutional mechanisms regulating the relationship of core political actors to the ministerial bureaucracy, less formal political aspects will be addressed.

### Powers of the *Bundestag*

Political control by the federal parliament over the bureaucracy is basically indirect through controlling the federal government, whose task it is in turn to control the ministerial bureaucracy. By electing the Chancellor and, if necessary, replacing him through a so-called constructive vote of non-confidence, as in 1982, the *Bundestag* first of all exerts its political power through personnel decisions. The other members of the political executive (and as a matter of course the civil servants) are not elected but appointed by the federal president on the suggestion of the Chancellor. Whereas ministers need not have a parliamentary mandate but usually are also MPs, parliamentary state secretaries (junior, non-cabinet ministers) have to be, and their term automatically expires with that of parliament or of their minister. Thus, formally the Chancellor has a high degree of appointment power, although actually this power is seriously limited under the conditions of a coalition government (Mayntz 1980) which puts the smaller partner in a veto position.

Because of the personal links between the executive and parliament in a system of party government, the dividing line between the two systems is rather that between the parliamentary opposition on the one hand and majority factions and the cabinet on the other. It is within his own faction and his party that the Chancellor must seek political consensus about the programme of his government and subsequent political support in its detailed execution. For, in a programmatic respect, the *Bundestag* is heavily involved owing to the fact that most programmes are legislated; at least they are indirectly legitimated through the federal budget and therefore depend on parliamentary budgetary power. Political responsibility is first of all that of the Chancellor to *Bundestag*; the ministers are formally only responsible to him. They are, though, also accountable to Parliament through answering questions, substantiating legislative proposals in their policy area and justifying budget claims.

About 400 bills are passed into law during the four-year legislative period. Most of these do not originate from the Parliament but in the executive branch of government and are drafted in the ministries. The *Bundestag* with its 662 members (since 1990) does not have the information-processing capacity to match the massive expertise of the federal bureaucracy. The scientific staff available since 1969 (Petermann 1990) and the personal assistant that each MP is entitled to have is far too small to engage successfully in policy development besides the management of constituency affairs. While the political agenda of the majority factions is largely identical with that of government as laid down in the voluminous coalition agreements, concepts of the major opposition factions tend to stem from party headquarters or those *Länder* governments which are under the control of the opposition in Bonn. Through party channels the opposition factions since the 1970s also instrumentalized *Länder* governments to block or to change federal legislation in the second chamber, the Federal Chamber, thus occasionally leading to 'divided government'.

The *Bundestag* has specialist standing committees which correspond to the departmental jurisdictions of the executive; here, personal expertise is accumulated over the years by individual members. Inquiry committees are constituted to uncover alleged political scandals in the executive, but tend to be inconsequential as they too are dominated by the majority. Enquête commissions, staffed by external experts, are established if there is a need, as recently in matters of technology assessment.

Overall, however, parliamentary political control is bound to remain selective because the 662 MPs and their staff are facing 25,000 bureaucrats in the ministries serving their ministers. But in judging the total control capacity one must not forget the other external control agents: the constitutional and administrative courts, the federal court of accounts, *Länder* governments, the media and 4000 interest groups organized on the federal level – actors who also form the political environment of the executive. In addition, according to the peculiar functional division of labour of German federalism, the federal government is only marginally involved in administrative routine matters typical of programme implementation at the *Länder* level. Federal government and individual ministries are basically occupied with drafting laws and issuing decrees and regulations for steering the implementation process. Nevertheless, although the ministries are responding frankly to informal opposition questions, all actors in Bonn agree, or even subjectively feel, that the opposition is informationally disadvantaged compared to the government factions.

Therefore, the question has to be asked about how the majority factions get along with the executive branch and how effectively they are exerting political control, albeit in reaction to executive policy initiatives. Owing to the fact that executive politicians are overwhelmingly faction members themselves or – to look at it the other way round – that 15 per cent of the government factions are co-opted by the Chancellor into executive positions, the information flow about policy matters is generally satisfactory. Nevertheless, because even within the ever-more-detailed coalition agreements conflicts regularly arise about policy details, consensus-building and daily political management tends to be hierarchical. Since 1966, when a grand coalition of the CDU and the SPD was formed, a system of informal co-ordinating circles of the coalition partners developed (Rudzio 1972), involving the Chancellor, key ministers and faction leaders. To the extent that the Chancellor and ministers are often also party leaders, they are ultimately in a position to impose their decisions on the factions; for the standing and the future political career of individual MPs strongly depends on being renominated by their parties.

The control problem, thus, shifts from Parliament as such to the coalition faction and again to the coalition leadership and ultimately arrives at the executive branch itself: do Chancellor, cabinet and individual ministers effectively control the ministerial bureaucracy?

## Bureaucrats and Politicians[1]

At the turn of the nineteenth century the tenured, professionally trained, appointed and salaried full-time civil servant who pursued a career to the top of the administrative hierarchy faced the elected, transitory amateur as his political master; after the introduction of equal suffrage the latter had often been brought up under working-class conditions. In the interim, both groups of politico-administrative actors have become assimilated, since politicians, as Max Weber observed, tended rather to 'live from politics than to live for politics'. Despite this professionalization of politicians, the career path of both elite groups remained quite distinct, with a predictable career and job security in the one case and more 'entrepreneurial', competitive, uncertain political careers and transitory hold on top positions in the case of politicians. To the extent that the notion of linkage rather than separation of powers is more apt, we notice that the actual threshold between politics and administration is located somewhere below the institutional borderline; the exact demarcation depends on the extent to which political criteria may be or actually are applied in staffing these positions, to what extent subjective role understanding is political rather than bureaucratic, and on the degree of civil servants' involvement in the policy process.

**Political Civil Servants**

After a government change, the only formal mechanism to streamline the federal higher civil service politically is temporary retirement of the officials at the very top of the hierarchy: state secretaries and division heads in the ministries as well as positions down to section heads in the foreign and intelligence services. Use of these instruments was made in particular during the only two fundamental government changes the Federal Republic experienced, in 1969 and 1982. In both cases roughly every second state secretary and every third division head in Bonn were temporarily retired (Derlien 1988). The cases of 1969 and 1982 demonstrate that the incoming governments carried on working with the majority of the administrative elite. Furthermore, most of the vacancies were staffed with candidates from within the ministries or experienced officials from *Länder* governments. At most, 10 per cent of the new appointments accepted by the civil service commission can be classified as outsiders.

In comparative perspective, the higher civil service in Bonn would take a middle position between the British and the US systems. While the first can be said to maximize permanency and expertise and takes political loyalty of the impartial civil service for granted, the US system of having political appointees with high intersectorial mobility is obviously to maximize political loyalty at the expense of expertise.

**Increasing Party-Politicization**

Another trend underlying formal civil service stability is increasing party-politicization (Mayntz and Derlien 1989). Although actively engaging in political parties is a civil right not withheld from the civil service, frequent membership of top civil servants in the governing parties could have a devastating effect on civil service morale and public trust in the impartiality of official conduct. Among the federal bureaucratic elite, party membership has spiralled from 28 per cent in 1970 to 36.7 (1972), 51.7 (1981) and 57.3 per cent (1987). Owing to temporary retirements in 1982–3, the dominant affiliation with the Social Democrats (1981: 30 per cent) was reversed and the majority of the civil service elite was affiliated with the Christian Democrats by 1987 (37.1 per cent). As there is a clear rank correlation of frequency of party membership (69 per cent of the state secretaries in 1987 were members of the governing coalition), non-party members and those with the wrong party book are demotivated as to their further advancement. Paradoxically, even those elite members who are engaged in the ruling political parties complain about increasing party interference in appointments (Mayntz and Derlien 1989, pp. 397ff).

There is, however, no performance indicator that the historically inherited system of matched expertise and loyalty is getting out of balance. On normative grounds, though, a prevalence of party membership over professional performance in appointments to elite positions would not merely be unconstitutional, but would also move the West German system dangerously close to that abolished in East Germany – with one decisive difference: in a competitive party system followers of all constitutional parties in principle have a chance to benefit from the spoils.

**Political Aspects of Role Understanding**

In continuing the line of reasoning about balancing expertise and loyalty with increased party-politicization, it is interesting to learn to what extent role understanding of the administrative elite in Bonn is technocratic or political. Although the majority of the administrative elite in 1987 as well as seventeen years earlier perceived their role as distinct from that of politicians (Mayntz and Derlien 1989, pp. 394f.), the majority today like the inevitable political aspects of their job very much (78.5 per cent), as opposed to only 45.2 in 1970 (Mayntz and Derlien 1989, p. 394). Only one out of four parliamentary politicians, including those of the majority factions, subscribes to this role understanding. In 1987 there was actually no difference between jurists and economists as to the positive assessment of the political side of their job. But relatively more jurists have come to enjoy the political nature of their job since 1970 than economists, who in the majority never had reservations. This political role understanding coincides with a low level of technocratic thinking (Aberbach *et al.* 1990) and a very modest degree of state-authoritarianism: a combination of etatist and elitist attitudes. In both respects, jurists take a middle position when compared to elite members with a different training background.

Not only do higher civil servants accept the political rules of the game they are involved in, they also ascribe more authority and accountability to executive politicians than they would claim for themselves (Mayntz and Derlien 1989, p. 395). Furthermore, working against the political programme of a new government is strongly rejected by 80 per cent and accepted by only 8 per cent. If civil servants believed that the government's programme contained incorrect or unsuitable points, 82 per cent would first try to talk to their superiors and then, nevertheless, would execute the orders. Almost one-third (27 per cent), though, would rather leave active service (15 per cent) or ask for transfer to another post (12 per cent) instead of carrying out orders they could not accept on professional grounds (Derlien *et al.* 1988, p. 26f.).

Consistent with insisting on their professional judgement, remonstrating and, if necessary, taking personal consequences is the fact that the administrative elite reject in their self-assessment the role of party politician or spokesperson of organized interests, but most strongly accept the roles of expert problem-solver, initiator of new projects and executor of politically set goals (Derlien *et al.* 1988, p. 14). These indicators suggest that, on the level of subjective role understanding, expertise as the most distinct role characteristic has not suffered from party-politicization. The latter may have contributed to the widespread political loyalty of the federal bureaucracy and acceptance of the political context they are operating in.

Thus again we observe a mechanism integrating various subsystems: this time the mechanism could be seen in the common party-political affiliation of bureaucrats and ruling politicians. Further, owing to a large share of juridically trained politicians, both elites have in common a strong affinity to the concept of the state as a reference point. Thus, at least the subjective role understanding of bureaucrats is shaped in such a way as to be compatible with that of their political masters.

# INTERNAL DYNAMICS OF THE MINISTERIAL BUREAUCRACY

To understand more fully why role understanding is rather political and why personnel policy is party-politicized, we must inspect the structure and the functioning of the machinery of government in more detail. For, despite ideologically biased confirmations to the contrary, the ministerial bureaucracy cannot function in the impartial and neutral way that field offices are obliged to do in application of the law; it is an active player in politics and necessarily functionally politicized (Mayntz and Derlien 1989).

### Structure of the Ministerial Bureaucracy

The elements of the executive branch can be derived from Article 65 of the federal constitution that combines three principles: (a) the *Chancellor principle* comprises the authority to decide on fundamental policy matters. Though seldom explicitly applied under conditions of coalition government, it was emphasized, for instance, in 1987 when Kohl decided against the modernization of short-range nuclear weapons. Further, the Chancellor principle entails organizational decisions such as the demarcation of departmental boundaries and his power of appointment. (b) the *departmental principle* states that individual ministers are responsible for running their departments; this implies the right to prepare programmes and to execute government decisions affecting their jurisdiction, but it also extends to personnel decisions.[2] (c) the *cabinet principle* states that Chancellor and ministers decide as a collegial body on important matters, in particular government bills submitted to the legislative branch. In helping to apply these principles ministers are supported by their departments, and the Chancellor as well as the cabinet principles are supported by the Chancellor's office, which functions both as a cabinet and as a staff for the head of government. The role of the Chancellor's office will be touched upon when I turn to discussing the co-ordination problem.

In 1992, besides the Chancellor's office there existed eighteen federal ministries. Variations in the number of ministries basically depends on political exigencies to accommodate party interests and to co-opt forces within the parties of the government coalition; for instance, after 1990 some (three) East Germans had to be included; or some female ministers or powerful regional party leaders had to be incorporated. In particular, the soft policy area of 'health, family, females, youth and senior citizens' (in a Bonn-mot: 'young healthy family') is the cake that can easily be divided, as recently, among three women ('three-maiden-ministry'). Consequently, the size of the ministries varies considerably between Defence with some 5000 officials, Finance with 1500, and Youth and Women with 200; the Chancellor's office employs some 500 people, among these 150 senior civil servants.

The ministries are all nevertheless structured according to the same principles laid down in the procedural code of the ministries. The basic organizational unit is the section; six sections are needed to form a division or, if necessary, to split a division into subdivisions. At the top of the administrative hierarchy stands the state secretary or – since the 1970s – in some ministries two state secretaries. They are, like the division heads, political civil servants as outlined above. Thus, there is a hierarchy of three echelons above the ministerial sections, and the control span comprises seldom more than six units. Deviations from this uniformity of structure occur occasionally as a result of personnel policy: 'Organization is the whore of personnel' would be a practitioner's comment.

## Staff Units

Unlike the French ministries with their cabinets, German ministries have no political staffs. The traditional view is that the ministry as such is the minister's staff. The staff units visible on organization charts are technical staffs: personal assistants to state secretaries and ministers (Wagener and Rückwart 1982), typists in the minister's bureau, a press spokesman and cabinet secretary to prepare the minister for all cabinet affairs. Indicatively, most of these functions are staffed with younger civil servants, who pursue an administrative career. Nevertheless, at the end of the 1960s, with increased emphasis on policy planning and analysis, most ministries created divisions for principal policy matters and policy analysis which actually serve staff functions. Their role in the department varies between research and documentation functions on the one and, if backed by a minister, priority setting on the other hand. In the latter case they are, however, likely to encounter conflicts with the regular line units (Mayntz and Scharpf 1975).

## FUNCTIONING

### Departmental Management

Managing a department with respect to organizing, staffing, budgeting and housekeeping is functionally differentiated and administratively prepared in the so-called central division of each department. In preparing the departmental budget proposal to the finance ministry or when personnel decisions are made, this central division interacts with the policy divisions in a matrix-like pattern. The same pattern can be found in interdepartmental relations on the level of government where certain ministries are functionally specialized to co-ordinate budgeting (Finance) or to deal with civil service principles (Interior) as their professional policy field. Of course, there are differences between ministers with respect to their management capabilities and interests, but in general the initiatives originate in the department and proposals are elaborated in close contact with the top civil servant, before a minister is informed or gets involved. It is, one could say, the privilege of the permanent state secretary, as opposed to the parliamentary secretary of state or the minister himself, to control management decisions and the maintenance of administrative resources. Only to the extent that these questions have an important bearing on substantive policy matters, is the minister asked for a decision or takes an active stand on them. Undoubtedly though, politicians are closely concerned with the appointment of their closest collaborators, the top administrators.

### Policy Development

A good deal of what a ministry does is – apart from some policy implementation and control of the implementation process – *devising new substantive policies and programmes*, which often have to pass cabinet and are legislated. Regardless of whether these new policies are innovative, or are incremental or pre-programmed by previous decisions, the initiative to deal with the problem, defining it, and devising (alternative) ways to its solution often originate in the operative sections at the bottom of the ministerial hierarchy. Of course, to a certain degree the decision-making process is fuelled by problems and policy proposals from party and election programmes; but already government declarations are regularly a *mixtum compositum* of political initiatives and bureaucratic suggestions (Böhret 1979). In any case, central political initiatives as well as decentralized bureaucratic proposals have to be mediated into the operating units and on to the political layer, respectively. Gearing both sides to one another is basically the function of the two top administrative levels in the hierarchy. For top civil servants this means either operationalizing policy goals, to specify the (basically normative) decision premises, and to anticipate constraints as well as political feasibility, or to filter decentralized initiatives through perceived or anticipated decision premises of the minister. Even routine matters, which normally would not involve the minister but be decided by officials, have to be evaluated with respect to potential political implications.

## Communication Patterns and Conflict Resolution

Matching political preferences and administrative professional and procedural expertise (*Fachwissen* and *Dienstwissen*, to use Weber's distinction) requires vertical communication. Contrary to the classical mechanistic model of hierarchical top-down decision-making and bottom-up reporting, the process of adjusting normative and factual decision premises is a dynamic, iterative process (Mayntz and Scharpf 1975, p. 100). In addition, it is highly selective, as the intensity of vertical communication varies with the stage in the process and with issue salience. Whereas entire divisions in a ministry may work on autopilot, there are issues of particular political moment, for which the minister is held accountable, with which he identifies, and in which he wishes to become renowned as a competent policy-maker. This means that the intensity of communication between division heads and the minister will increase.

Also, the arena of policy-making changes as we move up the hierarchy. Whereas the operative units basically communicate with sections in the same and other departments or with subordinate authorities to exchange information, top administrators are more likely to be engaged in parliamentary or cabinet committees (often accompanied by section heads to assist them) or – depending on the policy style of the government or the respective minister – may occasionally appear in public. So to an even greater extent, of course, does the politician. A German executive politician frequently spends only one-third of his working hours in his department. His function is predominantly to represent and 'sell' departmental policy in order to reach a consensus and to secure party support as his most important political resource.

Not only are top civil servants more involved in internal vertical communication, but the frequency of external contacts with other ministries, including the office of the head of government, with parliamentary bodies, interest-group representatives and press relations increases the higher the rank of a civil servant (Aberbach *et al.* 1981, pp. 209ff.).

This is so because top civil servants are involved in resolving conflicts which are engendered in lower level internal and external horizontal communications. The mechanism that shifts controversial matters up the hierarchy, which is well known from the process of settling budgetary disputes, also shifts power upward. To this extent, decision patterns follow the management-by-exception model. The typical form of conflict resolution, bargaining, implies changing the political preference structure; this power-shift mechanism thus serves to control politically lower-level co-ordination and transports consensus-building on to hierarchical levels. These levels are normally more informed about the politician's willingness and limitations to compromise, and are better legitimized to bargain.

Only the most essential matters, then, are referred to the minister for decision, whereas issues of minor political importance are accomplished by top administrators. This function of filtering the vertical flow of information presupposes that top administrators have developed the sensitivity to recognize what might be of political importance and should be reported to the political top.

**Policy Analysis and Planning**

After the government change of 1982 the term 'planning' was eradicated from the organization charts, because it was associated with the former Social Democrat Chancellors Brandt and Schmidt, and in particular Brandt's policy of internal reforms. In fact, a lot of devices discussed in policy science developed since the mid-1960s and were applied during Brandt's Chancellorship to modernize or, as I prefer to say, to formally rationalize the decision-making process. Medium-range financial planning was institutionalized in 1967 but never developed to the stage of integrated budgeting as in other countries; also, instead of determining the annual budget proposals it is rather derived from and actualized on the basis of the annual budget. In a number of policy areas forcasting is regularly practised, being most firmly established in economic policy and in the social insurance system regulated by the Ministry of Labor and Social Affairs. Cost-benefit analysis (seldom practised) and ex-post policy evaluation are obligatory since 1969 before important budgetary decisions are taken and where the *Bundestag* requested follow-up reports on the effects of important legislations (Derlien 1990a). The two-track system of budgeting and policy-making, as well as a lack of interest by the protagonists of the budgetary cycle, have left these elements rather unrelated to one another. Nevertheless, individual ministries have created considerable capacity for policy analysis and have located specialists in what was until 1982 frequently called the planning division.

Most of the research activities involved are, however, done outside the department, either in federal agencies or through commissioned research (Wollmann 1989). Further, the ministries make use of some 350 advisory committees; their utility varies between an alibi function – to symbolize government activity although one wants to postpone decisions – interest representation, and genuine presentation of knowledge not readily available in the departments. As all the interactions involved in policy analysis and formulation are basically orchestrated by the ministerial sections, it would add little to the description given so far to employ the concept of policy community or network.

## Policy Co-ordination

Since many policy initiatives originate in the ministries, co-ordination within and between departments is an essential prerequisite of comprehensive policies. As a rule, sections and divisions follow the principle of horizontal self-co-ordination laid down in the government manual. Every section can ask for participation, and as hardly any substantive issue is (or can be) kept secret in Bonn, this works quite well, notwithstanding incidents of 'negative co-ordination' (Scharpf 1972) in one case or another. Important matters involve politicians at an early stage of the decision process anyway; thus, in drafting the voluminous unification treaty in 1990, once the principal decision had been taken to expend Western law to East Germany, instead of negotiating every detail, the only thing for the departments to do was to enumerate the body of legislation to be transferred and to determine cases where temporal exceptions had to be made. Management of the process lay within the Ministry of Interior with the minister as chief negotiator (Derlien, 1993). Similarly, the co-ordination of German EC policy, although it involves a number of interdepartmental committees, is basically a routine affair, and lateral contacts between ministries in Bonn and general directorates in Brussels are frequent without apparently impairing the supremacy of politics (Derlien, 1979).

One important reason why horizontal self-co-ordination (including intermediate briefing of the minister and conflict-resolution by higher echelons) is working quite satisfactorily is that really important matters, such as bills and regulations, have to pass cabinet. This means that they also have to be reviewed by the Chancellor's office, particularly when they are part of declared government policy. As the departmental specialists in the Chancellor's office know anyway what their colleagues in the departments are doing, they can intervene at an early stage in programme development (Kaiser 1990); and as the officials in the department want to make sure that their drafts will pass cabinet or at least get on the agenda, they will keep the specialists in the Chancellor's office informed and make sure that all interdepartmental conflicts are resolved. Only in exceptional circumstances do controversial matters reach cabinet. In sum, despite the reform attempts between 1969 and 1975, the ministerial bureaucracy has not experienced spectacular changes but – some innovations notwithstanding – is still working in a rather traditional style. There is, though, a large practical and scholarly consensus that it is reliable, technically efficient and politically sensitive. Alleged deficits in policy design and policy innovation to a large extent have rather to be attributed to the various external constraints identified twenty years ago (Mayntz and Scharpf 1975) or to a lack of political guidance and initiative.

## CIVIL SOCIETY AND PUBLIC ADMINISTRATION

Although the state–society dichotomy of the authoritarian nineteenth-century state philosophy no longer applies to the second German republic, it might be descriptively useful to take this dichotomy as a starting point for reflecting on the mediation between citizens and those in political power, which in everyday life is experienced as administration (Max Weber). Except in the purely legal sense that citizens can go to the courts to sue a city, a *Land* or the Federal Republic as a juridical person, 'the state' and 'public administration' are abstractions and as little homogeneous actors as is 'civil society'. Empirically, there are merely interactions, communications and resource flows between individuals and collective actors playing roles that are defined as public or private. This is not to suggest that everything dissolves into more or less shapeless 'networks', for as within the politico-administrative system, these interactions, communications and resource flows are to a certain extent formally defined by duties and rights or, more generally, by institutionalized role expectations. Certainly, there are informal aspects of these exchange relationships, maybe even aspects that are more important in terms of power than those laid down in formal rules of constitutional and administrative law. However, the official must conform to the law that gives the citizen subjective public rights, just as officials can refer to and rely on their authority derived from public law (and ultimately 'the state's' monopoly of physical power to enforce the law). Therefore, when in what follows collective categories are descriptively employed, this is merely a technical device to reduce empirical complexity. Nevertheless, the state–society dichotomy and its conceptual correlates played an important role in German history as part of ideology and subjective role understanding of public servants as well as of the citizens.

### The Concept of *Rechtsstaat*

Essential for the modern understanding of state–society and official–client relationships is the legal differentiation between public and private spheres of life in the course of the nineteenth century, depersonalizing and limiting at the same time the power of the monarch and his servants, the bureaucrats. Further, since constitutionalism (1848) and equal suffrage (1919), representation and parliamentary procedure were the conditions under which, in Weber's terms, formal-rational domination was executed. This amounted at least to what can be called the 'rule of law' (*Gesetzesstaat*), in which public–private relations are governed by the law and nothing else. The modern notion of *Rechtsstaat* in addition encompasses the elements of independent juridical review of administrative decisions in special courts and the notion of immediately binding human rights, as well as a constitutional court to which alleged violation of basic constitutional rights can be referred. Obviously, this understanding of *Rechtsstaat* was deeply influenced by the historical experience of state practice under Nazi totalitarianism and has recently regained its practical significance since the East Germans joined the federal republic. For the GDR, contrary to official declamations of a 'socialist *Rechtsstaat*' was a blatant terror regime under which the individual was totally subject to an absolute one-party rule and a politically instrumentalized bureaucracy and judiciary. What East Germans now experience is not just freedom from arbitrary state intervention, but also the possibility of appealing to truly independent courts. The current number of roughly 80,000 administrative court appeals annually might grow considerably, once this institution has become more familiar in the eastern part of the country.

In the 1970s further legal safeguards were developed. Data-protection laws are to secure 'informational self-determination', and some of the *Länder* have institutionalized the Ombudsman in addition to traditional petition rights to parliaments. Until 1990 the federal parliament was confronted with some 5000 petitions per year. Also, there is a government commissioner for data protection and a parliamentary ombudsman for complaints by members of the armed forces.

## Direct Political Participation

Although the Federal Republic and her *Länder* are based on the principle of representative democracy limiting citizen participation to periodic elections, some of the old and new *Länder* in addition are familiar with mechanisms of direct participation in law-making: either the right to initiate laws or to decide about alternative bills. In local self-government, where the feedback between citizens and politicians may be less complicated, at least outside metropolitan areas, direct participation is traditionally possible in the southern part of the country.

In addition, since the 1970s *Bürger Initiatives* have been developed to put pressure on local governments and to have a say in devising infrastructural projects and in local planning matters in general. In development and urban planning, hearing procedures have been legally institutionalized since 1963, but limited to those directly affected by the suggested measures. With the rise of concerns about the state of the natural environment, this Bürger Initiative movement – along with other 'new social movements' – partly merged with environmentalist associations and ultimately the Green Party in the 1980s.

This was a development that originated in increasing criticism from the late 1960s of the traditional three-party system as the basic mechanism to mediate the political will of the citizen to parliaments and political executives. Ideologically, these movements also fancy the concept of direct democracy and cultivate the image of an extra-parliamentary opposition to the 'established political forces'. In the 1990s it goes along with the erosion of the traditional social basis of political parties (in particular the Social Democrats) and increasing scepticism about the conduct of politicians, in particular in granting themselves monetary rewards and in party-politicizing personnel decisions wherever they have any influence, be it in public broadcast corporations or in public administration. Ultimately, however, direct participation is legally limited to legislative matters on all three tiers of government, whereas the pure execution of (legislated) programmes must not be affected by these interventions.

## Official–Client Relationships

During the 1970s and 1980s in particular local governments tried to improve what is called in Germany *Bürgernähe*: an encompassing notion of having less geographical, political and social distance between the authorities and the citizen. Geographical distance became an issue during territorial local government reforms, but has lost its salience owing to improved means of communication (motor cars, telephone, banking system). As to political distance, apart from the *Bürger Initiatives*, most cities and larger rural communes allow for internal political decentralization by transferring to a lower level competencies in matters that solely affect specific neighbourhoods. What must be added here is the problem of the social distance in official–client relationships. Research over the last two decades has revealed several aspects. First, most citizens rarely have personal contact with public offices. Frequency varies with one's circumstances; the most frequent instances are when passports expire or a new car has to be registered. Of course, if we include contacts with public services like school, hospitals, railways or the post office the picture changes radically, but these contacts are normally not perceived as 'genuine' administrative contacts, that is, those involving paperwork and situations of dependency.

Secondly, certain social groups such as elderly people, social subsidy recipients or unemployed people are facing this dependency and have to engage in frequent interaction. Thirdly, the perception of social distance is a function of personal competence in administrative matters and basic positive or negative attitudes towards 'bureaucracy' or 'the state'. Thus, there is the helpless subject (*Untertan*) or the competent system critic (or the passionate voluntary bureaucrat, and so on). Also, it was shown that the conduct of officials is not impersonal in that it remains unaffected by the image one has of a client.

Altogether, it might be said, in particular in contrast to the authoritarian behaviour of former East German officials of all sorts, that administrators (and police officers) are very conscious of what is expected of them today and try to help – instead of rule over – subjects. Those exposed to direct client contacts often undergo special training; written communication tends to be formulated in a way that at least the average educated citizen can understand; cities, finance ministries and programme managers in general distribute a lot of brochures to help citizens find their way through offices and paragraphs. Also, in social security affairs the principle of active advice is institutionalized to find the optimal solution to a personal problem. In long-term retrospect, there may be justification in maintaining that bureaucrats have become much less reactive to demands and more responsive to public expectations. After all, every sixth person in the labour force is a public servant himself in need of an occasional licence plate, care for a grandmother, and so on. Nevertheless, public opinion in general tends to be critical about official–client relationships, in particular if the survey uses collective catchwords such as 'the bureaucracy' and does not ask for personal experience in specific contacts.

Under the heading of 'co-operative public action' a related phenomenon came to be addressed by administrative scientists in the 1980s: the interaction between public authorities and private economic enterprises. In particular in the implementation of environmental regulations aimed at reducing pollution, instead of imposing sanctions on polluters or closing down plants authorities have turned to co-operative strategies to find long-term solutions to the problem, to secure employment and to help the firms. However, the informal bargaining processes involved are of a two-edged nature because public offices can well come under corporate and political pressure to compromise where the law would require stricter solutions. And it is frequently in such cases that Bürger Initiatives act as watchdogs of the public interest.

## Corporatism and Administration

Civil society is not just the individual citizen or the private firm, but also associations of these to exert collective influence on policy-making. There are some 4000 federal associations officially recognized in Bonn, among these the powerful traditional pressure groups, such as trade unions and employer organizations, but also the tax-payers' association, the automobile clubs, social subsidy recipients and single parents. This interest group pluralism first of all operates *vis à vis* Parliament and ministerial bureaucracy in formal hearing procedures. Also, interest group functionaries work in the 350 permanent advisory bodies to the Bonn ministries. MPs, furthermore, are often members or officials of interest groups; thus about every second federal MP is a member of a civil service or a trade union. Naturally, associations have formed on the *Länder* level, too.

Corporatism has a long tradition in Germany, and many a public task was originally carried out by societal associations. Thus, even after putting them under state control in the nineteenth-century, the most important social insurance systems (health, accident, pension) are jointly run (and financed) by unionists and employer organizations in self-governing public law corporations under state supervision. And in the social affairs and labour courts, respective representatives are regularly on the bench. Often, the state virtually inspired the formation of associations in order to cope with problems. This intertwining is at the heart of the second typically German constitutional principle, that of *Sozialstaat*. Further, many professional groups are organized in public law corporations; in Bavaria, even the farmers' association is a public law corporation. That these institutions do not merely administer public tasks, for example, in further education for their clientele or in watching over professional conduct, but also tend to represent their interest, is a matter of course; and that governments employ them to support their policies may not be a surprise or such a new phenomenon as the literature on neo-corporatism suggests. But admittedly, the degree of interest-group centralization and the intensity of negotiations with government was remarkable in economic policy-making in the early 1970s starting from 1967, and in the second 'concerted action' on health cost control in the 1980s (Lehmbruch 1988).

Again, in the aftermath of the destruction of self-organizing civil society under totalitarian East German rule, it becomes evident how essential these corporations are (Anheier and Seibel 1990), in particular where their members act on a honorary basis, for example, in providing welfare assistance (Red Cross, Church organizations).

# CONCLUSIONS: A SPECIFIC ADMINISTRATIVE CULTURE?

Most of the theoretically significant traits of the German administrative system can be found in other countries, too. In all Western democracies, administration is bound by law. Nevertheless, one peculiar German feature is frequently seen in the legalism of the administrative culture. Although this need not mean much to the citizen, when political controls break down, as was the case under the Nazis, role understanding (and the kind of decision-making behaviour) might be different in Germany than in the UK or the US. The existence of administrative courts and the predominantly juridical training are leaving their imprint, although probably not as strongly as in France or Italy. Judging from the number of political issues which are referred to the constitutional court, it might well be the case that the legalist mode of thinking is more peculiar to politicians than it is to civil servants.

Probably more distinctive is the historical development of the relationship between politics and administration in Germany. Contrary to the Anglo-Saxon world, in Germany bureaucracy preceded democracy. This has had a lasting impact on the importance attributed to expertise and the low degree of intersectorial mobility from politics into administrative positions. Also, only the public offices at the apex are elective or staffed with appointed executive politicians. Finally, aspects of parliament–executive relationships display the 'strong state tradition', that is, the tradition of a strong bureaucracy (and military); for instance, the lack of comprehensive access of parliamentary investigation commissions to government records. Also, the absence of a Freedom of Information Act could be viewed from this perspective.

Thirdly, there is a relative resistance to fashionable ideas about reforming the public sector. Neither was PPBS with its derivatives adopted – the Germans settled for middle-range fiscal planning – nor has the civil service experienced a shake-up in recent years. Also privatization, as was mentioned above, did not become so important as it had in other countries. This is partly due to the construction of a federal system that leaves room for variation and heightens the barriers of the required political reform consensus; the more so as certain measures (privatizing postal and rail services, and a unitary civil service code) would require a two-thirds majority in the *Bundestag* and the Federal Chamber.

Fourthly, closely connected with and resulting from these elements of the administrative culture is the absence of bureaucrat-bashing by politicians. On the contrary, leading politicians of all parties have repeatedly appreciated the excellent work of the federal bureaucracy in drafting the unification treaty with East Germany and the service that 25,000 Western bureaucrats are presently doing in the East. This positive attitude among the political elite does not, of course, exclude ideologically based criticism of 'the state apparatus' and 'bureaucracy' among the bureaucratized intelligentsia in the universities.

Finally, party-politicizing the personnel policy of public administration is certainly not a new phenomenon in Germany, but the extent to which it has been done during the last two decades, and the frankness with which it is admitted, is new. On the one hand, the blame for this is put on the politicians; on the other hand, it might be asked if this tendency, together with the academization and professionalization of politicians, their frequent legal training and civil service background, does not contribute to a further bureaucratization of politics.

## NOTES

1. Parts of this paragraph are from Derlien (1987 and 1991).
2. Unless power of appointment is delegated to them, it is the federal president who ultimately appoints the political executive, including the Chancellor and the top civil servants in a formal act, based on the suggestions of the Chancellor (appointment of ministers and parliamentary state secretaries) or the respective ministers (parliamentary state secretary and civil servants) and cabinet consensus in the case of top civil servants.

## REFERENCES

Many of the facts and judgements contained in this article can be found elsewhere in more extensive descriptions; see, for instance:

Ellwein, T. and J. J. Hesse (1987), *Das Regierungssystem der Bundesrepublik Deutschland* (Opladen: Westdeutscher Verlag).
Johnson, N. (1973), *Government in the Federal Republic of Germany* (Oxford: Pergamon Press).
König, K., H. J. von Oertzen and F. Wagener (1983), *Public Administration in the Federal Republic of Germany* (Antwerp: Kluwer-Deventer).
Mayntz, R. (1978), *Soziologie der öffentlichen Verwaltung* (Heidelberg: Decker & Müller).
Rudzio, W. (1991), *Das politische System der Bundesrepublik Deutschland*, 3rd edn (Opladen: Leske und Budrich).
Siedentopf, H. (1988), 'Western Germany', in D. C. Rowat (ed.), *Public Administration in Developed Democracies: A Comparative Study* (New York and Basel: Marcel Dekker), pp. 315–38.

### References Cited in the Text

Aberbach, J. D., R. D. Putnam and B. A. Rockman (1981), *Bureaucrats and Politicians in Western Democracies* (Cambridge, Mass.: Harvard University Press).
Aberbach, J. D., H.-U. Derlien, R. Mayntz, and B. A. Rockman (1990a), 'American and West German Federal Executives: Technocratic and Political Attitudes', *International Social Science Journal*, 123, 3–18.
Abromeit, H. (1992), *Der verkappte Einheitsstaat* (Opladen: Leske & Budrich).
Anheier, H. K. and W. Seibel (eds) (1990), *The Third Sector: Comparative Studies of Nonprofit Organizations* (Berlin and New York: De Gruyter).
Böhret, C. (1979), 'Politische Vorgaben für ziel- und ergebnisorientiertes Verwaltungshandeln aus Regierungserklärungen?', *Schriften der Bundesakademie für öffentliche Verwaltung*, Sonderheft 4, 61–74.
Campbell, C. (1986), *Managing the Presidency: Carter, Reagan, and the Search for Executive Harmony* (Pittsburgh, Pa.: University of Pittsburgh Press).
Derlien, H.-U. (1987), 'Public Managers and Politics', in K. Eliassen and J. Kooiman (eds), *Managing Public Organizations* (Beverly Hills, Cal., and London: Sage), pp. 129–41.
Derlien, H.-U. (1988), 'Repercussions of Government Change on the Career Civil Service in West Germany: the Cases of 1969 and 1982', *Governance*, 1, 50–78.
Derlien, H.-U. (1990a), 'Genesis and Structure of Evaluation Efforts in Comparative Perspective', in R. Rist (ed.), *Program Evaluation and the Management of Government* (New Brunswick, N.J., and London: Transaction Publishers), pp. 147–76.
Derlien, H.-U. (1990b), 'Continuity and Change in the West German Federal Executive Elite, 1949–1984', *European Journal of Political Research*, 18, 349–72.
Derlien, H.-U. (1991a), *The Horizontal and Vertical Coordination of German EC Policy* (Finland: Hallinnon Tutkimus), pp. 3–10.
Derlien, H.-U. (1991b), 'Historical Legacy and Recent Developments of the German Higher Civil Service', *International Review of Administrative Sciences*, 57, 385–401.

Derlien, H.-U. (1993), 'German Unification and Bureaucratic Transformation', *International Political Science Review*, 14, 319–34.

Derlien, H.-U. et al. (1988), *CES II. Einstellungen der politisch-administrativen Elite des Bundes 1987* (Bamberg: Verwaltungswissenschaftliche Beiträge Nr. 25).

Ellwein, T. (1989), *Verwaltung und Verwaltungsvorschriften Notwendigkeit und Chance der Vorschriftenvereinfachung* (Opladen: Westdeutscher Verlag).

Hauschild, C. (1991), 'Die Modernisierung des öffentlichen Dienstes im internationalen Vergleich', *Verwaltungsarchiv*, 82, 81–109.

Kaiser, R. (1990), *Aspects of Managing the Centre of Government* (Paris: OECD Occasional Papers).

König, K. (1989), *Kritik öffentlicher Aufgaben* (Baden-Baden: Nomos).

Lehmbruch, G. (1988), 'Der Neokorporatismus der Bundesrepublik im internationalen Vergleich und die "Konzertierte Aktion im Gesundheitswesen"', in G. Gäfgen (ed.), *Neokorporatismus im Gesundheitswesen* (Baden-Baden: Nomos), pp. 11–32.

Lehmbruch, G. (1992), 'The Institutional Framework of Regulatory Change in West Germany', in K. Dyson (ed.), *The Politics of Regulation in Germany* (London: Dartmouth Publishers).

Mayntz, R. (1980), 'Executive Leadership in Germany: Dispersion of Power or "Kanzlerdemokratie"?', in R. Rose and E. Suleiman (eds), *Presidents and Prime Ministers* (Washington D.C.: American Enterprise Institute), pp. 139–70.

Mayntz, R. and H.-U. Derlien (1989), 'Party Patronage and Politicization of the West German Administrative Elite, 1970–1987: Towards Hybridization?', *Governance*, 2, 384–404.

Mayntz, R. and F. W. Scharpf (1975), *Policymaking in the German Federal Executive* (Amsterdam: Elsevier).

Petermann, T. (ed.) (1990), *Das wohlberatene Parlament: Orte und Prozesse der Politikberatung* (Berlin: Edition Sigma).

Rudzio, W. (1972), 'Die Regierung der informellen Gremien', *Sozialwissenschaftliches Jahrbuch für Politik*, pp. 339–67.

Scharpf, F. W. (1972), 'Komplexität als Schranke der politischen Planung', *Politische Vierteljahresschrift*, Sonderheft 4, 168–92.

Scharpf, F. W. (1991), 'Entwicklungslinien des bundesdeutschen Föderalismus', in B. Blanke and H. Wollmann (eds), *Die alte Bundesrepublik* (Opladen: Westdeutscher Verlag), pp. 146–59.

Scharpf, F. et al. (1976), *Politikverflechtung. Theorie und Empirie des kooperativen Föderalismus in der Bundesrepublik Deutschland* (Kronberg: Athenäum).

Wagener, F. and B. Rückwardt (1982), *Führungshilfskräfte in Ministerien* (Baden-Baden: Nomos).

Wollmann, H. (1989), 'Policy Analysis in West Germany's Federal Government: a Case of Unfinished Governmental and Administrative Modernization?', *Governance*, 2, 233–66.

# 5. 'Deprivileging' the UK civil service in the 1980s: dream or reality?

## Christopher Hood

### INTRODUCTION

One of the stated aims of the Thatcher government when it came to office in the UK in 1979 was to 'deprivilege the civil service', an institution which it saw as partly responsible for Britain's economic decline after 1945 (see Hennessy 1990, p. 628f.). The senior civil service had been much criticized, mainly from the Left, from the late 1950s onwards. Some (notably Balogh 1959) had blamed its 'generalist' tradition for poor economic management after the Second World War. Several ex-Labour ministers had claimed that senior civil servants, far from being mere technicians, belonged to what Castle (1980, p. 209) called 'the conventional change-nothing world of the top Establishment', favoured their own policy options and used their resources of information and 'system knowledge' to achieve those goals (cf. Crossman 1979; Benn 1989). But the Thatcher policy of 'deprivileging' the civil service marked a new line of attack from the right, incorporating the New Right critique of bureaucrats as self-interested empire builders (cf. King 1987, pp. 102–4). No other UK government since the Second World War – or perhaps ever – had expressed its policy towards the civil service in quite such stark and provocative terms.

The political goal of deprivileging the bureaucracy was much attacked as a gratuitous and morale-sapping insult to what was claimed to be a dedicated and hard-working public service. Some argued that the phrase – coming from a paper written by John Hoskyns in 1979, but said by some to have been coined by Sir Keith Joseph – was a needless irritant, serving only to poison relations between the senior civil service and the Thatcher government in its early years (see Hennessy 1990, pp. 628f.).

The aim of this paper is to assess to what extent and in what ways the UK government *succeeded* in deprivileging the civil service – for good or ill – over the 1980s. Such an assessment requires assembling pieces of evidence of varying quality and completeness from different sources, and can only be tentative. And even if all the evidence were readily available, debate would persist about the appropriate tests for the success or otherwise of a strategy for deprivileging a bureaucracy. As with most political catch-phrases, the meaning of the key terms - 'privilege' and 'civil service' is ambiguous.

Did 'civil service' denote all employees of central government departments - truck drivers and counter clerks as well as Treasury knights and departmental heads? Or was the 'civil service' in the phrase simply the conventional British shorthand for the relatively small number of top civil servants – the 200 or so topmost mandarins – on whom the overwhelming bulk of debate about, and criticism of, the UK civil service since the Second World War had concentrated? And did 'privilege' denote social status and perquisites in a narrow sense (benefits enjoyed by civil servants which were denied to most workers in the private sector), or automatic claims on resources in a broader sense: the 'favoured' position of organizations seen as able to be 'bankrolled' by taxpayers whatever the economic travails faced by the population as a whole?

Table 5.1  Aspects of 'deprivileging': 13 tests

|  | Civil service generally | 'Mandarins' |
| --- | --- | --- |
| 'Indirect' deprivileging (change background conditions and shrink overall resource base) | (1) Squeeze staffing ||
|  | (2) Squeeze core spending ||
|  | (3) Make most prestigious departments suffer more or as much as the rest ||
| | (4) Reverse 'double inbalance' pay structure ||
| 'Direct' deprivileging (frontal attack on pay, prerequisites and conditions) | (5) End pay comparability with the private sector and cut pay ||
|  | (6) End automatic pay increments and pay without reference to performance ||
|  | (7) End jobs for life ||
|  | (8) End free (inflation-proofed, non-contributory) pensions at age 60 ||
|  | (9) End 'inviolability' from accountability and responsibility ||
|  |  | (10) End automatic honours |
|  |  | (11) End 'revolving door' jobs on retirement |
|  |  | (12) Change exclusive social recruitment base |
|  |  | (13) Open up top jobs to lateral entry |

94    *Bureaucracy in the modern state*

The potential ambiguities of the word 'deprivileging' suggests that a distinction needs to be made between 'direct' and 'indirect' deprivileging. The term 'direct deprivileging' is here used to refer to frontal attacks on the pay, conditions and perquisites of civil servants. 'Deprivileging', for most British people, was probably understood in this direct sense as meaning an attempt to end those features of the civil service which marked them off from private-sector workers and aroused general resentment in the populace. Those features included: 'jobs for life' irrespective of performance or need; automatic salary increments; pay based on comparability with private-sector equivalents; automatic honours and 'cushy' private-sector directorships on retirement for the senior mandarins; 'free' (non-contributory, inflation-proofed) pensions at 60; the apparent 'inviolability of those who appeared to be able to deflect blame for every decision they made by invoking official secrecy, ministerial responsibility or 'the rules'.

'Indirect' deprivileging, by contrast, here denotes strategies for reducing the resources available to the civil service, its pay structure and social bases. In this less-conventional, 'indirect' sense, 'deprivileging' could have been taken as an attempt to take away the automatic tax-financed resource endowments of the civil service and squeeze its resource base. It might have been understood as an attempt to cut the most prestigous departments down to size. Or it might have been taken to mean an attempt to reverse what some (notably Sjölund 1989) have referred to as the 'double imbalance' of typical public-service pay structures: that is, the tendency for those in the lower hierarchical ranks to enjoy pay and conditions which are fairly generous compared to those of lower-rank workers in the private sector, while those at the top are relatively low-paid compared to senior private-sector managers. Not all of these elements lend themselves readily to empirical testing, but Table 5.1 indicates thirteen possible tests of direct and indirect deprivileging, for the civil service generally and its top mandarins in particular. Beginning with 'indirect' deprivileging, the tests are as follows:

- Deprivileging in the indirect sense of assaults on the civil service's claim to first call on the state's resources for its 'pay and rations'. An organization underwritten by the power to tax may be said to be 'privileged' in the indirect sense that it can maintain its organizational apparatus and volume-terms level of spending from the public purse, even if the market sector of the economy is facing inflation, slump or changed trading conditions. If civil service 'privilege' in this indirect sense was attacked, we would expect overall staff numbers (test (1)) and 'core budget' spending levels (test (2)) to be cut, forcing the civil service to respond to the same pressures to become leaner and cheaper that are experienced by 'unprivileged' organizations facing a hostile market environment. In addition, we might expect a special assault on the resource base of the most prestigious and powerful departments (test (3)) - those which traditionally have had

the most clout and influence in Whitehall. Hence we would expect the departmental 'aristocrats' of Whitehall, notably the Treasury, Cabinet Office, Foreign Office and Home Office, to be cut down to size more than the traditionally less glamorous departments such as social welfare, education or agriculture, or at the very least to experience the same degree of pain.
- Deprivileging in the sense of a particular squeeze on civil service pay and perquisites. We would expect to see at least a partial reversal of the 'double imbalance' civil service pay structure which was referred to earlier (test (4)). Deprivileging the bureaucracy in this sense would presumably at least mean squeezing the wages at the lower levels of the bureaucracy. It is arguable whether test (4) belongs in the realm of 'direct' or 'indirect' deprivileging, since it has elements of both. But, moving clearly into the realm of 'direct' deprivileging, we would expect civil service pay generally to be exposed to sharp downward pressures, and the abandonment of the tradition of basing civil service pay levels on comparability with private-sector pay, implicitly on Hegelian 'alimentation' principles (test (5)). We would expect fixed pay structures and automatic increments to be replaced by performance pay systems (test (6)). We would expect civil service 'tenure' – jobs for life – to disappear (test (7)), to be replaced by redundancy patterns like those of the private sector. We would certainly expect to see an end to the inflation-proofed (index-linked non-contributory) pensions which epitomized civil service 'privilege' in the UK in the 1970s era of high inflation (test (8)).
- Perhaps most important in terms of ordinary understandings of civil service 'privilege', deprivileging in the sense of a special assault on the upper ranks of the civil service. In addition to staff cutbacks and general pay and conditions changes of the kind outlined above, 'deprivileging' this group might include: cutting back on their *noblesse de robe* privileges: that is, their near-automatic expectations of medals, knighthoods and titles of nobility as regular career perks (test (10)); restricting their ability to gain lucrative private sector jobs through 'revolving-door' exits to firms which place a high price on the contacts and experience of ex-mandarins on resignation or retirement from the bureaucracy (test (11)); drawing them from less-privileged social and educational backgrounds than before (test (12)); and opening up their jobs to lateral entry in mid-career rather than restricting the top positions to an educationally advantaged career corps which entered as 'gilded youths' in their twenties (test (13)).

I argue that there seems to be enough evidence to conclude that some bureaucratic 'deprivileging' in the terms outlined above took place in the UK in the 1980s, but that it was somewhat selective, and that much of it consisted of 'indirect' deprivileging rather than frontal assaults. Staff cuts were accompanied by a 'retrenchment bonus' in financial terms, and both direct and indirect depriveleging applied mainly to the less-privileged groups and departments in the system rather than to the 'mandarins' and the more 'privileged' areas of the UK civil service.

## CIVIL SERVICE STAFFING CUTBACKS: *CUI MALO?*

In 1976 the famous Nobel prize-winning economist Milton Friedman gave a lecture in London in which he advocated various dramatic policy proposals, among which was the idea that one civil servant in six should be taken off the public payroll (Friedman 1977). At the time, Friedman's ideas were largely dismissed by the British policy *cognoscenti* in his audience as a far-Right fantasy (see Foster 1992, p. 108). But in the same year, under pressure for public spending cuts in exchange for a loan from the International Monetary Fund, the then Labour government announced its intention to cut civil service staff numbers (numbers began to fall in the following year) and the subsequent Conservative government adopted the same goal with greater ideological enthusiasm, becoming internationally known for its yearly programme of staffing cutbacks (see Dunsire and Hood 1989, pp. 17–20). By the start of the 1990s, reform in the UK had *outrun* Friedman's 1976 prescription. More than one civil servant in *five* disappeared from the staff count between 1979 and 1990, as Figure 5.1 shows.

These staff cutbacks 'deprivileged' the civil service in the indirect sense (test (1)) of reducing aggregate claims to staff resources. Such a large aggregate decline in staff numbers had not been seen for several decades. It is true that, in spite of the rhetorical hype about epoch-making change which surrounded the Thatcher government, the 1980s staff cuts in the bureaucracy were much less severe in proportionate terms than earlier twentieth-century shake-outs. (For instance, in the demobilization years after the Second World War there was an exodus of approximately one civil servant in two, and in the retrenchment years of 1920–8 more than one (white-collar) civil servant in three disappeared from the staff count; the effects of decolonization from the late 1940s to the 1960s are harder to document, but also amounted to a major shake-out.) It is also true that a substantial part of the staff cuts were 'paper losses', achieved through reclassification of staff in hiving off units to other parts of the public sector. Dunsire and Hood (1989, p. 152) estimate that such 'cosmetic cuts' never fell below 40 per cent of the total between 1980–1 and 1984–5, in spite of all the talk of 'conviction politics' in those years. It would be surprising if staff changes on such a scale did not contribute to a general atmosphere of contraction and unease in the organization, and many witnesses argued that civil service morale fell sharply in the early Thatcher period (see Hennessy 1990, pp. 680ff.).

*Figure 5.1  UK civil service staff numbers, 1974–92 (selected groupings)*

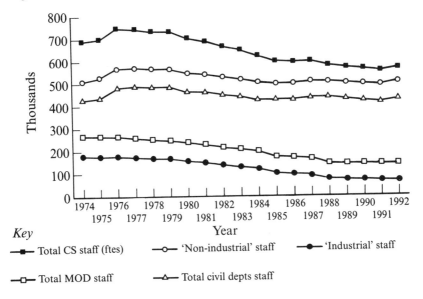

Source:  *Annual Abstract of Statistics*

Some parts of the civil service were more deprivileged in this indirect (test (1)) sense than others by the cutbacks. As can be seen from Figure 5.1, the bulk of those staff reductions are accounted for by reductions in the staff of the defence department rather than of the civil departments, and even there by cuts in blue-collar ('industrial') staff rather than in white-collar ('non-industrial') staff. Now blue-collar workers have traditionally been regarded by sociologists such as Mills (1951, pp. 240f.) as less 'privileged' in terms of prestige than white-collar workers (though at lower levels of white-collar work, such a judgement is highly debatable), and the idea of a 'class boundary between the blue-collar and white-collar categories' (Hyman 1983, p. 15) remains in the work of many later sociologists. If that conventional perception is accurate, it might seem that the civil service group which was most 'deprivileged' by the staff cutbacks consisted of those who were least privileged within the system to begin with. However, such a strategy of staff cuts was not an innovation on the part of the Thatcher government, and did not represent the radically new departure in dealing with the bureaucracy that Thatcherism is often argued to have heralded. Reduction in numbers of blue-collar staff in the civil service is a long-term trend in the UK. It predated the Thatcher era by several decades and occurred under both Labour and Conservative governments. It reflects a steady process of replacing contracting-out for direct bureaucratic employment in services involving blue-collar workers (see Dunsire and Hood 1989, pp. 73 and 85).

98                    *Bureaucracy in the modern state*

## CHANGES IN OVERALL CIVIL SERVICE COSTS AND THE CIVIL SERVICE 'RETRENCHMENT BONUS'

The fall in overall civil service staffing which is depicted in Figure 5.1 was not paralleled by a corresponding fall in aggregate government spending. Unlike government cutbacks in the 1920s era of retrenchment, the Thatcher cutbacks were cuts in staff, not spending in overall terms (Dunsire and Hood 1989, p. 15). Government Supply Estimates and Appropriation Accounts show that the money voted by Parliament to government departments increased by nearly 17 per cent in constant 1985 prices (using the Retail Prices Index) between FY 1975–6 and 1990–1 and showed no consistent fall relative to GDP. Rather than 'rolling back the state' in all its forms, government shifted to a different mix of resources, switching out of direct employment and spending more (out of a growing amount of overall government expenditure) on transfer payments and contracted-out services. The shift away from direct public service employment brought the UK into line with the more general OECD pattern (see Dunleavy 1989).

The direct cost of the civil service relative to total expenditure of central government authorized by Parliament fell substantially over the 1980s. Giving the civil service a smaller slice of the total spending cake for its direct costs could be counted as a weak form of indirect financial 'deprivileging' in the sense of test (2) in Table 5.1 – although such 'deprivileging' does not necessarily amount to much if that overall spending cake is itself growing. Again, this trend did not begin with the Thatcher government. It continued what seems to have been a long-term process dating from at least the early 1960s.

Figure 5.2 shows the cost of civil service pay and pensions as a percentage of net total estimates between FY 1961–2 and 1985–6. Beginning in FY 1985–6, separate central itemization of pay costs in the Treasury Guide to the Estimates was replaced by a 'running cost' regime, in which the budget for pay was merged with budgets for items such as travel and accommodation, on the grounds that managers needed more flexibility in allocating resources among different uses. These 'running costs' are thus not directly comparable to the figures shown in Figure 5.2, but as Figure 5.3 shows, running costs have also tended to decline as a proportion of supply estimates between their introduction in FY 1985–6 and 1992–3. It seems safe to conclude that running the civil service cost the UK government less over the period as a proportion of its total spending, and if that amounts to a form of indirect deprivileging, we must count it as a success, though it was not a reversal of previous trends. However, global spending levels and even spending on the civil service as a proportion of total spending are less relevant to test (2) of indirect deprivileging than what happened to the absolute level of spending on civil service pay.

*Figure 5.2* Cost of civil service pay and pensions as percentage of net total estimates, 1961–2 to 1984–5

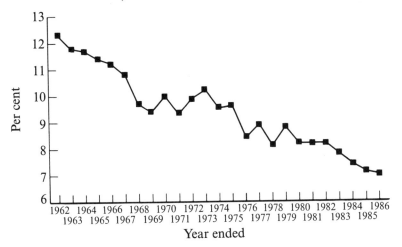

*Note*: Figures are for estimates, not outturn.

*Source*: Chief Secretary of the Treasury, *Memorandum on the Supply Estimates* (annual), 1961–2 to 1985–6.

*Figure 5.3* Civil service running costs as percentage of total supply estimates, 1985–6 to 1992–3

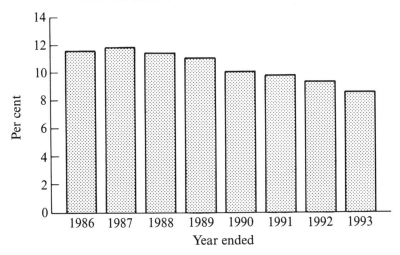

*Note*: Figures are for outturn; figures for 1993 are estimates.
*Source*: *Treasury Guide to Supply Estimates.*

Estimating what happened to the cost of the civil service in constant prices is much more problematic. In making such an assessment we encounter a technical debate among statisticians about which of several different deflators is most appropriate to apply to government spending generally, or to this category of government spending in particular. Here only the crudest measure is used, employing the Retail Prices Index (RPI) as a deflator.

It may well be argued that the RPI does not accurately reflect the basket of goods that government, as opposed to private citizens, has to buy. But this measure has the advantage that it closely fits the Thatcherite philosophy that government budgeting should be conducted according to the same constraints as ordinary domestic budgets (see, for example, Daly and George 1987, pp. 136f.), and hence tests 'privilege' according to the criteria most politically tuned to stated Thatcherite convictions. To use one of the several special 'government' indices might itself be argued to imply an assumption that government's needs are to be judged by rules and standards different from those of private individuals. Accordingly, Figures 5.4 and 5.5 express the figures on civil service pay costs depicted in Figure 5.2 (in this case beginning with FY 1966–7) in constant 1985 prices using the Retail Prices Index, and apply the same analysis to running costs as depicted in Figure 5.3 for FY 1985–6 to 1992–3.

Such figures are rough and ready, but they suggest that the long-term tendency for the cost of civil service pay and pensions to grow in real terms was checked

*Figure 5.4   Cost of civil service pay and pensions, 1966–7 to 1985–6 in constant 1985 prices*

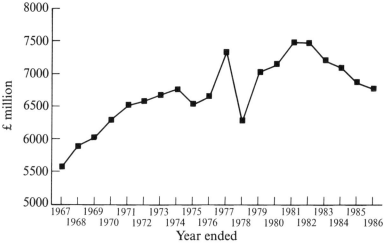

*Source:* Chief Secretary of the Treasury, *Memorandum on the Supply Estimates* (annual); and *Economic Trends* (annual).

for FY 1980–1 and reversed in the early 1980s. In terms of 'running costs' from FY 1985–6 to 1992–3 (Figure 5.5) the picture appears to be more one of stability than of a clear trend to reduction. Here, perhaps, is rather stronger evidence of successful indirect 'deprivileging' of the civil service in real cost terms (test (2)), forcing it to become leaner and cheaper in its own operations.

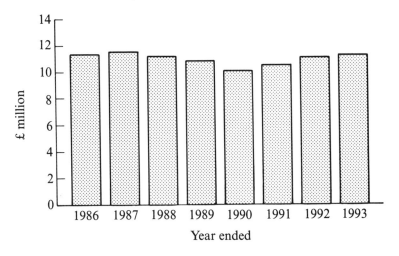

Figure 5.5   Civil service running costs, 1985–6 to 1992–3 in constant 1985 prices

Note: Figures are for outturns; those for 1993 are estimates.
Sources:   Treasury Guide to the Supply Estimates and Economic Trends.

The real cost of the civil service, measured in RPI terms, did not fall by nearly as much as the reduction in overall staffing depicted in Figure 5.1. In fact, the proportionate fall in civil service pay costs was only half or less of the percentage fall in staffing. This proportionate difference amounts to a 'retrenchment bonus' for the civil service over this period – that is, a tendency for staff and related costs to fall by a smaller proportion than the absolute number of staff in post, leaving more to be shared among those who remained. Or, to put it differently, the savings from staff retrenchment were shared between government and the bureaucracy.

Exactly where and how that 'retrenchment bonus' was spent is crucial for assessing the bureaucratic 'deprivileging' in the UK over the 1980s. Replacement of lower-paid staff by higher-paid or better-resourced staff is arguably a 'rational' response by a bureaucracy faced with retrenchment pressures expressed in overall staff cutback targets (as applied in the early Thatcher years), and reflects a classic problem of target-setting in a central planning system. And such a response perhaps explains the later shift in civil service management (from the late 1980s) away from the original stress on cutting staff numbers, expressed in simple annual 'body-count' terms, and towards the running-costs regime introduced from FY 1985–6. But such a shift in staff profile towards a more 'middle-heavy' civil service (see Dunsire and Hood 1989, p. 103) is at best an ironic outcome of attempts at indirect deprivileging.

## DEPARTMENTAL FORTUNES: THE UNTOUCHED, THE DEPRIVILEGED, THE PRIVILEGED AND THOSE OF MIXED FORTUNES

Test (3) of indirect deprivileging, as depicted in Table 5.1, concerns the extent to which the most prestigious departments in Whitehall, such as the Treasury and the Foreign Office, were singled out for special attention when government was wielding the axe. Was downsizing uniform across all departments of the civil service and did the traditionally most prestigious departments suffer along with – or more than – the rest? As a crude test, Appendices 5.A and 5.B show what happened to the staff and spending of selected central government departments and departmental groups over the period, taking four indicative years (1976, 1981, 1986 and 1991). These data upgrade the analysis of Dunsire and Hood (1989) and support their general conclusions about the distribution of 'pain' and 'gain' within the bureaucracy over the Thatcher period.[2]

This analysis shows that the traditionally 'privileged' departments do not stand out as major sufferers in resource terms over the period. Rather, the 'big losers' among the major departments were those in the industry, employment, trade and agriculture groups, whose staff numbers fell by 13 per cent between 1976 and 1991 and whose gross actual spending fell by almost 60 per cent over the same period in 1985 prices. The 'big gainers' in the major departments were the justice and law and order departments, which over this period saw their staff increase by nearly a third, their budgets nearly double in 1985 prices, and their budgets constitute a (moderately) rising share of total budget.

In between these clear patterns of bureaucratic gain and pain, several departments and departmental groups were losers in staffing terms, but gainers in overall budgets. The most dramatic example is the Defence Ministry. By 1991 it had lost close to 50 per cent of its total 1976 staff, but nevertheless ended the period with a budget one-fifth higher in 1985 prices than that for FY 1975–6, and with a larger proportion of the total budgetary cake than it had in 1975–6. The same pattern can be seen for the social policy departments (health, social security, education), the Scottish and Welsh offices ('prefectoral' departments with a guaranteed seat in Cabinet and well-placed to log-roll with their English spending counterparts against Treasury assaults on their resources) and the tax collectors. All of these departments show a pattern of staff cuts, to a greater or lesser extent, accompanied by real budget increases. Whether we count such patterns as amounting to 'privileging' or 'deprivileging' is debatable, and consideration of that issue will be postponed to the next section.

The pattern of resource shifts depicted here seems to reflect expected directions of change, given the political priorities of a Conservative government committed to increasing spending on 'law and order' and to decreasing 'intervention' by government in business (King 1987) – though the staff cutbacks in defence and the spending rises in welfare do not quite so closely fit those political expectations. But at the same time, it seems difficult to avoid the conclusion that the departments traditionally seen as most prestigious in the Whitehall bureaucracy – the Treasury and central agencies, the Home Office and the Foreign Office – have been remarkably proof against the staffing (and in some cases spending) cutbacks experienced by departments which are ordinarily regarded as lower down the Whitehall pecking order.

Of particular interest is the fate of the central agencies, those departments concerned with the central management and financial oversight of the civil service. Did these agencies 'share the pain' inflicted in staffing and spending cutbacks elsewhere, or did they make sure that the pain was directed elsewhere? The composition of central agencies changed considerably over the period (particularly with the dramatic abolition of the Civil Service Department in 1981 after a civil service pay strike in that year, its head despatched to early retirement and the House of Lords), and with changing ministerial responsibility for civil service management.

Central agencies as a group experienced no absolute staff cuts over the period considered here, saw their share of total spending and staffing increase, and ended the period with budgets double their 1976 level in 1985 prices. If central agencies imposed (indirectly) 'deprivileging' cuts on some other departments, they themselves seem to have been protected from such a fate.

## CHANGES IN CIVIL SERVICE PAY: DEPRIVILEGING THE BOTTOM AND REPRIVILEGING THE TOP?

Several of the tests of 'deprivileging' identified in Table 5.1 refer to changes in civil service pay and conditions. And such issues were certainly an item of much contention between the Thatcher government and the civil service unions, particularly in the early 1980s. Test (4), it will be recalled, refers to a reversal of a 'double imbalance' pay structure, and test (5) refers to pay cuts.

Figure 5.6 shows what happened to the pay levels of five selected grades of UK civil servants in constant 1985 prices (as measured by the retail prices index) over the period 1966–91, and also depicts the pay of the average UK worker in the same terms from 1972 (when average pay figures for the UK first appeared in their current form). Out of the five civil servant categories shown in Figure 5.6, two are intended to give an indication of what happened to 'top management' pay levels, namely: the top civil servant (the head of the civil service) and Grade 2 (the former Deputy Secretary grade). Two are intended to give an indication of 'middle management' pay levels, namely: Grade 7 (the former Principal grade) and Higher Executive Officer at the base level, to give an indication of 'middle management' pay levels. The final item shown on Figure 5.6, the pay of an 18-year-old Executive Officer, has been taken to give an indication of what happened to pay at the level of junior front-line workers in the civil service.

*Figure 5.6    Civil service and average pay trends, 1966–91 in constant 1985 prices*

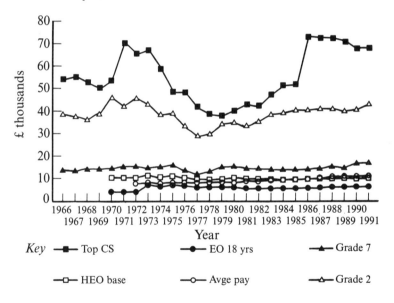

*Sources: Civil Service Yearbook* and *Economic Trends.*

The changes indicated by Figure 5.6 are precisely in the direction that would be expected if 'deprivileging' meant ending a 'double imbalance in pay' (test 4). Clearly, any squeeze on civil service pay levels seems to have occurred at the lower rather than the upper grades of the bureaucracy. Pay levels for the

HEO base and 18-year-old EOs generally fell in constant 1985 prices over the period from 1979 to 1991, and also fell relative to average workers' pay. In the upper ranges of middle management, Grade 7 civil servants did slightly better at the end of the period; but it is at top management level where the gains are clearest and where what we see for the 1980s looks more like 'reprivileging' than 'deprivileging'. Grade 2s experienced steady if undramatic rises in real pay levels; but the most dramatic pay increase was achieved at the very top, by the head of the civil service. As Figure 5.6 shows, the top civil servant enjoyed a spectacular pay rise in 1985–6 and ended the period very substantially better off than at the outset.

Other changes in pay and conditions are also consistent with reversal of a 'double imbalance' structure. For example, dramatic battles raged over the government's banning of trade union membership for staff at the Government Communications Headquarters in 1984 (Hennessy 1990, pp. 684f.). And for most of the civil service the expected result of test (5) – the ending of pay comparability with the private-sector – also came about. In 1981 the government scrapped the former system of 'pay research', in which systematic annual comparisons with private-sector equivalents had been conducted by a special semi-independent body as a basis for civil service pay negotiations. Instead, civil service pay was determined by a principle of paying what was needed to attract and retain staff, rather than on a 'fair comparison' or 'model employer' principle. Discretionary performance-related pay (test (6)) was also introduced into the civil service from 1984, amid strong condemnation from the First Division Association, the trade union representing senior civil servants (see Drewry and Butcher 1991, pp. 120ff.). At first it was introduced on an experimental basis for a few grades, but later became an established feature of the pay structure.

As far as the ending of 'jobs for life' (test (7)) is concerned, changes do seem to have taken place in the expected direction. Table 5.2, calculated from *Civil Service Statistics*, gives a breakdown of those who left the civil service in 1977, 1982, 1987 and 1992. As can be seen, the bulk of staff losses over that period always came from voluntary resignations, straightforward retirement and death. Early or ill-health retirement constituted a small but rising component of the total. The key figure from the perspective of 'deprivileging' is the 'other reasons' category, which comprises redundancy, compulsory early retirement, ending of the terms of fixed-period appointments and dismissals. As can be seen, this category of leavers rose steadily, changing from under 5 per cent of total leavers in 1977 to nearly 20 per cent in 1992. Unfortunately, published statistics do not break these categories down by grade, so we cannot say definitively whether civil service 'mandarins' were as much affected by these trends as those further down the line. However, it is noticeable that the UK, in contrast to Australia and New Zealand over the 1980s, did not abandon the concept of 'permanent heads' of government departments as a general rule, though it did introduce fixed-term appointments for other senior positions, which will be discussed later.

Table 5.2  Types of departures from the UK civil service as percentage of total leavers, selected years 1977–92

| Col. 1 Year | Col. 2 Total number leaving civil service | Col. 3 Vol resignations as % of Col. 2 | Col. 4 Deaths in office as % of Col. 2 | Col. 5 Age retirement as % of Col. 2 | Col. 6 Vol early/ ill-health retirements as % of Col. 2 | Col. 7 Other reasons[a] as % of Col. 2 |
|---|---|---|---|---|---|---|
| 1977 | 60,679 | 61.5 | 2.9 | 27.2 | 4.1 | 4.3 |
| 1982 | 46,251 | 51.3 | 2.8 | 33.8 | 4.8 | 7.1 |
| 1987 | 44,026 | 59.5 | 2 | 22.6 | 6.2 | 9.7 |
| 1992 | 29,602 | 41.3 | 2.4 | 25.4 | 11.6 | 19.3 |

[a] Includes redundancy, dismissal and compulsory early retirement.

Source: Civil Service Statistics.

Moreover (to anticipate the discussion of the next section), it is noticeable that the topmost ranks of the bureaucracy hardly suffered from the changes in pay and conditions which did meet our deprivileging tests. Union representation was not relevant to the topmost mandarins of the civil service, since pay levels at the very top are not arrived at by bargaining with trade unions, but by government responses to the recommendations of a separate top-level public pay body (the Top Salaries Review Body, recently renamed the Senior Salaries Review Body because some agency chiefs who enjoy very high pay levels are not within its purview). And while the Civil Service Pay Research machinery for the lower grades was swept away, the 'top people's' review body was untouched, and continued to deploy private-sector 'comparability' arguments in making its recommendations. Moreover, performance pay was not even introduced at the very top of the civil service, and its role for the 'sub-mandarins' could be argued to be a token one. Thus the *procedural* 'deprivileging' of civil service pay-setting – in the removal of the assumption that the civil service was automatically entitled to enjoy wages comparable to the private sector, rather than whatever the government as employer could 'get away with' – was instituted for the bottom and middle grades, but not for the top civil service grades.

Moreover, in the one striking area where the Thatcher government failed to 'deprivilege' the civil service as a whole, senior civil servants unavoidably had common interests with lower-level staff, unlike the position for pay determination. That is the outcome expected by test (8) - the removal of 'free' non-contributory inflation-proof pensions for civil servants at the age of 60. This system, introduced in its current form in 1971, withstood various attempted assaults over the Thatcher period (see Hennessy 1990, p. 683). Efforts at deprivileging most clearly failed in the one area where the interests of the top mandarins could not be easily uncoupled from those of middle management or lower staff. Indeed, it is worth noting that politicians (ministers and MPs) also enjoyed increasingly generous index-linked pensions under the same legislation, creating particular difficulties for deprivileging the less-privileged civil servants without also deprivileging those at the top.

There are various accounts of why senior UK civil servants in general seem to have collaborated enthusiastically in the Thatcher government's programme of public-sector cuts and restructuring. This collaboration sometimes surprises those who expect senior civil servants to act as staff- and budget maximizers, given the Thatcher government's perceived hostility towards civil servants as a breed and its aim to cut the bureaucracy and expose it to market pressure. One element behind this co-operation may have been the simple fact that for the first time in a decade, top civil servants, far from being 'deprivileged' in pay terms, saw their pay rise substantially, both relative to lower level civil servants and in constant price terms.

## TOP CIVIL SERVANTS: SOCIAL COMPOSITION, SHARE OF TOTAL STAFF AND WORKING CONDITIONS

As explained earlier, for many of the post-Second World War critics of the UK civil service, the key tests of deprivileging are those which apply to the topmost ranks of the civil service, and their fate over the 1980s therefore merits close attention. It might be supposed that a determined policy of 'deprivileging' this group would include:

- strategies for disproportionately cutting their numbers (test (1) in Table 5.1);
- reducing their pay (test (5)) or putting it on to a tough performance-related basis (test (6));
- replacing their traditional role as what Sisson (1976 p. 252) once described as 'Renaissance courtiers' around ministers by hands-on tasks of 'hard management', facing the discipline of a financial bottom line for large organizations under their command, and the associated bargaining (test (9));
- cutting back on automatic bestowal of honours and titles of nobility (test (10));
- reducing their opportunities for taking lucrative private-sector work after retirement on full index-linked pension at age 60 (test (11));

- drawing senior civil servants from different, less socially privileged backgrounds than before (test (12)); and
- opening up their jobs to lateral-entry competition (test (13)).

If that is an accurate description of what deprivileging might have meant for this group, changes along these lines seem to have been generally patchy and muted. It is true that numbers of top civil servants were cut at least in line with overall civil service staff cutbacks (test (1)), meaning that top managers do not seem to have increased as a proportion of total civil service staff over the period. Figure 5.7 shows numbers in the top three grades of the UK civil service as a percentage of total staff, suggesting that it was the middle rather than the top grades of the civil service which grew as a proportion of total staff as overall staff numbers fell (cf. also Dunsire and Hood 1989, p. 96).

*Figure 5.7* Grades 1–3 as percentage of total UK civil service staff, 1975–91

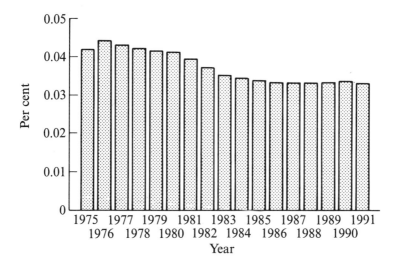

*Source:* Dunsire and Hood (1989, p. 96), updated from *Civil Service Statistics*.

General pay trends (tests (4) and (5)) have been discussed earlier; and we have seen that pay at the top of the civil service rose sharply while lower ranks saw their basic pay stagnate or fall. We have also seen that automatic reference to private-sector comparability arguments in pay-setting (test (5)) was removed for the bulk of the civil service while it was retained for the topmost ranks. (Even so, it is true that the top civil service management pay rises discussed earlier were moderate compared to rises in top professional and managerial salaries in much of the private sector over the 1980s and early 1990s, according to repeated reports of the Review Body on Top Salaries.)

Moreover, there is little evidence of a major shift towards performance-related pay at the very top (test (6)). Performance related pay, first introduced in 1984 on an experimental basis, was not applied to the topmost ranks of the UK civil service over the 1980s, though it was applied to chief executives of departmental agencies after 1988. Grade 1 civil servants did not receive performance-related pay. Grades 2 and 3 could receive discretionary pay points as a reward for sustained high performance, on the basis of an appraisal by their departmental head (subject to approval of the Head of the Civil Service for Grade 2s).

It is difficult to regard this pay regime as an indication of tough deprivileging managerialism. The total sum currently available for performance pay for Grade 2s and 3s is only 2 per cent of the paybill for those grades, meaning that the proportion of total pay that is at risk or at least 'in play' is very small in practice. Moreover, pay is *not* at risk in the sense that pay increases awarded for performance to Grade 2s and 3s can subsequently be removed; performance pay is a ratchet which only turns upwards. (Lower down the civil service, in the middle management ranks of Grades 5–7, an element of what is known as 'unconsolidated' performance-related pay – that is, one-off yearly bonuses which are not pensionable or consolidated into salary – was introduced in 1992–3, but these changes did not occur during the high noon of managerialist hype in the 1980s, and even now the 'unconsolidated' element only applies to the top 25 per cent or so of extended pay ranges which is currently largely uninhabited.) Hence it is difficult to see performance-related pay as much more than a token gesture to the new managerialism in the senior reaches of the bureaucracy.

As noted earlier, 'jobs for life' (test (7)) were not formally removed from UK departmental heads in the 1980s, unlike their Antipodean counterparts; nor was there a general move to adopt contract appointments, as occurred in New Zealand and Norway. However, all the chief executives of the departmental agencies which developed after 1989 as part of the 'Next Steps' programme of corporatizing the civil service, are appointed on fixed-term contracts of various types, and this change certainly modifies traditional concepts of career tenure at the top. Nevertheless, it would appear that those who are most at risk are those who come from outside the civil service, since regular civil servants can be appointed on contracts which enable them to return to the career civil service (see Treasury and Civil Service Committee, Fifth Report, HC 348 Session 1988–9: xiv, paras 31–2). So what seems to have happened in effect is a differentiation of the civil service, with 'permanent secretaries' of departments continuing to enjoy traditional tenure terms, while agency chief executives have much less job security (and those coming from outside the civil service have less security than their career civil service counterparts).

Could it be said more generally that the senior UK civil service was deprivileged as a result of being exposed to 'harder' management regimes over the 1980s (test (9)), with the government's adoption of 'new public management' measures and the strong emphasis on managerialism in the rhetoric of Thatcherism (cf. Pollitt 1993)? The development of a more managerial approach to the public sector, designed to put public servants under stronger pressure to produce demonstrable results (through devices such as performance measurement, league tabling, pay on performance, market testing) was one of the major elements in the image – and self-image – of Thatcherism in the 1980s.

But even this claim is debatable. It could be argued that over the 1980s at least, most of the 'managerial' thrusts struck harder at executive-level operations comprising middle and lower-level staff than at the policy work done by junior 'fast-streamers' and the topmost civil servants. Policy work was by and large not performance-measured or market-tested; no league tables appeared in this area, nor was there a 'Citizens Charter' for consumers of policy services. The most senior civil servants were not subjected to the performance pay regime applied lower down, and even for those who were subjected to performance pay there was comparatively little financial gain or pain linked to performance.

Senior civil servants have been able to deflect much of the pressures for tougher managerial discipline on to executive units, partially decoupling executive agencies from ministerial departments and placing themselves in the role of external overseers and developers for the 'policy framework' of executive work, while distancing themselves from hands-on managerial responsibility. Such a move fits with what Dunleavy (1991, p. 202) argues to be the preference function of rational bureaucrats. The claim (though Dunleavy does not use the analogy) is that senior bureaucrats are like police officers trying to avoid police patrol (that is, unpopular front-line work) and aiming instead to work behind the lines in a collegial setting at headquarters (cf. Jones 1980). Just as the 'beat ideology' of police chiefs often clashes with the reality of treating police patrol duties as a task for the raw recruit, the unpromotable misfit, or those put back into uniform as a punishment, so the 'management ideology' clashes with the reality of senior civil servants opting for policy work at headquarters.

Indeed, it can be argued that the main managerial innovation of the Thatcher/Major government – the introduction of a split between corporatized executive agencies and policy/oversight departments with the adoption of the 'Next Steps' programme after 1989 – was enthusiastically adopted by the senior UK civil service precisely because it made it possible for top civil servants to *avoid* being subject to the managerial rigours increasingly imposed on executive agencies down the line, and to continue to practise 'management avoidance' in their Sisson-type role of Renaissance courtiers.

If there was any 'deprivileging' embodied in the new managerialism, it was not strongly manifested in other areas. The policy of awarding medals and titles of nobility to senior civil servants as part of their *cursus honorum* (test (10)) does not appear to have changed radically until a 1993 declaration by the Major government that henceforward civil honours would be awarded on merit rather than as an automatic career entitlement for civil servants (the effect of this declaration has yet to be seen). A count of honours given to Permanent Secretaries and second Permanent Secretaries (Grade 1 and lA) in selected major government departments[3] in 1978, 1984 and 1990 indicates a slight decline in honours. All civil service knights and dames from the various orders of chivalry (mainly the Order of the Bath, the Order of the British Empire and the Order of St Michael and St George) totalled 27 in 1978, 22 in 1984 and 24 in 1990; and the incidence of the least prestigious CB (Companion of the Bath) also fell from eleven in 1978 to ten in 1984 and eight in 1990. But at most this change is a nibbling at the edges rather than a radical change of direction.

In addition, there was no attempt at all to deprivilege senior civil servants by tightening the rules restricting 'revolving-door' appointments of civil servants in the private sector after resignation or retirement (test (11)), and such activity was a prominent feature in the senior civil service over the 1980s and early 1990s, particularly as privatization and contracting-out made civil servants in areas such as prison policy more valuable to the private sector.

In social composition (test (12)) – the level of 'privilege' from which senior civil servants are drawn – it is far from obvious that the Thatcher government forced any major change to the upper echelons of the UK civil service, though the evidence is fragmentary. Theakston and Fry (1989), in a study of UK permanent secretaries (broadly, departmental heads) from 1900 to 1986, showed that those appointed to such positions, even in the 1980s, were increasingly career civil servants rather than people who had joined the civil service after working in other professions; that the proportion coming from private fee-paying schools remained unchanged from 1965 to 1985; and that the proportion coming from Oxford and Cambridge (traditionally, Britain's equivalent to the American Ivy League universities or Tokyo University in the Japanese system) increased slightly, being far higher in 1985–6 than it had been in 1900–19. There is no evidence of a sudden 'deprivileging' of the top group in the 1980s in these terms.

On movement towards greater lateral entry (test (13)) at the top of the civil service, we have already noted Theakston and Fry's evidence that up to 1986 there was no sign of 'outside' appointments at departmental permanent secretary level even approaching the levels of the early years of the century. However, as with 'jobs for life', the picture is rather different when chief executives of the corporatized executive agencies introduced within the civil service after 1988 are considered. As of 1993, 63 out of 93 chief executives had been appointed by open competition (that is, public advertisement open to all comers) and out of those 63 cases 34 had come from outside the civil service. Undoubtedly, this change represents a clear step towards lateral entry at the top of the civil service; but it makes all the more conspicuous the fact that similar steps have not been taken for permanent secretaryships or other senior appointments in departments, once more indicating that those positions have yet to be affected by the managerial precepts that have been imposed on those further down.

## CONCLUSION

This paper has not been concerned with whether an elected government *ought* to want to 'deprivilege' its public service, or whether the adoption of such a goal breaches one of the many shadowy conventions of liberal democracy in general or of the UK's unwritten constitution in particular. Leaving aside the question of whether the approaches to 'deprivileging' the civil service discussed earlier should be commended or deplored, it has merely attempted to examine the extent to which such changes actually occurred.

Such an assessment is not easy or straightforward. In commenting on intellectual developments in the UK over the last dozen years, Barker (1993, p. 138) judiciously recalls Mao Ze Dong's remark that it is still too soon to judge the effects of the French Revolution. Historians will still be debating the 'Thatcher effect' on the UK civil service many decades from now. As noted at the outset, the evidence on which this assessment is based is patchy and biased towards 'bureaumetric' measures rather than the kind of qualitative factors that can be drawn from an interview programme. But, for what it is worth, this evidence suggests that the Thatcher government's goal of 'deprivileging' the UK civil service was only partly realized. Table 5.3 gives a summary of the thirteen tests explored in this paper.

To the extent that the Thatcher government deprivileged the UK civil service, it seems to have had a much less dramatic effect on the senior ranks of the regular departments than might be expected either from inspection of the global staff cuts over the 1980s or from taking at face value the strong emphasis placed on 'managerialism' in the government's rhetoric on the public service over the period. In general, it seems to have been the less-privileged parts of the civil service which suffered the most and the most-privileged parts which suffered least. It is true that the development of the 'Next Steps' corporatized agencies has produced a new group of senior civil servants as chief executives who are in many cases relatively 'privileged' in pay levels but at the same time somewhat 'deprivileged' in conditions of tenure and pay structure. But outside this new and growing hybrid group, perhaps the senior civil service got the better of Mrs Thatcher after all, in so far as 'Thatcherism' seems to have been shaped in a way which largely preserved their privileges.

*Table 5.3   13 tests of deprivileging: summary of assessment*

|  | Civil service generally | | 'Mandarins' | |
| --- | --- | --- | --- | --- |
|  | Test no. | Observed | Test no. | Observed |
| 'Indirect' deprivileging (change background conditions and shrink overall resource base) | (1): cut in staff numbers | Yes, but staff cuts mainly on blue-collar staff | (1) | Yes |
|  | (2): cut in pay etc. costs | Yes, but pay etc. costs fell by only *c.* half the % fall in staff numbers |  |  |
|  | (3): high-prestige depts share the pain of cutbacks with others | No, Treasury, central agencies, FCO, Home Office, little damaged |  |  |
|  | (4): end DI pay pattern | Yes |  |  |
| 'Direct' deprivileging (frontal attack on pay, perquisites and conditions) | (5): remove comparability and cut pay | Yes, for lower (and to some extent middle staff) | (5) | No, top pay levels rose, TSRB survived |
|  | (6): end automatic pay increments and fixed pay | Limited | (6) | Minimal except for agency CEOs |
|  | (7): end jobs for life | Trend to rising redundancies | (7) | Mainly for agency CEOs, not top dept CS |
|  | (8): end free index-linked pensions at 60 | No | (8) | No |
|  | (9): end 'inviolability from accountability and responsibility' | To some extent | (9) | NS agency regime shielded top CS from hands-on m'gement & put pressure on agencies instead |
|  |  |  | (10): end routine honours | Modest but steady downturn |
|  |  |  | (11): end revolving-door jobs on exit | No |
|  |  |  | (12): change social basis of recruitment | No? |
|  |  |  | (13): open top jobs to lateral entry | Only for CEOs of agencies, not top dept CS |

## APPENDIX 5.A  STAFF OF SELECTED DEPARTMENTS, 1976–91: CHANGE OVER TIME AND PERCENTAGE OF TOTAL CIVIL SERVICE STAFF

|  | 1976 | as % of total staff | 1981 | as % of total staff | 1986 | as % of total staff | 1991 | as % of total staff | Change in staff from 1976 to 1991 as % |
|---|---|---|---|---|---|---|---|---|---|
| *Central agencies* | | | | | | | | | |
| Treasury | 1144 | 0.15 | 1006 | 0.15 | 3363 | 0.57 | 3008 | 0.54 | 162.94 |
| Cabinet Office inc. CSO | 685 | 0.09 | 591 | 0.09 | 1680 | 0.28 | 2570 | 0.46 | 275.18 |
| CSD inc. Parlt Counsel | 3738 | 0.50 | 3197 | 0.46 | | | | | |
| Total central agencies | 5567 | 0.74 | 4794 | 0.69 | 5043 | 0.85 | 5578 | 1.01 | 0.20 |
| *Regional depts* | | | | | | | | | |
| Scottish Office | 10850 | 1.45 | 10928 | 1.58 | 9817 | 1.65 | 10286 | 1.86 | −5.20 |
| Welsh Office | 1491 | 0.20 | 2357 | 0.34 | 2294 | 0.39 | 2326 | 0.42 | 56.00 |
| Northern Ireland Office | 276 | 0.04 | 219 | 0.03 | 172 | 0.03 | 196 | 0.04 | −28.99 |
| Total regional depts | 12617 | 1.69 | 13504 | 1.96 | 12283 | 2.07 | 12808 | 2.31 | 1.51 |
| *Environment and transport* | | | | | | | | | |
| DOE and Transport | 73063 | 9.77 | 58503 | 8.48 | 46642 | 7.85 | 38480 | 6.95 | −47.33 |
| *Social policy depts* | | | | | | | | | |
| DES and Arts/Libraries | 4142 | 0.55 | 3682 | 0.53 | 2464 | 0.41 | 2726 | 0.49 | −34.19 |
| DHSS and Health/ Social Security | 91563 | 12.24 | 98298 | 14.25 | 92727 | 15.61 | 83049 | 14.99 | −9.30 |
| Total social policy depts | 95705 | 12.79 | 101980 | 14.78 | 95191 | 16.03 | 85775 | 15.48 | −10.38 |
| *Industry, employment, trade, agriculture, energy* | | | | | | | | | |
| MAFF | 15636 | 2.09 | 13218 | 1.92 | 11009 | 1.85 | 9782 | 1.77 | −37.44 |
| Employment | 20995 | 2.81 | 23823 | 3.45 | 30428 | 5.12 | 44679 | 8.06 | 112.81 |
| MSC, Training Services Agency & ESA | 20862 | | 23672 | | 20793 | | | | |
| DTI and Trade/Industry/ Energy | 19662 | 2.63 | 17272 | 2.50 | 13682 | 2.30 | 12518 | 2.26 | −36.33 |
| Total industry etc. | 77155 | 7.53 | 77985 | 7.87 | 75912 | 9.28 | 66979 | 12.09 | −13.19 |
| *Defence* | | | | | | | | | |
| Ministry of Defence | 268248 | 35.86 | 232770 | 33.73 | 169462 | 28.53 | 140199 | 25.31 | −47.74 |
| *Foreign affairs* | | | | | | | | | |
| FCO inc. ODA/M | 10248 | 1.37 | 11515 | 1.67 | 9564 | 1.61 | 9912 | 1.79 | −3.28 |
| *Justice/law and order* | | | | | | | | | |
| Home Office | 32528 | 4.35 | 35482 | 5.14 | 37465 | 6.31 | 44097 | 7.96 | 35.57 |
| Lord Chancellor's Office | 9951 | 1.33 | 10022 | 1.45 | 10172 | 1.71 | 11223 | 2.03 | 12.78 |
| Total justice/law and order | 42479 | 5.68 | 45504 | 6.59 | 47637 | 8.02 | 55320 | 9.99 | 30.23 |
| *Tax collectors* | | | | | | | | | |
| Inland Revenue | 79081 | 10.57 | 76240 | 11.05 | 69261 | 11.66 | 65724 | 11.86 | −16.89 |
| Customs | 29285 | 3.92 | 26945 | 3.91 | 25159 | 4.24 | 27041 | 4.88 | −7.66 |
| Total tax collectors | 108366 | 14.49 | 103185 | 14.95 | 94420 | 15.90 | 92765 | 16.74 | −14.40 |
| Total civil service staff | 748000 | | 690000 | | | | 554000 | | |

*Note:* CSD = Civil Service Department; CSO = Central Statistical Office; DES = Department of Education and Science; DHSS = Department of Health and Social Security; DOE = Department of the Environment; DTI = Department of Trade and Industry; ESA = Employment Services Agency, FCO = Foreign and Commonwealth Office; MAFF = Ministry of Agriculture, Fisheries and Food; MSC = Manpower Services Commission; ODA/M = Overseas Development Administration (*formerly* Ministry).

*Source: Staff in Post and Civil Service Statistics.*

## APPENDIX 5.B  BUDGETS OF SELECTED DEPARTMENTS 1976 TO 1991: GROSS ACTUAL EXPENDITURE (GAE) FOR FOUR SELECTED YEARS ENDED 1976, 1981, 1986 AND 1991

| Year ended | 1976 GAE £m | % GAE of total GAE | 1981 GAE £m | % GAE of total GAE | 1986 GAE £m | % GAE of total GAE | 1991 GAE £m | % GAE of total GAE | Diff. between budgets of 1991 and 1976 as % of 1976 budget [in 1985 prices] |
|---|---|---|---|---|---|---|---|---|---|
| *Central Agencies* | | | | | | | | | |
| Treasury | 162.5 | 0.44 | 275 | 0.34 | 206 | 0.21 | 1589 | 1.09 | 191.76 |
| Cabinet Office inc. CSO | 31 | 0.08 | 60 | 0.07 | 95 | 0.10 | 208 | 0.14 | 100.20 |
| CSD inc. Parlt Counsel | 85.7 | 0.23 | 155.8 | 0.19 | | | | | −100.00 |
| MPO | | | | | 36 | 0.04 | | | |
| Total central agencies | 279.2 | 0.75 | 490.8 | 0.60 | 337 | 0.34 | 1797 | 1.23 | 92.04 |
| *Scottish Office and Welsh Office* | | | | | | | | | |
| Scottish Office | 2095.6 | 5.96 | 4328 | 2.58 | 5187 | 5.29 | 8313 | 5.71 | 18.36 |
| Welsh Office | 435.2 | 1.17 | 1062.2 | 1.31 | 2277 | 2.32 | 4179 | 2.87 | 186.51 |
| Total SO and WO | 2530.8 | 7.20 | 5390.2 | 3.12 | 7464 | 7.61 | 12492 | 8.58 | 47.28 |
| *Environment and transport* | | | | | | | | | |
| DOE and Transport | 9868.8 | 26.56 | 16486.5 | 20.31 | 14870 | 15.17 | 32656 | 22.43 | −1.27 |
| *Social policy depts* | | | | | | | | | |
| DES and Arts/Libraries | 1400.1 | 3.77 | 2941.6 | 3.62 | 3438 | 3.51 | 7243 | 4.97 | 54.35 |
| DHSS and Health/ Social Security | 8433.1 | 22.70 | 21122.9 | 26.02 | 34090 | 34.77 | 44969 | 30.89 | 59.10 |
| Total social policy depts | 9833.2 | 26.46 | 24064.5 | 29.64 | 37528 | 38.28 | 52212 | 35.86 | 58.43 |
| *Industry, employment, trade, agriculture, energy* | | | | | | | | | |
| MAFF inc. Intervention Board | 941.9 | 2.68 | 740.7 | 1.16 | 1242 | 1.27 | 699 | 0.48 | −77.86 |
| Employment | 599.6 | 1.61 | 1655.8 | 0.74 | 2831 | 2.89 | 3067 | 2.11 | 52.62 |
| DTI and Trade/Industry/ Energy/ECGD | 4889.7 | 13.91 | 6231.5 | 6.02 | 4215 | 4.30 | 5051 | 3.47 | −69.18 |
| Total industry etc. depts | 6431.2 | 18.29 | 8628 | 7.92 | 8288 | 8.45 | 8817 | 6.06 | −59.09 |
| *Defence* | | | | | | | | | |
| Ministry of Defence | 5476.4 | 14.74 | 11680.1 | 14.39 | 17993 | 18.35 | 22304 | 15.32 | 21.52 |
| *Foreign Affairs* | | | | | | | | | |
| FCO inc. ODA/M | 671 | 1.81 | 1361.7 | 1.68 | 1791 | 1.83 | 2558 | 1.76 | 13.75 |
| *Justice/law and order* | | | | | | | | | |
| Home Office | 1060.9 | 2.86 | 2272.6 | 2.80 | 3661 | 3.73 | 6041 | 4.15 | 69.90 |
| Lord Chancellor's Office | 92.5 | 0.25 | 275 | 0.34 | 496 | 0.51 | 1291 | 0.89 | 316.43 |
| Total justice/law and order | 1153.4 | 3.10 | 2547.6 | 3.14 | 4157 | 4.24 | 7332 | 5.04 | 89.67 |
| *Tax collectors* | | | | | | | | | |
| excl. Inland Revenue rates on govt property | 335.2 | 0.90 | 578.1 | 0.71 | 1018 | 1.04 | 1846 | 1.27 | 64.32 |
| Customs | 136.1 | 0.37 | 244.9 | 0.30 | 356 | 0.36 | 652 | 0.45 | 42.94 |
| Total tax collectors | 471.3 | 1.27 | 823 | 1.01 | 1374 | 1.40 | 2498 | 1.72 | 58.14 |
| Total gross actual spend | 37156.7 | | 81193.4 | | 98032 | | 145598 | | |

*Note*: Abbreviations used as in Appendix 5.A, plus ECGD = Export Credits Guarantee Department; MPO = Management and Personnel Office.
*Source*: Supply Estimates and Appropriation Accounts.

## NOTES

1. I am grateful to Andrew Dunsire, Desmond King and Jon Pierre for valuable comments on an earlier draft of this paper.
2. In this case, however, attention is directed only at the major departments and excludes several of the smaller departments included in the earlier analysis.
3. That is, MAFF, Cabinet Office/MPO(1974)/CSD(1978), Customs and Excise, Defence (civilian staff only), Education and Science, Employment, Energy, Environment, Office of Fair Trading, Foreign and Commonwealth Office, Health and Social Security, Home Office, Inland Revenue, Lord Chancellor's, Overseas Development, Industry/Prices and Consumer Protection/Trade/Trade and Industry, Transport, Treasury, Treasury Solicitor, Northern Ireland Office, Scottish Office, Welsh Office.

## REFERENCES

Balogh, T. (1959), 'The Apotheosis of the Dilettante: the Establishment of Mandarins', in H. Thomas (ed.), *The Establishment: A Symposium* (London: Blond), 83–126.
Barker, R. (1993), *Politics, Peoples and Government: Themes in British Political Thought Since the Nineteenth Century* (London: Macmillan).
Benn, T. (1989), *Against the Tide: Diaries 1973–77* (London: Hutchinson).
Castle, B. (1980), *The Castle Diaries, 1974–76* (London: Weidenfeld & Nicolson).
Crossman, R. H. S. (1979), *The Crossman Diaries: Selections from the Diaries of a Cabinet Minister, 1964–1970* (London: Methuen).
Daly, M. and A. George (1987), *Margaret Thatcher in Her Own Words* (Harmondsworth, Middx.: Penguin).
Drewry, G. and T. Butcher (1991), *The Civil Service Today,* 2nd edn (Oxford: Basil Blackwell).
Dunleavy, P. J. (1989), 'The United Kingdom: Paradoxes of an Ungrounded Statism', in F.G. Castles (ed.), *The Comparative History of Public Policy*, Cambridge: Polity Press, pp. 242–91.
Dunleavy, P. J. (1991), *Democracy, Bureaucracy and Public Choice* (Brighton: Harvester).
Dunsire, A. and C. Hood (1989), *Cutback Management in Public Bureaucracies* (Cambridge: Cambridge University Press).
Foster, C. D. (1992), *Privatization. Public Ownership and the Regulation of Natural Monopoly* (Oxford: Basil Blackwell).
Friedman, M. (1977), *From Galbraith to Economic Freedom*, IEA Occasional Paper 49 (London: Institute of Economic Affairs).
Hennessy, P. (1990), *Whitehall* (London: Fontana).
Hyman, R. (1983), 'White Collar Workers and Theories of Class', in R. Hyman and R. Price (eds), *The New Working Class?: White Collar Workers and Their Organizations* (London: Macmillan), pp. 3–45.
Jones, J. M. (1980), *Organizational Aspects of Police Behaviour* (Farnborough, Hants.: Gower).
King, D. S. (1987), *The New Right: Politics, Markets and Citizenship* (London: Macmillan).
Mills, C. W. (1951), *White Collar* (Oxford and New York: Oxford University Press).
Pollitt, C. (1993), *Managerialism and the Public Services: Cuts or Cultural Change in the 1990s?,* 2nd edn (Oxford: Basil Blackwell).

Sisson, C. H. (1976), 'The Civil Service After Fulton', in W. J. Stankiewicz (ed.), *British Government in an Era of Reform* (London: Collier-Macmillan), pp. 252–62.

Sjölund, M. (1989), *Statens Lönepolitik, 1966–1988* (Stockholm: Allmänna Förlaget).

Theakston, K. and G. Fry (1989), 'Britain's Administrative Elite: Permanent Secretaries, 1900–1986', *Public Administration*, 67, 129–47.

# 6. Japan: divided bureaucracy in a unified regime

## Ellis S. Krauss

## INTRODUCTION

The image of the public bureaucracy in Japan has evolved to the status of myth in many parts of the world. The myth has depicted a bureaucracy with only the stereotypically best characteristics of the civil services of the West: the elite status, elan and power in policy-making of French bureaucrats, the efficiency of the German administrator, the shared world view and informal establishment networks with civil society of the British civil servant, and the public-spiritedness and autonomy from politics of the Swedish official. All this, of course, has also been wrapped up with an almost mystical Asian ability to produce unparalleled economic growth from the private sector. On all the dimensions of state–society relations covered in this volume, policy-making, internal organization and relations with civil society, Japan of the myth seems to be the stellar model that has managed to have it all.

As with most myths, there is a kernel of truth to all these characterizations; as with all myths, portions of it, and especially the cumulative impression of public administration it conveys, are distorted and exaggerated. Most importantly, the ideal portrayal of Japan's bureaucracy omits many of its equally true aspects. One can also build a case that public administration in Japan has been as subject to manipulation by politicians as the Italian civil service, has been as penetrated by interest groups as the American bureaucracy, and is as fractured by inter-agency rivalry and conflict as any administration anywhere.

Which is the 'real' Japanese bureaucracy? Both views, of course, depend on where one looks and what one is looking at. In particular, it is important to realize, and this is one of the themes of this chapter, that the admired aspects of Japanese public administration are often purchased and facilitated by its less-known but equally valid 'weaknesses'.

This chapter will attempt to give a brief but balanced view of Japan's public bureaucracy and its relationship to policy-makers, internal organization and dynamics, and connections to civil society. In the conclusion I shall return to the theme of how these dimensions are related to each other to produce a complex reality of public administration that often differs from the myth.

## OVERVIEW

The framework for the pre-war civil service was established by Japan's modernizing political elite during the Meiji era (1868–1913) (Koh 1989, pp. 10–31). The small oligarchy that led Japan during this entire period founded a modern civil service as well as a training school for public administrators (Tokyo Imperial University's Faculty of Law) during the 1880s. In conformity with the dominant idealogy that this oligarchy used to legitimize the state and mobilize the population for industrialization, the bureaucracy was considered the servants not of the public, but of the Emperor, and responsible not to the nascent parliament (the Diet) but to the Cabinet who was in turn theoretically appointed by the Emperor. The ideological conception was of a public administration separate from and above politics and elected representatives, serving the imperial state for the public good. It is no coincidence if this is reminiscent of the Prussian model of bureaucracy, as the Meiji state was intentionally modelled on the nineteenth-century Prussian state. This civil service led the successful economic modernization of Japan during this period.

While the Emperor ruled in theory, in practice the small oligarchy of about eight men who founded this state rotated the main Cabinet positions among themselves or their immediate disciples for all of this period and thus directly controlled the civil and military services. With the death of the original oligarchy by the 1920s and the rise of both political parties and popular demands for democracy, the Diet became a more representative institution, and the Cabinet, and thus the bureaucracy, more penetrated by elected politicians and parties. The ideal of the elite, neutral and non-political civil service continued, however. The gradual consolidation of power from within the state by the military bureaucracy during the 1930s – using foreign and domestic challenges as the pretext – and finally the Pacific War that began in 1937 with Japan's invasion of China, ended the trends toward more democratic accountability for the civil service.

The American Occupation of Japan (1945–52) carried out a major restructuring of Japan's social and political system. One of its major goals was to 'democratize' Japan, substituting popular sovereignty for imperial sovereignty, creating a democratic polity, and establishing a post-war Constitution as the legal framework. The National Diet – elected by universal suffrage – constitutionally was made the 'supreme organ of state power'. The national bureaucracy also was made directly responsible to a Cabinet chosen by the majority party in the Diet. For the first time, public administration was to be embedded in the legal framework of responsibility to a civilian Cabinet and prime minister, who in turn were selected by and responsible to elected party politicians in a sovereign parliament; this was the same system as had evolved in the other industrialized democracies of Western Europe.

Further, to accomplish 'democratization', the Occupation carried out purges of politicians and officials who had been too closely identified with pre-war nationalism and military rule. The Americans introduced their own ideas of democratic civil service, and bureaucrats were required in 1950 to take and pass a new civil service examination based on those principles or lose their posts (Koh 1989, pp. 56–8).

Nevertheless, the national bureaucracy was the least-changed of Japanese political institutions (Pempel 1982, pp. 15–16). Its personnel were the least-purged in democratic reforms, and the Occupation's civil service examination was known as the 'paradise examination' because parts of it were simpler than the prewar variety and because it had no time limit and one could take it leisurely with many tea breaks and still pass. Few of the test-takers, including pre-war bureaucrats, failed – over 80 per cent are estimated to have passed (Koh 1989, p. 57). After the end of the Occupation more rigorous examinations were reintroduced. Further, the Occupation reforms concentrated more on raising bureaucratic efficiency than on fundamentally altering the elite and discretionary character of the civil service (Pempel 1992, p. 20). Thus today, as in the pre-war era, the Japanese civil service recruits a highly elite bureaucratic cadre selected according to meritocratic criteria, as will be described below.

More altered was the local administration. Pre-war governors of prefectures – the intermediary unit between centre and local government – were appointed by the central government, and in general the aim was to depoliticize local government into an administrative arm of the central state. The American Occupation attempted to decentralize local government and devolve administrative functions such as police and education down to the lowest level, much as in the US. After the end of the Occupation some of these reforms were reversed, giving some responsibility to the prefectural level and recentralizing some others, such as textbook selection or rural policing, to the national state. Longer-lasting reforms were the election of governors, mayors and local assemblies and the placing of local administration under the purview of these elected officials (Steiner *et al.* 1980).

The national legal and structural framework introduced by the Americans has been little altered during the past forty-plus years. Ministries and several agencies constitute the national civil service. The twelve main ministries are organized along functional lines; for example, Finance, International Trade and Industry, Construction, Education, and so on. Agencies are of two types. Some are just sub-units of a ministry, such as the Small and Medium-sized Enterprise Agency of the Ministry of International Trade and Industry, and function essentially as a constituent part of it. Other agencies, however – particularly those technically located in the Office of the Prime Minister (such as the Economic Planning Agency, the Defence Agency, and others) are to all intents and purposes the same as ministries. The Cabinet consists of the twenty individuals who head the twelve ministries and also the agencies in the prime minister's office (some of the latter often holding dual portfolios).

A few ministries and agencies have been added during the post-war period – Economic Planning, Science and Technology, Environment, among others – and a few have had name changes or revised functions – the Ministry of Home Affairs from a similar agency, and the Management and Co-ordination Agency from the Administrative Management Agency, for example (Koh 1989, p. 63). None of these changes has been controversial.

The personnel of the government are governed by the National Civil Service Law originally adopted under the Occupation, and administered by the National Personnel Authority (*jinjikyoku*). One controversial aspect of personnel administration has been an Occupation proscription against strikes by public employees, a law that the public-sector unions have been trying to change for 40 years, thus far without success.

The size and scope of the various levels of government in Japan have not been central political issues in Japan as they are perennially in the US. Indeed, Japan has the smallest public-sector bureaucracy of any of the advanced industrialized nations, with government employees comprising less than 5 per cent of the total population and less than 10 per cent of the work-force (Pempel 1992, p. 21). Approximately 1.2 million persons work for the national government, of which about 420,000 are actually general administrative staff. The rest are employed by the Defence Agency (that is, the military), the education system (including national university professors and staff), or one of the five government enterprises (posts, the mint, forestry, and so on) (Pempel 1992, p. 21). The size of the public sector grew considerably in the post-war period, but much of that growth was in the local government system. The percentage of central government public employees per employed population has actually declined considerably since the 1950s. During the 1980s, especially, the number of public employees at the national level declined – due in large part to the privatization of formerly public corporations, to be discussed below – while the number of prefectural and city, town and village employees (the only sub-national levels of government in Japan) remained about the same (Yano Memorial Society 1991a, Figure 41-9 and Chart 41-7, p. 450).

In terms of finances, the revenues and expenditures of central government have expanded enormously along with Japan's affluence: central government income and expenditures are nearly a hundred times greater than they were in 1950, for example (Yano Memorial Society 1991b, chart 7–12, pp. 387–8). As a percentage of national income, however, the tax burden of under 19 per cent for the central government and 28 per cent overall is among the lowest of the industrialized nations (Yano Memorial Society 1991a, Figure 41-7 and Chart 41-5, p. 448). National debt rose greatly in the 1970s, partly as a result of major new welfare programmes and partly because of Liberal-Democratic Party (LDP) spending to try to stem the rise of opposition strength at the local and national levels. Indeed, Japan's dependency on bonds (that is, debt percentage) rose to over 30 per cent of the budget in the late 1970s and early 1980s; by 1991, however, the debt percentage was down below 10 per cent (Yano Memorial Society 1991a, Chart 41-1, p. 445).

Keeping the size of central government small in Japan is the result of intentional government policy. The drastic reduction in debt in the 1980s was the result of fiscal austerity programmes undertaken by the LDP and the Finance Ministry once the conservatives' electoral strength had rebounded after the 1980 election. Personnel growth too has been checked by policy. In the 1960s, the government's First Administrative Reform was carried out, which placed a ceiling on national government growth. As a result, the number of national government employees in 1979 numbered the same or less than before the reforms (Pempel 1982, pp. 255–295). A Second Administrative Reform was carried out in the 1980s with the aim of privatizing the largest public corporations and redistributing some functions among national and local governments. This reform was more controversial than the first and will be discussed more extensively below.

A second controversial issue for a brief period in the 1970s was that of the degree of local autonomy that should be granted to sub-national units. Although the national government collects two-thirds of all government revenues in Japan, the local (prefectural and city, town and village) units account for two-thirds of the expenditures of government. The difference is made up by local transfers from the centre to the local level. The centre can also mandate the local authorities to implement some of the national activities.

For many years when conservatives dominated the local executive and assembly posts, the fiscal and policy leadership of the central government, also under long-term conservative (LDP) rule, was unquestioned. In the 1970s, however, along with the rise of citizens' movements protesting against pollution and Leftist parties capturing the local government of many urban areas, one of the rallying cries was for more local autonomy and the devolution of power down to the local level. Local governments also took more policy initiatives during this period as well (Steiner *et al.* 1980). With the LDP's policy response to controlling pollution and the partial recapture at least of many urban local governments, this issue is no longer as salient as it once was.

In general, Japan's public administration has changed greatly since pre-war days, yet none the less probably exhibits more continuity than one would expect, given the upheavals of the war and the Occupation and the enormous social changes of the post-war era. The responsibility of civil administration to democratically elected officials, rather than to the Emperor, has become well-established, and is probably the greatest change in the legal and contextual framework of public administration since the pre-war era. The fact that such issues as privatization of public services and decentralization of administration have at various times in the post-war period become important and controversial issues is also a major break with historical tradition representing the new, democratic legal context.

The greatest structural and functional changes, however, have probably occurred more at the sub-national than the national level. Further, the elite, non-partisan and meritocratic status of, particularly, national bureaucrats, the leadership role, but small size, of the central government, and a conception that the bureaucracy should serve the public interest have remained as basic continuities from the pre- to the post-war and throughout the past 40 and more years since the Occupation's democratizing reforms.

## POLICY-MAKERS AND POLICY-MAKING

As mentioned above, the post-war Constitution of Japan clearly established the national Diet as the 'supreme organ of state power'. No policy can become law without the approval of the elected representatives of the public in the House of Representatives (HOR) and the House of Councillors (HOC). One party, the conservative LDP, controlled the majority of seats (although not necessarily a majority of the popular vote) in the more important HOR until 1993, and thus in the Cabinet; effectively this means that proposals had to be approved by the politicians in the LDP if they were to have a chance of becoming government policy and law. Administrative officials thus had to operate within a clear legal framework of parliamentary sovereignty and Cabinet responsibility, and within the political context of one-party dominance, in the post-war period.

The reality of the political–administrative relationship, however, was far more complicated and subject to debate among political scientists than the formal environment might indicate. The question of the role and power of bureaucrats in policy-making has been a central focus for political scientists. For many years, indeed, the two most popular models of the post-war Japanese political system saw the bureaucracy as *the* single dominant power in policy-making, or at least as one of the three main pillars of an exclusive 'ruling triad' governing coalition of the bureaucracy, the LDP and big business (see Muramatsu and Krauss 1984, pp. 127–9, for a description of these models).

Those who saw bureaucrats as being dominant in policy-making pointed to several dimensions of their role and activities in the process. One was simply the legacy of their pre-war function and status and the authority that it gave to the administrative elite, especially in the immediate post-war era when democracy was not yet institutionalized, political elites were new to the job of governing, and private-sector elites were dependent on the state for resources to revive the Japanese economy after its wartime devastation. The continuity in administrative personnel and structure gave bureaucracy an advantage and a leading role in making policy for reconstructing the economy and society.

Partly as a result, the bureaucracy came to play a major role in the policy-making process. Most of the bills – for the quarter century after the LDP became the majority party in 1955, about 60 per cent – considered by the Diet were Cabinet-sponsored legislation – were initiated and formulated in the bureaucracy (Richardson and Flanagan 1984, p. 347). A typical bill formulated in the bureaucracy would then be considered in the various policy-making bodies of the LDP, especially its Policy Affairs Research Council (PARC). The functionally organized divisions of PARC have close relations with their ministerial counterparts, and bureaucrats were often called to testify about bills in PARC meetings. A party-approved (and often modified) bill would then go to the Cabinet for (unanimous) final approval before being introduced into the Diet committees to testify about a bill.

Further, in contrast to the US or Italy, for example, the Japanese Diet passed far fewer laws and they were of a much more general nature, relying on the civil administration to interpret and apply the law in specific ways. Whereas the US Congress may pass 1000 bills in a session (a small percentage of the number actually introduced, however), and the Italian parliament 400, the Japanese Diet typically passed only just over 100 bills. The laws, furthermore, were written very generally and, while setting limits and guidelines for application, allowed the bureaucracy to carry out the details of implementation within that framework. The bureaucracy thus gained some degree of power through the small number and vague nature of Japanese laws.

The influence of the bureaucracy, it has been argued, is not only in its overt role. The administrative elite also came to penetrate and influence the LDP. Thus, an average of about one-quarter of LDP Diet members (and a higher proportion of Cabinet ministers) in the post-war period have been former higher civil servants who have received LDP endorsement and successfully run for office after retirement or resignation from the bureaucracy. This practice is called *amakudari* ('descent from heaven'), reflective of the status of the bureaucracy (Johnson 1975, p. 7) and is similar to the French bureaucracy's *pantouflage*. Thus, even before it undertook to implement policies, the bureaucracy was intimately involved in each stage of the policy-making process, from formulation to enactment. Even the parts played by the party and government were indirectly influenced by the bureaucracy as so many of the key politicians were former bureaucrats with the orientation of and connections to the agencies they used to serve.

Finally, the ability of the Ministry of International Trade and Industry (MITI) to formulate, gain passage of and implement an industrial policy that allowed it effectively to pick 'winners and losers' among various industrial sectors without partisan political interference, was in particular seen as evidence of the bureaucracy's autonomy from politicians (Johnson 1982).

Beginning in the 1980s, however, a different and more complex view of the role of the bureaucracy began to emerge among both American and Japanese political scientists specializing on Japan. For one thing, no matter how much desired by the bureaucracy, no bill would ever be introduced into the Diet unless the ruling party achieved a consensus over the policy and approved it. Secondly, it could be pointed out that the LDP and its leaders had various powers of control over the bureaucracy, including informal veto power over the promotion of the highest-ranking civil servants in each ministry. Thirdly, the parachuting of former bureaucrats into the LDP could be seen as a two-edged sword: rather than just giving agencies a spokesman in the party, it also brought policy-making skills and expertise to the LDP, allowing it to influence policy and manipulate the bureaucracy more effectively.

Indeed, both case studies and survey data began to show that the role played by politicians in influencing policy-making was by no means insubstantial. Thus, in surveys conducted in both 1976 and 1986, Michio Muramatsu found that *both* politicians and bureaucrats themselves tended to accord the Diet an important role in policy-making (Muramatsu and Krauss 1984, 1988).

In addition, using questions very similar to those that Aberbach *et al.* (1981) used to classify the roles of the higher civil servants in Western Europe and the US, Muramatsu's 1976 survey discovered that, as in the other Western democracies, 'the role of politicians and bureaucrats has been converging, but there are still differences in their contributions and emphases in the policymaking process' (Muramatsu and Krauss 1984, p. 134). There was a tendency for bureaucrats to define their roles, and also for politicians to perceive them, as primarily providing information and technical expertise to politicians, and secondly, as brokers and managers of social interests. The notion that bureaucrats were either mere implementors of decisions made by politicians, or leaders defining directions of national change, the role usually ascribed to political leaders, received less support. Thus Japan's civil servants, like those in other Western democracies, do perform several important functions in the policy-making process; but so also do politicians.

Furthermore, many scholars have argued more recently that, particularly since the 1970s, the senior politicians of the LDP have been increasing their influence and role in the policy-making process (for example, Muramatsu and Krauss 1984, 1987; Pempel 1987). The long-term rule of the LDP has increased the influence of the ruling senior LDP politicians and leaders. Particularly important in this respect has been the rise of *zoku* (policy 'tribes') within the divisions of the LDP's PARC, who are specialists on particular areas of policy. The senior LDP leaders of these *zoku* rival the higher civil servants in knowledge and expertise on policy-making and also have excellent connections both to the parallel ministries and to the major interest groups in that policy arena. They are thus able to wield major influence and co-ordinating power over the 'iron triangle' of LDP PARC divisions/Diet committees, bureaucratic agencies and major interest groups in decisions affecting the policies in that area. Their co-ordinating ability is said to be increasingly necessary also because of the intensifying conflict and fragmentation of co-ordination among bureaucratic agencies in the expanding number of issues that cross bureaucratic jurisdictions (Pempel 1987; Muramatsu and Krauss 1987).

More recent studies have shown that the role of bureaucrats and politicians may be quite complex, differing not only by policy area but also within policy areas and across time (Anderson 1992, pp. 53–4). Thus, a detailed study of the role of *zoku* within the educational policy area has shown that their role may vary with the type of issue, from little more than 'cheerleaders' for bureaucratic-led policy-making to leading roles as influential brokers moving policy forward (Schoppa 1991).

The relative emphasis in the roles of bureaucrats and politicians also may shift over time. Muramatsu's follow-up survey in 1986 showed that after a decade of growing power of private-interest groups and international pressure on Japan, there was an increase in the number of bureaucrats who perceived their main role as co-ordinating social interests, and in the proportion, particularly of the highest civil servants, who perceived it as changing society in desirable directions (Muramatsu and Krauss 1988).

Even more striking evidence that the relative roles of bureaucrats and politicians may fluctuate over time was a major study of several policy-making areas – small business, agriculture, regional and other policy areas – during the postwar period that has also concluded that in times of 'crisis', when LDP majorities have been threatened by external events, the party takes the lead in using policy to compensate societal groups and shore up its weakened support base (Calder 1988).

In a related vein, the question of the extent of the bureaucracy's autonomy is a similarly complicated issue. On the one hand, it has been portrayed as quite autonomous, efficient and effective in applying rational, technocratic decisions to policy, particularly in the important area of industrial policy (Johnson 1982). On the other hand, industrial policy (and perhaps economic policy in general) may be an exception – in most other policy arenas, the bureaucracy is much less autonomous and much more subject to intervention and interference by politicians (Campbell 1990, pp. 128–33). A 1986 survey of bureaucrats, for example, found differences in attitude between the 'economic' bureaucracy, represented by MITI, the Ministry of Finance and the Economic Planning Agency, and the other ministries including in attitudes concerning politics and technocratic solutions, with the latter being more 'politicized' and less technocratic (Aberbach *et al.* 1991). The same survey found that the economic ministries had much greater contact with the higher levels of government leadership, especially the prime minister, than the 'political' ministries, the latter having greater interaction with the *zoku* sectorial interest politicians (Muramatsu 1987).

Indeed, in any policy area in which the LDP had fairly high political stakes – agriculture, construction, education, transportation, for example – the policy-making arenas bore far more resemblance to the American case of politicians and interest groups having greater influence than bureaucrats, with the latter essentially 'captured' or 'colonized' by the former elites. The Japanese electoral system, with its multi-member districts pitting LDP politicians against each other, induces great pressures on representatives to deliver concrete public goods to their constituencies. Thus, one reason industrial policy may be an exception is that – especially given the employment system of large firms, which avoids layoffs of employees except as a last resort – there are few direct and immediate constituency benefits that can be provided by strategic industrial policy. Politicians are more likely to become involved in other policy areas with more potential for pay-offs to the voters (Krauss 1992 pp. 53-54; Krauss and Pierre 1993, pp. 170–5).

As this review of the literature suggests, the actual role of the bureaucracy in policy-making and its relation to politicians in that process is far more complex than might be assumed. The civil service is a major player in the policy-making game and, as in other Western democracies, is no mere implementor of decisions made by political leaders. Nevertheless, as in these other democracies, politicians and parliamentary institutions also play a significant role in formulating and making policy. Further, the relative influence of the civil service will vary across and within issue areas and over time, and the extent of political interference in administration also varies greatly by the type of ministry. In general, the political leaders' relative influence and its integration with administration seems to have increased over time with the institutionalization of the LDP as the perennially ruling party. With the advent of shifting coalition governments in 1993, however, and the partial diminution of LDP power, relative influence of bureaucrats and politicians may be changing yet again.

## PUBLIC ADMINISTRATION AS ORGANIZATION

At the heart of Japan's public administration system, as in its private-sector organizations as well, is the process of recruitment of personnel. Although special and some technical personnel will be hired by evaluation procedures other than examination, most general administrative personnel, and especially higher civil servants, are hired by competitive examination (Koh 1989, pp. 82–6). There have been various changes in the labelling and categorization of the examinations over time, but in general there are separate types for higher, middle and lower civil servants. Since the 1970s, the number taking the higher civil service examination has ranged between about 30,000 and 50,000 persons. The ratio of those passing this difficult examination to those taking it has ranged between 1.3 and 6 per cent. In 1976, for example, of more than 44,000 applicants taking the highest grade examination, only slightly over 1100 passed; whereas in 1988, of the 28,000 candidates, more than 1800 passed (Koh 1989, Table 6, p. 80). Naturally, there is also a self-selection process involved in application, with only the brightest graduates of the best universities most likely to present themselves, so that the small success rate among such a pool of applicants represents an elite group indeed.

Not everyone who passes the examination, however, is employed as a higher civil servant. Only about half of those who passed will actually apply to a particular ministry for a job and succeed in getting through the subsequent interview process which they must also satisfy if they are to be hired (Koh 1989, p. 80). Overwhelmingly, those passing the examination and being hired are graduates of the national university system. Although the number of private university graduates is increasing, between 80 and 90 per cent of those hired are national university alumni. In particular, Tokyo University, the post-war elite successor to the Tokyo Imperial University set up in the Meiji era to train bureaucrats, still provides about a third of those who successfully pass the examination; and its rival from the Kansai area, Kyoto University, provides more than 10 per cent (Koh 1989, Table 9, p. 87). This means that nearly half those who pass the examination are from these two universities alone.

To have a degree in law is also an advantage: whereas only about 15 per cent of those who pass the examination have law backgrounds, over 40 per cent of those hired have that background. And about two-thirds of those who pass the examination with law backgrounds are from the Tokyo University Faculty of Law (Koh 1989, Tables 12 and 13, pp. 95 and 97). Clearly, entering the Faculty of Law at Tokyo University is the career ladder to the higher civil service in Japan. Tokyo University, or 'Todai' as it is called, itself recruits only the 'best and the brightest' of Japanese youth by competitive examination.[1] In these terms, the Japanese bureaucracy strongly resembles the French bureaucracy, with its elite status and recruitment from particular prestigious schools that specialize in training the administrative elite. Obviously this recruitment from such a limited range of universities, combined with attempts by each ministry in the interview/selection process to hire those it believes will fit in with its existing personnel, give each ministry a fairly homogeneous staff.

Ministries and agencies do differ in their status and thus in their ability to recruit the best of the best who apply. Generally, the 'economic' ministries – the Ministry of Finance (MOF) and the Ministry of International Trade and Industry (MITI) are the most prestigious and get some of the best recruits. Interestingly, these ministries are known to be less penetrated by the external influence of politicians and interest groups, compared with the more 'political' ministries that providing subsidies, patronage and 'pork-barrel' distributive goods to electoral constituencies, such as the Ministries of Agriculture, Construction, Transportation, Posts and so forth.

Once in a ministry, the bureaucrat is likely to stay there for most of his career. If he leaves the ministry at all, it is likely to be only for a short-term (perhaps two-year) posting to another agency or for study abroad.

The patterns of advancement for the Japanese bureaucrat are relatively fixed, and emphasize a career ladder that promotes individuals on performance but only within the context of a group seniority system. One of a 'class' of young bureaucrats who entered the ministry at the same time will reach the first higher official level, that of section chief, in his early forties or late thirties. Later, a few of his other classmates may also reach that post. From among those who become section chiefs, a few will become bureau heads, department heads, perhaps counsellors; finally, only one will usually become Administrative Vice-Minister, the highest career administrative post, usually in his early fifties (Muramatsu 1981, pp. 69–74). It is customary for all other members of that person's 'class' to retire from the civil service when one of their number is appointed Administrative Vice-Minister.[2]

Career 'lifetime employment' in the same ministry and conscious efforts at socialization are said to encourage particular loyalty and identification with the civil servant's ministry (Campbell 1984, pp. 315–17). The *esprit de corps* of Japanese ministries, particularly the more prestigious economic ministries, is acknowledged to be quite high.

Consensus is emphasized in internal decision-making, including the famous *ringisei* system by which everyone involved in a decision from the lowest ranks and upwards must 'sign off' on it with their seals, but there is also a great deal of informal consensus-seeking as well (Craig 1975, pp. 17–24). Formal mechanisms are also used to mitigate conflict between agencies over resources. In deciding increases or cuts in agencies' budgets, the norms governing Ministry of Finance recommendations have emphasized 'fair shares', that is, relatively equal increases or decreases for similar programmes within different ministries, thus minimizing interministerial conflict over budget allocations (Campbell 1975, pp. 71–100).

On the other hand, the negative consequence of intra-agency *esprit de corps* and consensus, and of conflict-avoiding norms in budget allocations, is interministerial conflict and rivalry over policy jurisdictions. A major problem of Japanese government, therefore, is said to be co-ordination across ministries (Campbell 1984, pp. 298–9) as bureaucrats, perceiving and pursuing their own agency's goals and agenda, engage in 'turf' battles over jurisdiction. The perpetual rivalry between MOF and MITI is legendary, and lately MITI and the Ministry of Posts have engaged in highly publicized conflict over who was to have jurisdiction over new forms of telecommunications (Johnson 1989). The latter conflict is particularly interesting as it involved a ministry, Posts, usually identified as a less-prestigious 'political' ministry, attempting to gain status by entering into the area of industrial policy (towards telecommunications), and thus provoking MITI to defend its 'turf' (Johnson 1989). In general, as long as a policy problem is contained within the clear jurisdiction of one agency it seems that it can be approached, dealt with and managed. Policies that span agency boundaries, on the other hand, seem to escalate into public battles fairly easily, and often require resolution by the senior leaders of the LDP, as happened in the 'telecom' war just described.

The greatest changes in internal administration in the post-Occupation period have been imposed on the civil service by politicians in response to the LDP agenda or international pressure. I have already mentioned the First Administrative Reform of the 1960s. Here, further personnel expansion of the central government was to be stopped and the size of government reduced, but the administrative service also needed to be able to respond flexibly to changing societal needs. To accomplish the former goal, the main ministries and agencies were told to cut one bureau each, and total personnel was reduced 5 per cent over a three-year period through attrition. Positions saved by the across-the-board cut were to be put into a pool of positions that could be tapped by ministries and agencies to meet their needs, but on a competitive basis (Pempel 1982).

By these techniques, the reform mitigated bureaucratic resistance because all agencies were being treated equally and no lay-offs were carried out. Flexibility was left to the administrative apparatus also because each ministry and agency was left to determine which bureau should be cut. That agencies could remain flexible to national needs was also ensured by linking acquisition of further personnel to competitive justifications from a central pool (Pempel 1982, pp. 264–6). As mentioned above, this reform has successfully restrained the grown of the central government in Japan for the past 25 years.

The Second Administrative Reform (discussion below based on Muramatsu 1987, pp. 312–13, 318–24, 328–32, 336–38) was part of the strategy of Nakasone Yasuhirō for making government smaller and more efficient. Using special councils of experts appointed by the prime minister, Nakasone intended to propose and implement new policies while overcoming expected resistance from the bureaucracy to the changes. The purposes of the Second Administrative Reform were, first, to reduce central government spending that had built up such large budget deficits in the 1970s. This was accomplished, as explained above, mostly through stringent capping of, and later actual reductions in, ministry and agency budgets. Pension plans were also reorganized. A second goal was to streamline administration, especially to aid management of and by the Prime Minister's Office. The main organizational means to do this was to combine the former Administrative Management Agency and the Prime Minister's Office into one Prime Minister's Agency (*sōmuchō*). A third goal was to privatize some of the huge public corporations and thus reduce the government's and increase the private sector's role in the economy, partly in response to international pressure for a more dynamic economy to ease the trade crisis. This last aspect of administrative reform will be discussed in more detail below, in the next section.

One way in which the above goals were accomplished was by Nakasone's careful attention to forestalling and countering bureaucratic resistance. Public deliberative bodies appointed by Nakasone advisors from the academic world and business were created, first, to propose the changes, and then, later, to coordinate their implementation. In the process, these public bodies legitimized the reforms with great publicity. Early in the process, the bureaucracy's suggestions and reactions to nascent proposals were sought to reduce resistance later on, and many Administrative Vice-Ministers especially were brought into the implementation process. Finally, in pursuing administrative reform, Nakasone allied himself with both the powerful leaders of the corporate world and the economic ministries, such as the Ministry of Finance, that supported administrative reform, in order to overcome resistance from the other agencies and the LDP *zoku* whose client groups would be most changed by the reforms.

The reforms have been carried out over a period of years and monitored by special advisory committees to ensure their implementation.

## ADMINISTRATION AND SOCIETY

The word 'civil servant' had little place in traditional Japanese concepts of bureaucracy. In the Tokugawa period (1603–1868) prior to modernization, when *samurai* warrior elites were in the process of being converted into stipendiary feudal administrators, one saying that summed up the relationship between administration and society was 'officials honoured, people despised'. Modernization under the aegis of an imperial bureaucracy did little to offset these attitudes. The postwar democratization, however, has raised the status of 'the people' considerably and made administrators more into the 'civil servants' that they are. Nevertheless, the position of the higher national bureaucrat – with its stringent access through prestigious universities and difficult examinations – retains a cachet and status that was unchallenged until recent economic growth and more democratic attitudes gave to the roles of top business executives for major firms and Diet members equivalent status.

If attitudes toward individual national bureaucrats are still respectful, so the image of the bureaucracy in general is generally positive as a relatively incorruptible and effective institution; in particular contrast to American political culture with its deep and innate assumption of governmental incompetence and inefficiency. For example, a 1977 survey found the bureaucracy to have the second highest rating of trust of any institution in Japanese society, with over three-quarters of the sample saying it could be, or probably could be, trusted – a much greater proportion than for the national Diet, the government, big business and labour unions, and somewhat higher than the courts, police, newspapers and commercial television. The only institution attaining trust from a higher percentage of the population was NHK, Japan's giant public broadcasting organization (NHK Hōsō Yoron Chōsajo 1981: Chart 2, p. 46).

Further, a 1972 replication of the *Civic Culture* study (Almond and Verba 1967) in Japan (Nakamura 1975) found that, unlike the high percentage of Britons and Americans who would turn to their elected representatives or their friends and neighbours to change a law they didn't like, the Japanese, like the Germans, were more prone to turn to the bureaucracy. Nonetheless, attitudes towards public administration are not unambivalent. Thus, another survey on Japanese political culture found that between one-fourth and one-third of the Japanese respondents did not necessarily expect to be treated equally by their public administration, and 63 per cent thought that they needed personal contacts to reach a government official, compared to only about a quarter of Americans, and more than half of those thought it would be difficult or impossible to find such a connection. These personalist, particularist and cynical attitudes are both a reflection and a cause of the pronounced lack of political efficacy among citizens in Japan (Richardson and Flanagan 1984, pp. 179–80).

There is no tradition of an ombudsman in Japan, although the concept achieved some attention from intellectuals in the 1970s during the height of the concern over citizens' movements against pollution, local autonomy and enhancing citizen access to local governments. Many local governments did expand their citizens' complaints apparatus at the time. Further, an office of Trade Ombudsman was established in the Cabinet Secretariat in the 1980s to provide foreign firms with a window to complain about bureaucratic obstacles to trade. Nevertheless, the ombudsman role is not well institutionalized in Japan's domestic public administration.

Organized interests have a far greater influence on the bureaucracy than do individuals but, similar to the relationship between politicians and bureaucracy, for many years the predominant image was one of bureaucratic-led state dominance of the private sector, most notably in the area of industrial policy and economic growth (Johnson 1982). Especially in the early post-war period, MITI had great formal powers, such as over currency exchange, with which to exert leverage for compliance to its wishes from the private sector. With liberalization after the 1960s, however, MITI lost these key formal powers and had to rely instead on 'administrative guidance' (Johnson 1982, pp. 242–74).

Administrative guidance refers to the range of administrative means available to the bureaucracy in Japan to implement its decisions *vis-à-vis* the private sector. This may entail the Cabinet or a specific agency issuing a formal ordinance that has the force of law. More usually, however, it may involve sending written 'communications' with the bureaucracy's interpretation and advice concerning a particular policy, or informal verbal communication attempting to persuade industry to co-operate with the Ministry's ideas of what should be done. Even after losing some of the formal legal mechanisms for inducing private industry compliance, therefore, MITI was seen to be able to gain it by using administrative guidance (Johnson 1982, pp. 242–74).

Recently, however, similar to the changing view of policy-makers and the bureaucracy, many observers believe that the expanding resources and global reach of Japanese business have decreased the relevance of the government to big business and that the latter has become far more autonomous from bureaucratic influence – without the formal powers of the earlier postwar period, even the more informal influence of 'administrative guidance' may be losing its effectiveness as well.

Some scholars argue that the case of administrative leadership has actually never been as great, or the government–business relationship as two-way, as has been depicted, in any case. Thus, Richard Samuels, in a landmark historical study of the history of the energy sector, argues that while the state has repeatedly tried to assert control in the energy field over the private sector, it has just as repeatedly failed against private-sector resistance. Rather, business has traded 'jurisdiction for control', giving the state nominal supervisory powers but retaining some real power over activities through a process of 'reciprocal consent' with the state (Samuels 1987, pp. 260–1). Recent attempts by MITI, in the cases of steel minimills and VCR standardization, even with the support of major firms in the industry, to impose their preferences on recalcitrant smaller firms who have a market advantage have also failed (Noble 1989).

John O. Haley, a legal scholar, contends that administrative guidance itself is not a sign of bureaucracy's extension of power, but rather its lack. He argues that administrative guidance is only a particularly Japanese form of the informal enforcement that all bureaucracies have. Further, administration in Japan lacks formal regulatory powers and therefore, where it has no ability to compel or coerce, bureaucracy must negotiate and compromise (Haley 1987, esp. pp. 352–7).

Haley's emphasis on bureaucrat–private-sector negotiation raises the possibility that neither a model that views a strong state able to impose its will on private industry, nor one that sees bureaucracy as irrelevant to the outcomes, is the most applicable to Japan. Indeed, the most salient aspect of bureaucratic–civil society relations in Japan may be how difficult it is to separate the boundaries of the two. The density of institutionalized formal and informal networks between state and society in Japan – not only in the area of industrial policy and large enterprise, but also in other policy sectors – is quite striking, even in comparative perspective.

Private-interest groups are highly and hierarchically organized in almost every sector of society, and these associations in turn have close and frequent interaction with the state bureaucrats supervising that field, through the multiple formal advisory bodies (*shingikai*) attached to each agency and composed of non-governmental experts and representatives from organizations in that field, and through more informal contact. Bureaucrats and major interest-group leaders at times may also be connected through old school, marriage or friendship ties, as well. The practice of *amakudari*, by which former bureaucrats retire to a second profession, also sends many former higher civil servants into the business world, further cementing government–business connections. Policy, as frequently as not, turns out to be the product of what Samuels has aptly labelled 'reciprocal consent' between bureaucratic and societal elites (Samuels 1987, p. 260). This characteristic of Japan has led another author to refer to Japan as having a 'societal' or 'network' state, with a close and organic relationship between civil administration and society (Okimoto 1988, p. 314).

Thus, if industrial policy represents an area where the MITI is relatively more autonomous from interference by policy-makers and partisan pressures than others, it is not insulated from societal groups such as business, but neither is the Ministry the captive of any interest group. The very success of industrial policy in Japan may well stem from the close mutual information and goal-sharing of business and bureaucratic elites unperturbed by great contrary pressures from politicians, labour or small business. Officialdom's task of policy implementation is also eased when the societal groups are intimately involved in the process of creating the policy (Krauss 1992, p. 51; Krauss and Pierre 1993, p. 173).

The question of corporatist arrangements naturally comes to mind. There are corporatist tendencies in various dimensions of the relations between the state and private organizations, but again these vary greatly in kind and degree by sector and level. There are overarching 'peak' associations of business such as *Keidanren* (the Federation of Economic Organization), which is an influential representative of business to the government on macroeconomic policy, and *Nikkeiren*, which represents large enterprises' unified stance toward labour. Labour too has a few federations of unions. Because of business's close relationship to the formerly perennially ruling party and labour's usual affiliation with the previously perpetually out-of-power opposition parties, however, labour has not been brought into formal bargaining arrangements with business and government (Pempel and Tsunekawa 1979). Business may co-ordinate its wage posture with top political leaders informally before bargaining with union representatives during the annual 'spring labour offensive', but there are no formal tripartite bargaining mechanisms.

More-institutionalized corporatist tendencies have probably been greatest at the mesocorporatist level of specific sectors. One salient example is agriculture, where, especially in the earlier postwar period, a large association of agricultural co-operatives representing nearly all of Japan's farmers, the Ministry of Agriculture and the LDP were integrally involved in bargaining and administering a complex system of price and distribution mechanisms for rice (Donnelly 1984; Pempel and Tsunekawa 1979). Trade association–bureaucratic relationships are well-organized and close in other fields and in each manufacturing sector as well, even if not to the same extent as agriculture, but again the channels are institutionalized with the 'bargaining' usually behind-the-scenes and less formalized.

The role of administration and its ties to interest groups also varies by policy area. In some, such as agriculture and the setting of rice prices, the bureaucracy is like a broker between the interest groups and their LDP politician-supporters who are pushing for a higher price, and the top political leaders of the LDP (in alliance with another part of the bureaucracy, the Finance Ministry) who are trying to restrain prices (Donnelly 1984). In other cases, the bureaucratic ministry may be lined up against the LDP politicians and interest groups, and in still others one ministry, as I mentioned above, may be involved in a 'turf battle' with another, each using its affiliated interest groups and politicians as supporters (Muramatsu and Krauss 1987, pp. 543–8). Finally, although labour may be relatively shut out of the institutionalized channels to the governing party because of its alliance with the opposition, it does have some input through the bureaucracy (Muramatsu and Krauss 1990, pp. 292–6).

There is one generalization that emerges from the otherwise complex sectoral patterns: the ties between social groups and administration may become more institutionalized with time, and the more institutionalized the group the closer the relationship to the bureaucracy. Thus, a survey of interest-group leaders found that the older and more institutionalized the interest group the more they tend to go to the bureaucracy for help; whereas the less institutionalized groups with new policies to push tend to go to political parties. Parties and politicians promote emerging interests; bureaucracies respond to established ones (Muramatsu and Krauss 1987, pp. 539–40).

As mentioned above, under the Nakasone administration (1982–7), one of the major goals of administrative reform was to privatize some of the mammoth public corporations and thus to energize the economy in response to foreign demands for greater imports during a time of budget constraints. There are over 100 public corporations in Japan, employing almost one million persons in 1974 (Johnson 1978, p. 38). Two of the largest were the Nippon Telephone and Telegraph Corporation (NTT) and the Japan National Railways (JNR). First the JNR was privatized and broken up into several separate companies, with 61,000 employees retired or transferred off the payroll. One of the additional benefits of privatization of the JNR was to create a more difficult and less politicized environment for the National Railway Workers' Union who have long been a bulwark of the opposition Japan Socialist Party (Muramatsu 1987, pp. 312–13).

Later, NTT stock was also partially sold off by the government, making it the world's largest private firm. Many public corporations remain, but the fact that the government was able to successfully 'privatize' the largest further reinforces the nature of the Japanese state as small in size, but by no means diminutive in ability.

## CONCLUSIONS

The myth of Japanese public administration contains some aspects of reality. Japan's civil service is an elite, respected, dedicated corps of bureaucrats, connected by formal and informal networks to private elites, who play a major role in policy-making. Politicians, especially the long-ruling LDP, however, were also major players in policy-making, and have imposed organizational reforms on the bureaucracy. Social interest groups have had close ties to administration and, in some areas in alliance with their LDP allies, have had the ability to determine policy to a greater extent than the ministries.

Perhaps from this more complex view of Japan's public administration we can tease out a few generalizations related to Pierre's framework in this volume comparing the influence of national style, sectorial properties and issue properties. The first is that there are distinctive aspects of national style to Japan's overall public administration. In politico-administrative relations, the important role of the bureaucracy in policy-making and also its close ties with the LDP were certainly created by Japan's own developmental history, but also by the long-term rule of a single conservative party and the fusion of party–administrative functions that occurred as a result. So too is national style a factor in state–social-group relationships, with Japan's particular emphasis on highly institutionalized formal and informal connections and channels of communication between the private sector and bureaucracy. The standardized recruitment and socialization processes of all bureaucrats, with its resulting loyalty to particular ministries and cross-ministry fragmentation, but across-the-board conflict management mechanisms used to contain the worst excesses of administrative conflict, also stand out as part of the national style.

Within this framework, however, what is evident is the importance of sectors in determining variations, especially in politico-administrative relations and state–client relationships. The Japanese electoral system that forced many LDP representatives to run against their colleagues, and thus put a premium on constituency services, helped to bifurcate the Japanese bureaucracy into two styles. The 'political' ministries dealing with agriculture, construction, transportation, posts and other constituency-related goods, were highly penetrated by LDP policy-makers and also by the client interest groups they were supposed to be supervising. On the other hand, the economic ministries, dealing with the 'higher politics' of finance, trade and economic growth, were accorded somewhat greater prestige, autonomy and influence in the policy-making process partly because they do not deal with immediate constituency goods but rather basic financial stability and the long-term goal of economic growth and trade, of less immediate interest to politicians. The consequences of Japan's rather unique electoral system and long-term conservative rule thus make the influence of sectorial properties much greater in politico-administrative and state–client relationships than one might expect.

Most especially, it is important to note that many of the vaunted strengths of the Japanese bureaucracy are intimately connected to its weaknesses. Its elite recruitment and internal *esprit de corps* also produce its factiousness; its autonomy from politicians in economic policy-making is made possible by a great degree of partisan politicization in non-economic areas; its national interest goals are not only constrained, but also achieved, even defined, by dense informal networks with private societal groups.

Thus, Japan may resemble France, Sweden and Germany in many respects; but it also has important elements of the US, Italy and the third world. Many of the threads are found in the cloth of other nations, but their particular weaving has produced a Japanese tapestry of public administration.

## NOTES

1. The dominance of 'Todai' was even greater in the past, and there are no figures on the proportion of its graduates actually hired, or on promotion figures, especially to the highest levels. Thus, Todai's dominance may be even greater than the current statistics of exam-passers indicates. Thus, in one survey of national bureaucrats, about 84 per cent of upper-level bureaucrats, and 78 per cent of middle-ranking bureaucrats were educated at Tokyo University. Kyoto University, the similarly elite and long-standing national university rival to Tokyo University, also provides a disproportionate share of the bureaucracy (about 10 per cent of higher, and 5 per cent of middle bureaucrats) (see Muramatsu 1981, p. 56).
2. This practice is said to be based on the principle that the incumbent in that post should be the most senior member in the ministry. Retiring at such a relatively young age, almost all higher bureaucrats then seek out second careers, sometimes in politics, as we have seen, but more usually in big business, as will be discussed below.

## REFERENCES

Aberbach, J. D., R. D. Putnam and B. A. Rockman (1981), *Bureaucrats and Politicians in Western Democracies* (Cambridge, Mass.: Harvard University Press).

Aberbach, J. D., E. S. Krauss, M. Muramatsu and B. A. Rockman (1990), 'Comparing Japanese and American Administrative Elites', *British Journal of Political Science*, 20, 461–88.

Almond, G. and S. Verba (1967), *The Civic Culture* (Princeton, N.J.: Princeton University Press).

Anderson, S. (1992), 'The Policy Process and Social Policy in Japan', *PS: Political Science and Politics*, XXV, 36–43.

Calder, K. (1988), *Crisis and Compensation: Public Policy and Political Stability in Japan, 1949–1986* (Princeton, N.J.: Princeton University Press).

Campbell, J. C. (1975), 'Japanese Budget Baransu', in E. Vogel (ed.), *Modern Japanese Organization and Decision-making* (Berkeley, Cal.: University of California Press), pp. 71–100.

Campbell, J. C. (1984), 'Policy Conflict and its Resolution within the Governmental System', in E. S. Krauss *et al.* (eds), *Conflict in Japan* (Honolulu: University of Hawaii Press), pp. 294–334.

Campbell, J. C. (1990), 'Bureaucracy', in T. Ishida and E. S. Krauss (eds), *Democracy in Japan* (Pittsburgh, Pa: University of Pittsburgh Press), pp. 113–38.

Craig, A. (1975), 'Functional and Dysfunctional Aspects of Government Bureaucracy', in E. Vogel (ed.), *Japanese Organization and Decision making* (Berkeley, Cal.: University of California Press), pp. 3–32.

Donnelly, M. (1984) 'Conflict over Government Authority and Markets: Japan's Rice Economy' in E. S. Krauss *et al.* (eds), *Conflict in Japan* (Honolulu: University of Hawaii Press), pp. 335–74.

Haley, J. O. (1987), 'Governance by Negotiation: a Reappraisal of Bureaucratic Power in Japan', *Journal of Japanese Studies*, 13, 343–57; also published the same year in K. B. Pyle (ed.), *The Trade Crisis: How Will Japan Respond?* (Seattle: Society for Japanese Studies), pp. 177–91.

Johnson, C. (1975), 'Japan: Who Governs?: An Essay on Official Bureaucracy', *Journal of Japanese Studies*, 2, 1–28.

Johnson, C. (1978), *Japan's Public Policy Companies* (Washington, D.C.: American Enterprise Institute).

Johnson, C. (1982), *MITI and the Japanese Miracle* (Stanford, Cal.: Stanford University Press).

Johnson, C. (1989), *MITI, MPT, and the Telecom Wars: How Japan Makes Policy for High Technology* (New York: HarperBusiness/Ballinger).

Koh, B. C. (1989), *Japan's Administrative Elite* (Berkeley, Cal.: University of California Press).

Krauss, E. S. (1992), 'Political Economy: Policymaking and Industrial Policy in Japan', *P.S.: Political Science and Politics*, XXV, 44–57.

Krauss, E. S. and J. Pierre (1993), 'Targeting Resources for Industrial Change', in R. K. Weaver and B. A. Rockman (eds), *Do Institutions Matter?: Government Capabilities in the United States and Abroad* (Washington, D.C.: Brookings Institution), pp. 151–86.

Muramatsu, M. (1981), *Nihon no Kanryōsei* [Japan's Bureaucratic System] (Tokyo: Toyo Keizai Shinposha).

Muramatsu, M. (1987), 'In Search of National Identity: the Politics and Policies of the Nakasone Administration', *Journal of Japanese Studies*, 13, 325–8; this special issue was republished in the same year in K. B. Pyle (ed.), *The Trade Crisis: How Will Japan Respond?* (Seattle: Society for Japanese Studies).

Muramatsu, M. and E. S. Krauss (1984), 'Bureaucrats and Politicians in Policymaking: the Case of Japan', *American Political Science Review*, 78, 126–48.

Muramatsu, M. and E. S. Krauss (1987), 'The Conservative Policy Line and Patterned Pluralism', in Y. Yasuba and K. Yamamura (eds), *Japan's Political Economy,* vol. 1: *The Domestic Transformation* (Stanford, Cal.: Stanford University Press), pp. 516–54.

Muramatsu, M. and E. S. Krauss (1988), 'Japanese Bureaucrats Revisited: Changes in Influence and Role in Policymaking', paper presented to the International Political Science Association Triennial Meeting, Washington, D.C., August.

Muramatsu, M. and E. S. Krauss (1990), 'Social Coalition and the Dominant Party System in Japan', in T. J. Pempel (ed.), *Uncommon Democracies: The Politics of One-Party Dominance* (Ithaca, N.Y.: Cornell University Press), pp. 282–305.

Nakamura, K. (ed.) (1975), *Gendai Nihon no seiji bunka* [The Political Culture of Contemporary Japan] (Kyoto: Minerva Shobo).

NHK Hōsō Yoron Chōsajo (1981), 'Nipponjin no terebikan' survey, December 1977, reproduced in Tokunaga Masa?, *NHK fushoku kenkyū* (Tokyo: Chūmonsha).

Noble, G. W. (1989), 'The Industrial Policy Debate', in S. Haggard and C. Moon (eds), *Pacific Dynamics: The International Politics of Industrial Change* (Boulder, Col.: Westview Press), pp. 53–95.

Okimoto, D. I. (1988), 'Political Inclusivity: the Domestic Structure of Trade', in T. Inoguchi and D. I. Okimoto (eds), *The Political Economy of Japan,* vol. 2: *The Changing International Context* (Stanford, Cal.: Stanford University Press), pp. 305–44.

Pempel, T. J. (1982), *Policy and Politics in Japan: Creative Conservatism* (Philadelphia, Pa.: Temple University Press).

Pempel, T. J. (1987), 'The Unbundling of "Japan, Inc.": the Changing Dynamics of Japanese Policy Formation', *Journal of Japanese Studies*, 13, 287–91; later published the same year in K. B. Pyle (ed.), *The Trade Crisis: How Will Japan Respond?* (Seattle: Society for Japanese Studies).

Pempel, T. J. (1992), 'Bureaucracy in Japan', *PS: Political Science and Politics*, XXV, 19–24.

Pempel, T. J. and K. Tsunekawa (1979), 'Corporatism without Labor?: the Japanese Anomaly', in P. C. Schmitter and G. Lehmbruch (eds), *Trends Toward Corporatist Intermediation* (Beverly Hills, Cal., and London: Sage Publications), pp. 231–70.

Richardson, B. M. and S. C. Flanagan (1984), *Politics in Japan* (Boston, Mass.: Little, Brown).

Samuels, R. J. (1987), *The Business of the Japanese State: Energy Markets in Comparative and Historical Perspective* (Ithaca, N.Y.: Cornell University Press).

Schoppa, L. J. (1991), 'Zoku Power and LDP Power: a Case Study of the Zoku Role in Education Policy', *Journal of Japanese Studies*, 17, 79–106.

Steiner, K., E. S. Krauss and S. C. Flanagan (eds) (1980), *Political Opposition and Local Politics in Japan* (Princeton, N.J.: Princeton University Press).

Yano Memorial Society (1991a), *Nihon kokusei zue, 1991* [Japan's Circumstances in Figures] (Tokyo: Kokuseisha).

Yano Memorial Society (1991b), *Sūji de miru Nippon no hyakunen* [100 Years of Japan Seen in Statistics] (Tokyo: Kokuseisha).

# 7. Governing the welfare state: public administration, the state and society in Sweden

## Jon Pierre

### OVERVIEW

Post-war Sweden will probably go down in history as the epitomy of the welfare state. The political belief that the state could and ought to play a key role in the redistribution of wealth and that the public sector was the superior provider of social services was the ideological framework for the emergence of an extensive and widely renowned welfare state. The unprecedented expansion of public services covering all essential spheres of life was orchestrated by the Social Democratic Party (SAP), a socialist party in ideology but whose *Realpolitik* has been based on a firm belief in private industry and economic growth.

Alongside the notion of the welfare state Sweden has become equally, or more, famous for its system of interest representation and mediation with regard to labour-market policies and industrial policy. This system, generally referred to as 'the Swedish model', was one of the pillars of the Swedish post-war political economy and has attracted a large number of foreign scholars (Hancock 1972; Heclo and Madsen 1987; Katzenstein 1985; Weaver 1987). Although the public administration's role in this model is quite marginal, organized interests are important societal actors in the context of the public bureaucracy's relationships with civil society, as we shall see later in this chapter.

A major challenge embedded in the process of developing welfare state politics and programmes was the creation of the administrative instruments required for the implementation of these programmes. Thus, the post-war period has seen agencies rapidly expanding their domain and competence as well as staff and expenditures. In a longer perspective, it is not until fairly recently that cutback programmes have been implemented due to the financial crisis of the state.

It is probably not very controversial to assert that welfare state politics has been instrumental in enhancing the overall wealth of the Swedish people. On most indicators, the overall standard of living in Sweden is among the highest in the world. The school system, the medicare system, and the overall high level of skills in the population are all attributed to welfare state politics.

At the same time, Sweden is often described, and rightly so, as the highest-taxed country in the world. Despite recent tax reforms, the public sector still accounts for a very large share of the Swedish economy. According to recent estimates this figure is as high as almost 70 per cent of the total GNP (SOU 1993:16, pp. 6ff.). Some observers – most of them non-Swedes – have pointed to another downside of the welfare state. In order to conduct extensive redistributive policies, the state requires information about its citizens; information which according to these observers sometimes ought to be reserved for the private sphere of the life of the citizens (Hancock 1972; Heclo and Madsen 1987; Huntford 1972).

Another critical point raised by these critics is that as welfare services have extended beyond merely providing a minimum standard of living they have tended to reduce the significance of individual choices, priorities and responsibilities. According to this perspective, welfare-state politics and services are addictive among the population. After a while, citizens come to expect the public sector to cater to all their needs, and personal initiative hence becomes less important. To be sure, not everyone would subscribe to this critique but is is none the less important enough to deserve mentioning.

The formal organization of the Swedish political system is that of a unitary state with extensive local government autonomy. Local government has a very long tradition in Sweden. Following a period of relative centralization after the Second World War, the period from 1970 onwards has witnessed a series of reforms aiming at decentralizing authority and responsibility within a wide range of sectors of public service. Thus, while Sweden remains a 'centralized unitary state' (Söderlind and Petersson 1992, p. 24), the important role of local government in the delivery of public services and as an independently elected tier of government must not be overlooked.

At the nation state level, Sweden presents a case of bureaucratic autonomy which singles it out in any international comparison. Due to a distinct separation between the formulation and the implementation of public policy, political control of the bureaucracy is conspicuously vague and indirect. We shall return to this phenomenon below.

At the local level, 286 municipalities (*kommuner*) play a key role in the delivery of public services in a wide range of areas.[1] In less than 20 years the number of municipalities was decreased from 2500 to fewer than 300. This process of merging small municipalities into larger political and administrative structures was triggered by a strong need to beef up local governments so that they could deliver the services regulated by the Parliament (the *Riksdag*) and the Cabinet.

The combination of relatively autonomous agencies at the national level and a longstanding tradition of local government autonomy, coupled with a corporatist style of policy-making, sets an interesting point of departure for a discussion on problems related to the governance of the Swedish welfare state. Furthermore, the institutional particularities of the Swedish case raise some intriguing broader questions about how the public administration relates to the sphere of policy-making and to civil society. What have been the roles of policy-makers and executive agencies in the process of welfare state expansion? What types of challenges to the public administration have been entailed in, first, the expansion of the welfare state and later, the cutback programmes? To what extent has the public administration remained a politically neutral actor in the implementation of Social Democratic politics?

## THE STRUCTURE OF THE PUBLIC ADMINISTRATION

The organizational structure of the Swedish state public administration reflects the institutional separation laid down in the Constitution between policy formulation and policy implementation. Thus, policy planning and deliberation is executed by the departments (*departement*). Policy implementation, on the other hand, rests with agencies (*ämbetsverk*).

Over time, the organization of government has developed towards an increasing number of agencies and their staff, while the departments have remained fairly constant in these respects. The departments have a small staff; the total number of employees in 1991 was only some 1800.[2] The agencies, on the other hand, are significantly bigger organizations. Today there are some 70 central agencies, with a total of 390,000 employees. The process of expansion came to a halt in the 1980s. For the past few years there has been a steady process of reorganization of the agencies, including mergers, abolitions and staff reductions (Söderlind and Petersson 1992, pp. 66ff.; Vedung 1992).

Both departments and agencies are organized along functional lines. Thus, there are departments for social welfare, defence, communications, and so on. This organization is largely mirror-imaged among the agencies. The number of departments is decided exclusively by the prime minister, who at any time and at his own discretion can increase or reduce that figure. The number of departments has varied significantly during the past twenty years. However, for the past ten years or so the number of departments has remained about twenty. The issue of how to organize the system of departments is indirectly linked to the process of government formation; members of Cabinet are normally also heads of a department. Therefore, at times the number of departments appears in part to have been guided at least as much by the politics of forming coalition governments as by considerations concerning the optimal way to organize the government.

At the departmental level, there are two exceptions to the system of functional organization. First, there is the prime minister's staff (*statsrådsberedningen*), which dates back only to the mid-1960s. Prior to that, the prime minister, interestingly, was one of the poorest-staffed ministers. Partly in order to ameliorate this problem, and partly to create a body close to the top political leadership which was not bogged down in the day-to-day work of running a department, the prime minister's staff was created to function as a sounding board and think-tank within the government.[3] Today, the staff has developed into an important instrument for long-term policy planning, communication and co-ordination of the government's work (Larsson 1986).

The second exception to the functional organization of the departments is the Department of Home Affairs (*civildepartementet*). This department was abolished by the first non-socialist government in 1976 but reinstalled when the Social Democrats resumed power in 1982. During the 1980s, the Department of Home Affairs came to play a key role in the politics of 'renewal of the public sector', enforced by the Social Democrats. We shall return to this later in this chapter.

The departments are headed by a minister, normally – but not always – a senior representative of the party or parties constituting the government. There are a few exceptions to this rule. Throughout the postwar period there have been a limited number of ministers without a (stated) party affiliation. However, given the overall strong presence of the political parties in the Swedish system of government and policy-making, there is a strong tendency to avoid appointing non-partisan ministers.

The number of political appointees is quite small, both within the departments and to an even lesser degree within the agencies. Within the departments, the minister and his senior secretary are politically appointed, as are information officials, spokesmen, and so on. In addition, in some cases the heads of sections within the departments are recruited on political grounds. Finally, when there is a coalition government, the departments become divided among the parties comprising the government. To ensure policy co-ordination and concerted action, it is considered necessary to have a political appointee present within those departments where their respective party does not hold a senior position. For instance, if the minister is a Conservative, it is likely that his senior secretary will be recruited from the same party. In those cases, the other parties in the Cabinet will be represented within the department by a junior political appointee. Within the agencies, the number of political appointees is even smaller. Heads of agencies are sometimes but not always recruited on political grounds rather than on professional merit.

There exists one additional element of the state public administration that should be mentioned. There are a number of (previously) state-owned companies that have operated in areas such as the telecommunications, railway transportation, and so on. Many of these companies were for a very long period of time agencies engaged in non-profit business operations (*affärsdrivande verk*). A number of these state-owned companies have already been privatized; more privatizations are planned within the next few years.

There appears to be some variation with regard to the amount of discretion which different agencies enjoy. Those engaged in the provision of services within core welfare state sectors, such as social welfare, education and housing, are probably less autonomous than agencies in the industrial development or the foreign aid sectors. In some cases there seems to be an understanding that agencies should be given substantial discretion in order to function properly and not become politicized (Krauss and Pierre 1993).

Given the uniqueness of the autonomy of the Swedish public administration and in order to understand its politics, we have to look at how this system evolved. The origins of the Swedish system of government dates a couple of centuries back in time, to the Swedish Age of Greatness in the seventeenth century (Söderlind and Petterson 1992, pp. 52f.; Ruin 1991, pp. 67f.). One of five 'administrative colleges', the Chancery, was assigned matters related to foreign affairs as well as forwarding matters deliberated by the other colleges. The Chancery was the predecessor of the departments; the other colleges developed over time into agencies. Later, the limited executive powers over the bureaucracy became an efficient means of reducing the powers of the monarchy, in the wake of a long period of absolutist rule in Sweden.

Today, a minister cannot instruct an agency how it is to deal with a particular issue. In fact, the only contacts which are allowed to take place between the senior levels in departments and agencies are said to be informal. The good news from the point of view of the minister is that although he does have some means of influencing the public bureaucracy – as we shall see below – he cannot be held personally responsible for the bureaucracy's actions. As Larsson (1993, p. 239 (present author's translation)) aptly puts it,

> [I]t is quite easy to see why the political elite is so fond of the model. In the Swedish public administration model influence and accountability do *not* go hand in hand; the elite has an influence which does not correspond with the same amount of responsibility.

The extraordinarily high degree of autonomy which the public administration enjoys in relationship to policy-makers remains, as Petersson (1989, p. 67) puts it, 'one of the major mysteries of the Swedish public life'. Part of the mystery stems from what appears to be a contradiction in the Swedish Constitution. On the one hand, the Constitution rules that agencies are autonomous institutions. On the other hand, the Constitution states that these agencies operate under the Cabinet. In addition to these legal ambiguities, the Constitution declares that 'the government rules the country', a task which clearly accords to the government substantial influence over the public administration.

Another part of the mystery – slightly less mysterious – is how the architects of the Constitution perceived the government's ability to 'govern the country', given its limited capabilities even to govern the public bureaucracy. The historical development of the model proceeded without very many reflecting on the functional aspect of the system, let alone the problems of governance it creates. On the other hand, there are certain positive aspects of the system, for example, professionalization of the civil service. We shall return to these aspects later.

A third element of the mystery – even less mysterious – is the ways and strategies employed both by department officials and bureaucrats to circumvent the odd constitutional ruling according to which they are not supposed to have any frequent *ex officio* communication with each other. A number of studies have shown that such contacts are quite frequent, if not as frequent as in those systems where such communication is not ruled unconstitutional.

Clearly, it would be misleading to assume that the formal separation between departments and agencies is an accurate description of the actual *modus operandi* of these institutions. First of all, while the departments are prevented from intervening in specific policy matters within the agencies, they still have some means of controlling them. Some of these capabilities are contingent on formal decisions by the *Riksdag*. Thus, normally based on proposals from the departments, the *Riksdag* can at any time change the legal framework of the agencies. Furthermore, the *Riksdag* enjoys the power of the purse *vis-à-vis* the agencies and can target resources for specific programmes. Thirdly, the government appoints the heads of agencies, presumably on a strictly non-partisan basis but normally with an understanding that the candidate should combine some degree of expertise in the area with a greater or smaller degree of understanding of the government's policy objectives.[4] In addition to these control instruments there are a couple of other but less important techniques.

The general observation is that the government and the *Riksdag* have only indirect instruments at their disposal to control and guide the agencies. Indeed, as a study conducted in the 1980s concluded, if the government wishes to change the course of an agency's actions it appears easier to create a new agency and give it the staff, budget and instructions necessary to accomplish that than it is to change the behaviour of an already-existing agency (SOU 1983:39, pp. 58f.).

Secondly, regardless of the empirical case we are observing it seems inconceivable that implementing agencies should not have an input at the earlier stages of the policy process (Heclo 1974). Given the complexity of most current politics, policy and administration must interact at some level and at some phase of the policy process in order to make the process work.

Thirdly, agencies host a highly specialized expertise which is of tremendous value to the departments as they draft governmental proposals to the *Riksdag*. Departments also have an interest in having a channel to the agencies in order to fine-tune the implementation of policies prepared by the departments themselves.

Finally, agencies have a strong interest in influencing the policy process in its very early stages, because that is often where the key decisions are made.[5] Thus, both departments and agencies have strong interests in maintaining informal contacts in order to exchange ideas, information, and so on.

Empirical data corroborate this theory. Informal contacts between departments and agencies are very frequent indeed. In 1968, 63 per cent of the contacts at senior level between departments and central agencies were made 'once a week or more frequently'. Initiatives were equally frequent on both sides (Molin *et al.* 1979, pp. 85f.). Contacts were typically informal in nature. Twenty years later, in 1988, the pattern is virtually the same; among department employees, 'close to 62 per cent are in contact with at least one central agency at least once a week' (Petterson 1989, p. 71). Although the two studies use slightly different survey populations their results are fairly comparable.

This seemingly remarkable stability in the network intensity between the departments and the central agencies must be interpreted against the background of an overall growing bureaucracy between the late 1950s and late 1970s. Thus, if we were able to calculate contacts relative to the number of departments and central agencies (not to mention the number of employees) we might find that this relative network intensity had declined slightly. Unfortunately, however, the data available do not allow such a recalculation.

Time seems to be running out for the formal Constitutional model of division of labour in other respects as well. According to the theory of the model, departments should be involved mainly in policy deliberation and long-term planning. The agencies, on the other hand, were assumed to concentrate their energy on the implementation of public policy. Consequently, departments should be bigger in staff than the agencies. The outcome, however, became pretty much the opposite, as mentioned earlier. Departments are today fairly small organizations. Agencies, conversely, soon developed into huge structures and became centres for much of the administrative expertise. That said, the cutback programmes which were implemented during the 1980s and early 1990s reduced the staff size of most agencies. Indeed, a couple of agencies were simply abolished, as was the case with the National Agency for Education (*Skolöverstyrelsen*).[6]

What have been the political consequences of this separation of policy-making and policy implementation? First, it has probably fostered and sustained a high degree of *Rechtsstaat* ideals among Swedish civil servants. In theory at least, civil servants have been guided by an ideal of 'neutral competence' (Aberbach and Rockman 1993), remaining detached from partisan conflict. However, as we shall see, elements of the public administration appear to be more politicized than the theory of the organization would predict. Secondly, the Swedish organization has encouraged professionalization among the government's staff. Insulated from strong political pressure, civil servants have been able to develop a high degree of professionalized expertise which in turn has been conducive to delivering high-quality public services. Finally, autonomous central agencies are better equipped to implement policies which are not biased in favour of special-interest groups, such as private business and organized labour. In other words, the risk of this type of politicization of public policy is smaller, compared to systems where agencies operate closer to the departments (cf. Rockman and Weaver 1993).

However, the detachment of public bureaucracy from the sphere of policy-making also raises a number of questions concerning the governability of elected officials over the bureaucracy and the accountability of the public bureaucracy (Peters 1978, p. 232). In this context it should be remembered that Swedish politics in general and policy-making in particular is distinctively structured by the political parties and their organizations. Thus, any political accountability for bureaucractic actions or non-actions would eventually become a matter of responsibility for the party or parties in government, not the individual ministers.[7]

The positive aspect of the model is that both departments and central agencies appear to have developed elaborate but informal networks exchanging information and ideas between the two types of institutions (Jacobsson 1984). These informal contacts seem to be just as necessary to make the system work as are formal contacts *faux pas*. Needless to say, while it is usually possible to tell a formal contact from an informal one with some degree of certainty, it is virtually impossible to decide what separates the exchange of ideas and information from the exercise of subtle political pressure.

## POLITICO-ADMINISTRATIVE RELATIONSHIPS

Given the clear constitutional separation of policy formulation and policy implementation, the relationship between policy-makers and bureaucrats in the Swedish public administration displays a couple of features not found in any of the other countries covered in this volume. In addition to the Constitutional idiosyncrasies of the Swedish case, the politico-administrative relationship there takes on some special characteristics due to the long tenure of the Social Democratic party.

It hardly comes as a surprise to any scholar of public administration that elected officials have sometimes lamented the public bureaucracy's – and indeed even the departments' – capabilities to obstruct or stall the formulation and implementation of new policies. This problem has taken on some special features in the Swedish model. Moreover, it has also taken on different forms in different time periods and in different political contexts.

Before we go into that discussion, there are a couple of systemic factors which need to be mentioned. First, in Sweden, to a greater extent than in most other countries, the mechanics of the system seem to work against political change. Almost by definition, a public administration insulated from direct political control is not very amenable to continuous political management; that is with policy-makers carefully monitoring the implementation process and giving new instructions as soon as the agencies' operations deviate from the political objectives. In the Swedish model, agencies become inclined to stick to the principle of business as usual. Changes in the *modus operandi* of the agencies are probably more likely to occur as a result of professional considerations than because of political directives.

Secondly, with regard to the significance of the political attitudes of the bureaucrats in their interaction with politicians we can see two different general scenarios. The first highlights the elected politician who is determined to bring about change facing the non-political bureaucrat. The other scenario features the Conservative politician's encounter with a nominally non-political bureaucrat but with clear Social Democratic preferences. In both cases, a misfit occurs between what the elected official wants to do (or does not want to do) and what the bureaucrat perceives as the best way of conducting his and the agencies' business. In both cases, the interface between the politician and the bureaucrat is influenced more by party politics than the Constitutional model would lead us to believe. And in both cases it is the elected politician who appears to come out the loser, because of his shorter tenure, limited personal expertise, and his restricted formal powers to impose new ideas on the bureaucracy.

Many of these features of Swedish public administration and its relationship to elected politicians can be related in part to the significant role of political parties in Swedish political life. In part, it can also be attributed to a political-administrative culture not very different from the Weberian school of thought according to which civil servants are supposed to act strictly within the boundaries set by the legal framework and in the interest of the state and the citizens without making any partisan or politicized judgements. In short, the Swedish case displays very clearly the problems of maintaining a Weberian, non-political bureaucracy in a highly politicized society.[8]

In order to approach this problem we must briefly look at the Swedish specificity of politico-administrative relationships from a historical and conceptual point of view. Here, Mellbourn (1979, p. 51) offers a distinction between two different bureaucratic ideal models of non-political civil servants; civil servants 'below politics' and 'above politics'. The former category refers to the civil servants of the pre-democratic era. This type of civil servant operated within an administration which enjoyed tremendous powers in society, to some extent because of the absence of any other significant loci of power (Ehn 1993, p. 17). The latter model of non-political civil servants – those 'above politics' – highlights a non-political bureaucrat in a democratic and politicized society. In this type of society the public administration is the executive branch of a partisan, parliamentary government, something which gives a very different meaning to the concept 'non-political', compared to the previous age. For civil servants 'above politics', society outside the bureaucracy has a number of 'competing power centres', primarily political power centres, and consequently it becomes the norm to stand above any partisan division.

Beyond these systemic factors and bureaucratic roles there also exist a number of shorter-term contextual factors which have a strong impact on the relationship between policy-makers and the bureaucracy. The Swedish political system has a strong tradition of non-political civil servants guided by ideals of legality and legal security; in Mellbourn's language, civil servants 'above politics'. However, this was a model which would prove susceptible to the tremendous changes taking place in Sweden around the turn of the century.

During the nineteenth century, in Sweden the powers of the monarch were gradually transferred to representative pre-party alliances and coalitions among elected members of a pre-democratic parliament. Political conflict at this level occurred mainly between Liberal and Conservative groupings in the *Riksdag*.

With the advent of political democracy in the early twentieth century, the relationship between policy-makers – now recruited from the leaderships of political parties of increasing organizational strength – and the bureaucracy became strained. Once universal suffrage was introduced (male in 1911, female in 1921) and a parliamentary system of government was established (in 1917), the notion of a public bureaucracy insulated from these significant political changes became an important problem. Later, as the party system was consolidated in the 1930s with the reformist Social Democratic party emerging as the dominant political force, the problem of a nominally non-political bureaucracy – staffed by presumably mainly non-Socialist bureaucrats – became an obstacle to the introduction of more radical policies. Put differently, the bureaucratic ideal of the time – to stand 'below politics' – remains an honourable civil servants' *esprit de corps* but one which is of little help to a government wanting to put new and radical political ideas into practice.

As a result, the Social Democrats tried to find ways within the Constitutional framework to infuse some political control over the bureaucracy. In some policy areas, particularly labour-market policies, the Social Democrats launched policies which greatly differed from prevailing concepts, both in terms of their budgetary size and in their institutional ramifications (Rothstein 1986).

Clearly, this was both a short-term and a long-term problem with short-term and long-term solutions. The short-term solution to the problem was to create new institutional structures and staff them with bureaucrats sympathetic towards the new policies. Thus, the government created an agency for labour-market affairs. A large number of those who staffed the agency had some connection either with the Social Democratic Party or with the Confederation of Labour (LO) (Rothstein 1986). Over time, Social Democratic sympathizers were recruited to the public administration to guarantee that policies were implemented adequately. Thus, a public bureaucracy evolved which was fairly well in tune with the predominant strategy among the political elite.

This subtle politicization of the departments and agencies became obvious in 1976 when the non-Socialist parties formed their first government after 44 consecutive years of Social Democratic rule. At the level of the departments a number of tenured senior officials had very clear Social Democratic political sympathies. Bert Levin, a Liberal, newly appointed deputy minister at the Department of Education, describes the problem facing the new government in 1976 thus (Levin 1983, p. 91, present author's translation):

> When Jan-Erik Wikström [newly appointed minister of education] and I walked into the department of education we were met by a forest of red party needles [the common Social Democratic badge at the time]. Six of eight tenured senior officials were active Social Democrats ... In several sections of the department the Social Democratic dominance was overwhelming.

Other non-Socialist ministers have also testified to the Social Democratic predominance in the departments as a significant obstacle to policy reassessment and change (cf., for example, Ahrland 1983). The problem is that the officials whom Levin identified as Social Democrats were not political appointees but tenured senior officers and could hence not be replaced by non-Socialist political appointees. However, over time, and given the higher degree of turnover in government, we are likely to see a decreasing politicization of the departments' and agencies' staff. Within the departments, coalition governments pose a special type of problem, since the coalition partners have to divide the departments among them. This means that some parties in the coalition are not represented at the senior level of all the departments. The coalition governments usually handle this problem by appointing a representative for those parties who are not managing a particular department. At the level of the agencies the problem of depoliticizing the staff may take even longer because even fewer are politically appointed compared to the departments.

To sum up the discussion so far, we can see that both scenarios of different types of 'misfit' relationships between politicians and bureaucrats described earlier have occurred in Sweden. In the early 1930s reformist Social Democrats were confronted by cadres of non-political civil servants. Conversely, in 1976, non-Socialist ministers and deputy ministers experienced significant resistance from tenured senior executive officers with strong Social Democratic sentiments.

These two incidents raise some intriguing questions about the politics of a presumably non-political public bureaucracy. The design of the system is such that in theory these 'misfits' should not occur. Moreover, had it been the case that departments and agencies had been more politicized by design, that is, had they had a greater number of political appointees, then the misfit problem would have been resolved simply by replacing the political staff with other political appointees. One conceivable solution would be to increase the number of political appointments in the departments and the agencies, but none of the political parties seem to support that idea.

We conclude this brief discussion on different politico-administrative relationships in the Swedish context with a couple of general points. First, the Swedish public administration stands out as an extraordinarily autonomous bureaucracy in a formal, constitutional sense. In order for policy-makers to have an influence on the public administration beyond the indirect channels granted by the Constitution, one of the very few means available is to change recruitment to the agencies. However, political appointments are very few indeed, particularly at the junior and middle levels of the organizations.

Secondly, for parties of social reform, non-political bureaucracies and civil servants may pose an even bigger obstacle than a more politicized bureaucracy. This is because in a politicized bureaucracy the number of political appointments and positions is fairly high and thus there can be quick replacement of personnel in such positions.

Finally, over time different informal techniques have evolved to try and ensure that policy-makers have a stronger political control over the bureaucracy. At the same time, however, other measures seem to have worked in the opposite direction. For the past fifteen to twenty years, much of the legislation has been so-called 'frame legislation' (*ramlagar*). In this type of legislation, the *Riksdag* states the long-term objectives of a particular policy or legislation, and then leaves it to the bureaucracy to work out the finer details of the programme. This type of legislation – which replaces more specified rules – has been prominent in policy areas such as social welfare, medical care and planning.

Moreover, in order to support long-term planning the *Riksdag* recently decided to adopt a longer budget cycle than the usual one-year cycle. In 1989, a three-year budget cycle was introduced (Osborne and Graebler 1993, p. 329). From 1993 onwards, the budget system has become more differentiated. The plan is to assign different budget cycles to agencies within different policy sectors. Thus, agencies operating in policy areas where the nature of policy problems changes fairly quickly will have one-year budget cycles, while agencies within more stable policy areas may have up to six-year budget cycles. This system is more consistent with the general shift from input control to output control in Swedish budgetary process and will significantly help facilitate long-term planning and will relieve many agencies of the annual hassle of submitting budget proposals. At the same time, it has further reduced political control over the agencies.

## THE ORGANIZATIONAL DYNAMICS OF PUBLIC ADMINISTRATION

Two concepts have dominated the politics of public administration in Sweden during the past decade: de-sectorization and decentralization (Mellbourn 1987; Söderlind and Petersson 1992). Clearly, both these strategies have targeted the local governments but none the less they have had significant ramifications in public administration, too.

In order to understand the forces of change within Swedish public administration it is important to approach this topic in a broader societal perspective. In particular, we need to understand the role of the public bureaucracy in bringing about social change and the development of the welfare state.

The greater political, economic and social significance of a public administration is to a very large extent a mirror-image of that of the state. This appears to be particularly the case in Sweden, where the public bureaucracy generated much of its legitimacy from two sources. One was the redistributive role of government, as outlined by the Social Democratic notion of the politics of welfare and social justice.

The other is related to what is often referred to as 'the Swedish Model': a system of interest representation and intermediation at the peak organizational level (cf. Weaver 1987). Here, the role of the public bureaucracy was much more marginal. The Swedish model essentially served to leave substantial autonomy to major organized interests in the labour market to handle their disputes with a minimum of state interference. However, the Swedish model and the initial development of the welfare state shared a strong belief in top-down politics, hierarchy and regulations. By the early 1990s, there were many indications that this hierachial patterns of political and social control had surrendered to increasingly strong horizontal networks. This was one of the general findings of a Royal Commission on democracy and the distribution of power in the Swedish society (SOU 1990:44).

This development is quite evident within the public administration. Due to the extensive decentralization and a simplification of state grants to the municipalities, agencies have come to play less-important roles in the central–local relationship. In the previous system, agencies controlled vast financial resources *vis-à-vis* the local governments and used these resources to control the delivery of public services at the local level. The new system of state grants has far fewer strings attached to these resources. Municipalities receive a bloc grant and can to a very large extent use that money at their own discretion.

It goes without saying that this reform undercut much of the agencies' powers and indeed their entire existence in the public administrative system. As a result, agencies have, with varying success, tried to redefine their *raison d'être*. Today they describe their role as mainly 'servicing' local authorities (Montin 1993). Another philosophy which has emerged during the past few year is 'management by objectives' and evaluation in the central–local relationship. Agencies define what should be the overall goals for their respective policy areas and then monitor carefully what happens at the local level. While this softer approach by the agencies towards the municipalities has been applauded at the local level, it remains unclear what means of control will be employed should the evaluations indicate that local governments are not working towards the formulated goals.

Simultaneously with the cutback programmes at state level and the cuts in state grants to the local governments there has been a number of projects aimed at relaxing much of the regulation pertaining to the municipalities. One such project was the so-called 'free-commune experiment'. Since the experiment was mainly concerned with state–local relations, we shall not go into it in any greater detail here.[9] However, what is interesting about the experiment in the current context is how it was handled at the national level, particularly with respect to its effects on interdepartmental relationships. The experiment was conducted by the Department of Home Affairs. The basic idea was to let a selection of municipalities and county administration indicate which regulations they thought should be discontinued. Their applications were deliberated both by the Department of Home Affairs as well as the functional departments. While many of these departments did not oppose the idea of deregulation *per se*, they frequently opposed such measures within their own specific jurisdiction. As a result, there were a number of 'turf battles' between the Department of Home Affairs and the functional departments which had to be settled at Cabinet level (Mellbourn 1987; Strömberg 1990).

Despite these frictions at national level, the experiment – coupled with other reforms – have helped to bring about effective decentralization and also to create cross-sectorial institutions at the local level. Since the departments and agencies are still largely sectorial/functional, we see an organizational confusion emerging. The public administration and the municipalities appear to be operating today in a less concerted fashion than, say, ten years ago. The next few years will probably show what the long-term consequences of these problems will be.

## PUBLIC ADMINISTRATION AND CIVIL SOCIETY IN SWEDEN

Some of the most important changes in the Swedish public administration during the past ten to fifteen years have concerned its changing interaction with civil society. A number of public services have been decentralized. Furthermore, several aspects of local governments have been deregulated; private organizations have been encouraged to engage in the delivery of public services at the local level, and so on. The legal framework of the public administration has also been revised to strengthen the relationship of citizens with the public administration (Gustafsson 1987).

As we mentioned earlier, most of these reforms have occurred at the local level.[10] However, since one of the agencies' most important functions has been to control the local governments in areas such as education and social welfare, these reforms have had strong reverberations at national level. The agencies are searching for a new role in this new system of central–local relationships.

However, state–society relations at agency level are just as important as those at the local level of the political system. Given the (previously) strong sectorization of public administration, agencies have forged coalitions with organized interests in their respective sector. As a result – as a Royal Commission (SOU 1993:16, p. 166 (present author's translation)) recently described it – 'agencies and functional departments have often operated as embassies of special interest groups'. The political autonomy of the agencies has probably encouraged this development; with tighter political control over departments and agencies there would be fewer opportunities for these institutions to play the role of special interests' embassies.

The long-term consequence of this close relationship between segments of the public administration and organized interests has been a further reduced governing capacity from the point of view of the *Riksdag* and the cabinet (SOU 1993:16). Moreover, organized interests have been successful in influencing the agencies, who in turn have attempted to influence the *Riksdag* and the departments through informal channels. This path of societal influence over the state has been deemed so significant that a Royal Commission in the 1980s described the situation as 'politics backwards'. Instead of the textbook model of policy-making and implementation, 'politics backwards' denotes a process by which organized interests and agencies influence the *Riksdag* and departments while the political parties play the part of generating legitimacy for decisions and actions made elsewhere (Larsson 1993 p. 228; SOU 1983:39).

This corporatist trait of public administration has for a long time been institutionalized in the agencies' boards where organized interests have enjoyed representation. Lately, this type of bureaucratic management – officially referred to as 'laymen boards' – has come under attack. Critics argue that the model institutionalizes sectorization and undercuts political control. As a result, a Royal

Commission in 1985 recommended that the role of the 'laymen boards' should mainly be just advisory (SOU 1985:40). In 1992 a governmental bill (prop 1991/92:123) suggested that the laymen boards within agencies operating in the labour market area should be abolished. More recently, another Royal Commission recommended that these boards should be abolished for the majority of agencies (SOU 1993:58) and be replaced by collegial boards (cf. Petersson and Söderlind 1992, pp. 68ff.). Through this sequence of reforms the presence of organized interests at the top level of the agencies has lost much of its significance.

Much of the interaction between civil society and public administration occurs through institutionalized channels of civic control of the public bureaucracy. An important case in point is the so-called Principle of Publicity (Herlitz 1958; Vedung 1992, p. 75). According to this principle, all documents in public authorities are avaliable to the public. There are of course exceptions to this rule, for example, documents pertaining to national security and defence, certain financial policy issues, the privacy of individual citizens (for instance medical records), and so on. Also, some material which is produced within the authority and where the decision-making process is not yet complete may be witheld from public access. However, the important element of the principle is that unless documents are classified – and the rules allowing classification are quite restrictive – they are public and accessible to the public as soon as they have been catalogued. It is probably a unique feature of Swedish public administration that any citizen can walk into the offices of a public authority and enquire what mail senior officials have received. Unwillingness to produce such material might induce the citizen to submit a letter to the ombudsman – originally a Swedish word – who will investigate the incident.

The Principle of Publicity, the ombudsman system, and the developed mechanisms for appealing against public administrative rulings have helped to create the image of Swedish public officials working in a 'goldfish bowl' (Peters 1978, p. 208).[11] Swedish public administration is probably more open to civil society than most other public bureaucracies. The reforms conducted during the 1980s, such as a revision of the Public Administration Act, have further strengthened the position of the citizen in his/her relation with the public authorities (Pierre 1993).

## CONCLUSIONS

In a comparative assessment of Swedish public administration, its autonomy comes out as the most striking feature. Thus, a key question is to what extent this autonomy of the agencies has impeded policy-makers' capacities to govern the public bureaucracy.

In order to get a grip on this question we must once again look at the historical political development. For a very long period a chief objective among the Social Democrats was to develop the institutional means necessary for the development of the welfare state. To that end, they were unlikely to encounter any major opposition from the bureaucracy. On the contrary; the combination of a steady influx of resources and the absence of tight political control of the bureaucracy led to increasing professionalism within the public administration. In addition, over time the number of civil servants with Social Democratic political sympathies appears to have increased. This opened up intra-party channels as a potentially important option to control the bureaucracy.

It was not until non-Socialists entered government in 1976 and a powerful fiscal crisis hit the country in the late 1970s that bureaucratic autonomy began to be noticeable. First of all, non-Socialist ministers frequently reported tacit opposition both from non-political departmental staff but also from the agencies as they tried to alter the course of public policy. Secondly, the cutback programmes implemented to attack the fiscal crisis of the state triggered bureaucratic resistance which proved more complex than would probably be the case in political systems with a stronger political control over the agencies.

More speculatively, regarding the future of the Swedish model of separation of policy formulation and policy implementation, it seems likely that there will probably be intensified proposals to modify the system in the future. To understand the political legitimacy of the system and the political forces sustaining it we must once again look at the Swedish case in its historical context. With the advent of the Social Democratic government in the 1930s there followed a period of rapid extension of the public bureaucracy. The political insulation of the bureaucracy was at this time seen by the non-Socialists as a constitutional safeguard against Social Democratic politicization of the public administration. As the non-Socialists came to power in the late 1970s indications soon appeared that they were beginning to see the apolitical agencies as awkward. With an increasing turnover in government between Socialists and non-Socialists there may be stronger incentives to increase political control over the bureaucracy. Not only would that help make the public sector more governable, it would also strengthen the political accountability of the bureaucracy.

In many ways, increasing the political presence in the executive branch of government would also help to bring the different elements of public administration closer together. It is an interesting irony to note that while many efforts have been made to make public bureaucracy more accessible to the public, it still largely remains constitutionally off-limits to elected politicians. Indeed, many of the changes and reforms implemented during the 1980s and early 1990s have aimed at moving public administration even further from the realm of policy-making and political representation. Those of us who follow these developments with considerable interest wonder how far an allegedly non-political public administration can be depoliticized without policy-makers losing all political control over it.

## NOTES

1. The regional level of the political system comprises both the directly elected counties (*landsting*) and also a state regional administration (*länsstyrelser*). The counties are chiefly involved in the provision of medical care. The state regional administration is a cross-sectorial body that oversees the implementation of state programmes, co-ordinating the region's economic development and representing the county before nation state institutions.
2. According to Vedung (1992, p. 75) the number of departmental employees is 2900.
3. Another important – perhaps the most important – reason why the prime minister's staff was created was related to national security and was brought up in the findings of a Commission in the wake of one of Sweden's biggest spy scandals, the so-called Wennerström incident. The Commission found that the prime minister was so understaffed that important information concerning suspicions that Wennerström was a Soviet intelligence agent never reached Prime Minister Erlander.
4. Since partisan appointments are not unconstitutional but rather are ruled out by practice, it becomes difficult to ascertain to what extent some appointments are based on political grounds. This became an issue when tighter political control over the agencies was proposed (SOU 1985:40; Governmental Bill 1986/87:99).
5. This holds particularly true in Sweden where so-called Royal Commissions – groups of experts and representatives of organized interests – are often used to lay down the principles of new policies and to generate consensus around those proposals. However, a recent study on the Royal Commissions suggests that these committees became more conflictual during the 1980s and less able to create consensus on their policy proposals. These conflicts have become increasingly frequent both between government and opposition but also between different elements of the public bureaucracy (Johansson 1992, pp. 223f.).
6. In some cases of agency abolition, their functions were transferred to other agencies. The process of abolishing agencies sometimes highlighted Kaufman's (1976) theory of the immortality of public organizations. Thus, when the Agency for Higher Education was abolished, no less than five agencies – a couple of which were created for this purpose – took its place.
7. This model of acountability also relates back to the process of government formation in Sweden. Once the prime minister is accepted by the *Riksdag* he appoints at his own discretion the other ministers and merely informs the *Riksdag* of these appointments.
8. The term 'politicized' in this context refers to the combined outcome of a number of factors, e.g., a large public sector, extensive redistributive policies, a policy process to a very significant extent shaped by partisan cleavages, a high degree of party cohesion in Parliament, strong party organizations, and strong links between those organizations and organized interests. All these factors are directly or indirectly derived from the significance of parties in the state and also in civil society.
9. For reports in the English language on the free-commune experiment, see Gustafsson 1987; Montin 1993; Pierre 1993; Rose 1990; Stewart and Stoker 1989.
10. At the local level, public actors have increasingly engaged in what Kooiman (1993, p. 2) calls 'new social-political forms of governing'. These include different forms of public–private joint ventures in the process of policy implementation (cf. Gustafsson 1987). Since most of these joint projects occur in those areas of local government services which are not directly related to implementation of nation-state programmes we shall not go further into them in the present context.
11. Peters has this expression from Herlitz (1958).

# REFERENCES

Aberbach, J. D. and B. A. Rockman (1993), 'Civil Servants and Policy Makers: Neutral or Responsive Competence?', paper delivered at the Annual Meeting of the American Political Science Association, 2–5 September.

Ahrland, K. (1983), 'Nej, fru statsråd!' [No, Minister!] *Statsvetenskaplig Tidskrift*, 65, 145–52.

Ehn, P. (1993), 'Svenska Högre Statstjänstemän 1971–1990: En Attitydstudie', [Swedish Civil Servants 1971–1990: A Study of Attitudes] paper delivered at the Swedish Political Science Association's Annual Conference, Gothenburg, 4–5 October.

Governmental Bill no. 1986/87:99, 'Ledning av Den Statliga Förvaltningen' [The Management of the Public Sector].

Governmental Bill no. 1991/92:123, 'Om Slopande av Intresserepresentation i Vissa Statliga Myndigheter' [On the Abolition of Interest Representation in Selected State Authorities].

Gustafsson, L. (1987), 'Renewal of the Public Sector in Sweden', *Public Administration*, 65, 179–92.

Hancock, M. D. (1972), *Sweden: The Politics of Postindustrial Change* (Hinsdale, Ill.: Dryden Press).

Heclo, H. (1974), *Modern Social Politics in Britain and Sweden* (New Haven, Conn.: Yale University Press).

Heclo, H. and H. Madsen (1987), *Policy and Politics in Sweden: Principled Pragmatism* (Philadelphia, Pa.: Temple University Press).

Herlitz, N. (1958), 'Publicity of Documents in Sweden', *Public Law*, 17, 54–9.

Huntford, R. (1972), *The New Totalitarians* (New York: Stein & Day).

Jacobsson, B. (1984), *Hur styrs Förvaltningen: Myt och Verklighet kring Departementens Styrning av Ämbetsverken* [How the Civil Service is Managed: Myth and Reality in the Departments' Control of Agencies] (Lund: Studentlitteratur).

Johansson, J. (1992), *Det Statliga Kommittéväsendet* [The Royal Commissions] (Stockholm: Department of Political Science, University of Stockholm).

Katzenstein, P. J. (1985), *Small States in World Markets* (Ithaca, N.Y., and London: Cornell University Press).

Kaufman, H. (1976), *Are Government Organizations Immortal?* (Washington, D.C.: Brookings Institution).

Kooiman, J. (1993), 'Social-political Governance: Introduction', in J. Kooiman (ed.), *Modern Governance* (Newbury Park, Cal., and London: Sage), pp. 1–8.

Krauss, E. S. and J. Pierre (1993), 'Targeting Resources for Industrial Change', in B. A. Rockman and R. K. Weaver (eds), *Do Institutions Matter?: Government Capabilities in the United States and Abroad* (Washington, D.C.: Brookings Institution), pp. 151–86.

Larsson, T. (1986), *Regeringskansliet* [The Cabinet and its Ministries] (Lund: Studentlitteratur).

Larsson, T. (1993), *Det svenska statsskicket* [The Swedish Government] (Lund: Studentlitteratur).

Levin, B. (1983), 'En Skog av Röda Nålar: Om politiseringen av departement och förvaltning' [A Forest of Red Needles; On the Politicization of Departments and Agencies,] in B. Rydén (ed.), *Makt och Vanmakt* [Power and Powerlessness] (Stockholm: SNS Förlag), pp. 91–100.

Mellbourn, A. (1979), *Byråkratins ansikten* [The Faces of Bureaucracy] (Stockholm: Liber).

Mellbourn, A. (1987), *Bortom det Starka Samhället* [Beyond the Strong Society] (Stockholm: Liber).
Milner, H. (1989), *Sweden: Social Democracy in Practice* (New York: Oxford University Press).
Molin, B., L. Månsson and L. Strömberg (1979), *Offentlig Förvaltning* [Public Administration] (Stockholm: BonnierFakta).
Montin, S. (1993), 'Swedish Local Government in Transition', (Örebro: Department of Politics, University of Örebro, and Gothenburg: Department of Political Science, University of Gothenburg), mimeo.
Osborne, D. and T. Gaebler (1993), *Reinventing Government* (New York: Plum Books/Penguin).
Peters, B. G. (1978), *The Politics of Bureaucracy* (New York: Longman).
Petersson, O. (1989), *Maktens Nätverk* [The Networks of Power] (Stockholm: Carlssons).
Pierre, J. (1993), 'Legitimacy, Institutional Change, and the Politics of Public Administration in Sweden', *International Political Science Review*, 14, 387–401.
Rockman, B. A. and R. K. Weaver (eds) (1993), *Do Institutions Matter?: Comparing Capabilities in the U.S. and Abroad* (Washington, D.C.: Brookings Institution).
Rose, L. (1990), 'Nordic Free-commune Experiments: Increased Local Autonomy or Continued Central Control?', in D. S. King and J. Pierre (eds), *Challenges to Local Government*, Sage Modern Politics Series, vol. 28 (Newbury Park, Cal., and London: Sage Publications), pp. 212–41.
Rothstein, B. (1986), *Den Socialdemokratisha Staten* [The Social Democratic State] (Lund: Arkiv Förlag).
Ruin, O. (1991), 'The Duality of the Swedish Central Administration: Ministries and Central Agencies', in A. Farazmand (ed.), *Handbook of Comparative and Development Public Administration* (New York and Basel: Marcel Dekker), pp. 67–80.
Söderlind, D. and O. Petersson (1992), *Svensk Förvaltningspolitik* [The Swedish Politics of Public Administration] (Stockholm: Fritzes).
SOU 1983:39, 'Politisk Styrning – Administrativ Självständighet' [Political Control – Administrative Autonomy] (report of the Royal Commission on the Public Administration [*Förvaltningsutredningen*]).
SOU 1985:40, 'Regeringen, Myndigheterna och Myndigheternas Ledning' [The Government, the Authorities and the Management of the Authorities] (report of the Royal Commission on the Guidance of Administrative agencies ['*Verksledningskommittén*']).
SOU 1990:44, 'Demokrati och Makt i Sverige' [Democracy and Power in Sweden] (report of the Royal Commission on Democracy and the Distribution of Power in Sweden [*Maktutredningen*]).
SOU 1993:16, 'Nya Villkor för Ekonomi och Politik' [A New Situation for the Economy and Politics] (report of the Royal Commission on the Crisis in the Swedish Economy ['*Ekonomikommissionen*']).
SOU 1993:58, 'Effektivare Ledning i Statliga Myndigheter' [A More Efficient Management of State Authorities] (report of the Royal Commission on the Management of Agencies).
Stewart, J. and G. Stoker (1989), 'The "Free Local Government" Experiments and the Programme of Public Sector Reform in Scandinavia', in C. Crouch and D. Marquand (eds), *The New Centralism: Britain Out of Step with Europe*, London: Political Quarterly Publishing, pp. 125–42.

Strömberg, L. (1990), 'Det svenska frikommunförsöket 1983–1989' [The Swedish Free-Commune Experiment 1983–1989], in K. Ståhlberg (ed.), *Frikommunförsöket i Norden* (Åbo: Åbo Akademi), pp. 65–88.

Vedung, E. (1992), 'Five Observations on Evaluation in Sweden', in J. Mayne *et al.* (eds), *Advancing Public Policy Evaluation: Learning from International Experiences* (Amsterdam: Elsevier Science Publishers), pp. 71–84.

Weaver, R. K. (1987), 'Political Foundations of Swedish Economic Policy', in B. P. Bosworth and A. M. Rivlin (eds), *The Swedish Economy* (Washington, D.C.: Brookings Institution), pp. 289–317.

# 8. Public administration in developing countries: Kenya and Tanzania in comparative perspective
## Goran Hyden

## INTRODUCTION

In trying to bring comparative analysis back into public administration, it is worth recalling that it was in a confrontation with the administrative needs of developing countries that the first wave of such scholarly work was attempted some 30 years ago. As one of the true 'elders' of this specific field of study, Milton Esman, noted in a recent reflective volume, the challenge then was that mainstream public administration, by virtue of its pronounced technocratic orientation, needed strong infusions from politics and the other behavioural and social sciences if it was to become relevant to the development needs and aspirations in rapidly changing third world environments (Esman 1991, p. 2). As has been well documented in many places (for example, Savage 1976; van Wart and Cayer 1990; Caiden and Caiden 1990), little came out of this bold move by its flagship, the Comparative Administration Group, chaired by Frederick Riggs. In the early 1970s, it had essentially folded: its *Journal of Comparative Administration* had closed; Duke University Press had brought to an end its publication series of CAG papers. Public administration returned to being the least universalist and least comparative of all the major fields in the social sciences. For nearly 20 years, two types of publications have been allowed to dominate the field: (a) descriptive case studies of public administration in individual countries; and (b) prescriptive analyses based on the model and practice of administration in the US or Western Europe. Political science and public administration parted company, as did theory and practice.

It is significant that recent efforts to restore a comparative perspective to the study of public administration (Leonard 1987 and 1991; Dwivedi and Henderson 1990; and this volume) place it in its political context, much as the research of the 1960s did. The difference is that the ambitions today are more humble and realistic. Instead of trying to come up with a single 'grand' theory, what may become a second generation of comparative public administration studies position themselves at a 'middle-range' level and accept that a range of theoretical perspectives may usefully inform such studies.

This chapter differs from the others in this volume in that it is not country-specific but cast more broadly to reflect the insights of the literature on public administration in developing countries. In order to give the presentation some empirical concentration, it refers primarily to two East African countries: Kenya and Tanzania. The analysis of these cases is enhanced by references to other experiences that differ in their degree of proximity. Thus, for example, other anglophone countries in Africa and Asia will feature more often than others. The rest of the chapter is organized into four sections. Following a brief introduction of the two case countries, it will proceed to discuss in turn: (a) the relations between policy-makers and administrators; (b) the principal changes attempted within the public service; and (c) the relationship between the public service and civil society. It concludes by drawing some of the implications for future studies.

## KENYA AND TANZANIA: A BRIEF BACKGROUND PROFILE

Located in East Africa on the shores of the Indian Ocean, Kenya and Tanzania share a similar historical experience. In pre-colonial days both were subject to influence from trade and settlements established by Persians, Arabs and the Portuguese. Although much of the hinterland was unaffected, slave trade in the eighteenth and nineteenth centuries opened up routes into the interior and facilitated the spread of Kiswahili, the *lingua franca* that had developed as a result of contacts between the Arabs and Bantu speaking peoples on the coast. The colonial experience was primarily with the British, although Tanganyika – the mainland part of the country – had originally been colonized by Germany. After its defeat in the First World War, however, it had to turn it over to the League of Nations – the precursor of the United Nations – which in turn gave it to Great Britain to administer on its behalf as a trust territory.

Because of its pleasant highland climate, its wildlife and agricultural potential, East Africa attracted a fair number of settlers from Britain and other parts of Europe. Land, especially in Kenya, which was the crown in the British chain of colonies in Africa, was taken from the Africans and given to the new settlers. The latter were huddled into 'reserves' and used as cheap labour. Commerce was given to immigrants from India and Pakistan, who came to make up a sizeable minority in both countries. Thus, colonial society was essentially three-tiered, with Europeans at the top, Africans at the bottom, and Asians sandwiched in between. Following the Mau Mau rebellion in Kenya and the Meru Land dispute (that was taken to the UN) in Tanganyika in the 1950s, land was returned to the Africans at independence. Europeans either left the country or moved into other types of business. The stronger presence and greater political clout of the settlers in Kenya, however, left it with a much better physical and institutional infrastructure in place than neighbouring Tanganyika, which became Tanzania in 1964, three years after independence, when it entered into a union with the then independent islands of Zanzibar.

Tanzania is slightly larger than Kenya both in area and population. In 1990 the former had just over 25 million people, the latter 24 million. Ninety per cent of the population live in the southern third of Kenya, which therefore has pockets of very high population density, most of it on relatively fertile volcanic soil. As a result of very rapid population growth in the 1970s and 1980s – close to 4 per cent per annum – plots have been subdivided but, even so, many people have been forced on to more marginal lands or into the urban slums. Northern Kenya is arid or semi-arid and occupied by nomadic peoples. Tanzania's population is concentrated on its physical periphery, typically in the highlands and on the shores of the big lakes – Nyasa (Malawi), Tanganyika and Victoria. The central parts of the country are arid or semi-arid with only a small population. Unlike Kenya, communications, therefore, have always been a big problem in that country. The Germans built both railways and roads that still form the core of the national transportation network, and a new railway and roads were built after independence to open up the south. These investments notwithstanding, the physical infrastructure in Tanzania is still undeveloped.

The economy of both countries is heavily dependent on agriculture. Its exports come mainly from such commodities as: in Kenya, primarily coffee and tea; in Tanzania, cloves, coffee, cotton and sisal. Neither country has any mineral deposits to speak of, though iron, coal and natural gas are exploited on a limited commercial basis in Tanzania. Kenya is more industrialized than Tanzania. In particular, it has an impressive range of domestic industries processing agricultural produce, both dairy and horticultural products. Its foreign trade is also more diversified: it includes exports of both flowers and fruits to the European and Middle Eastern markets and some manufactured products to neighbouring countries. Kenya also earns considerably more in revenue from tourism than does Tanzania, although some of the most scenic wildlife reserves in the world – Ngorongoro Crater and Serengeti – are located there.

Politically, the two countries have followed separate paths since the late 1960s, when President Nyerere of Tanzania launched his country's socialist blueprint – the Arusha Declaration. His older counterpart in Kenya, Jomo Kenyatta, remained committed to his country's special form of 'African socialism', which amounted to no more than an endorsement of capitalist practices. This ideological split exacerbated existing personal differences between the two leaders and their immediate followers. As a result, the East African Community – a regional organization running the railways, harbours, postal and telephone services of the two countries, plus Uganda – collapsed in 1977 and the borders between the two countries remained closed for six years. Since then relations have been normalized and at the time of writing (1994) are good.

In sum, it should be said that economically Kenya is further ahead than Tanzania, but in spite of its poverty and economic stagnation – largely as a result of overambitious socialist policies – Tanzania has been more politically stable. There was a coup attempt by the air force in Kenya in 1982 and the recent transition from one-party to multi-party politics has been characterized by ethnic violence and government repression. In Tanzania, by contrast, there has been no similar serious attempt to overthrow the government (although a military mutiny in 1964 scared Nyerere); nor has the ongoing transition to multi-party politics there been as turbulent.

## RELATIONS BETWEEN POLICY-MAKERS AND ADMINISTRATORS

### Context

Any discussion of this topic needs to consider the fact that the state in African countries, with a few exceptions such as Ethiopia and South Africa, is an entity that was created by foreign powers. It is not the product of 'home-grown' interaction with society. This legacy was particularly significant in shaping relations between policy-makers and administrators in the first years of independence. There were two aspects of this legacy that became important. The first was that the colonial state had been principally concerned with maintaining law and order. Investments in development activities were the exception, at least until the 1950s (Adu 1969, pp. 17–18). The second was that the African civil servants who had worked for the colonial power were viewed with suspicion by the nationalist leaders (Mutahaba 1989, pp. 121–5). Could they really be trusted to implement the nationalist project effectively?

These factors made the new political leaders anxious to revamp the public service and develop a new relationship with the civil servants. They wanted an administration that could promote development, not just prevent troubles. They wanted it involved in a positive way that helped legitimize the new regimes. Such were the sentiments in the early years of independence. But what would such a development administration look like?

Judging from the academic literature that helped to shape the debate on this topic, three separate models emerged. The first of these acknowledged that at least senior administrators stand with one foot in politics when they help formulate policy and advise politicians. In this model, the *political* role of public servants is being particularly emphasized. Even in the implementation of policies, they decide what information is relevant and they interpret policies and rules in ways that make important differences to members of the public (Lindenberg and Crosby 1981). In performing this political role, they exercise a lot of discretion *vis-à-vis* their political masters and/or the public. Their control of policy and programme implementation may, deliberately or inadvertently, produce consequences substantially at variance with those intended by the political leadership (Esman 1991, p. 41). Many leaders of the new states, however, wanted a politicized civil service without such discretion. They wanted them more 'red' than 'expert', to use the language of Mao Tse-tung. These leaders often went out of their way to cancel general orders and regulations put in place by the colonial rulers on the assumption that they stood in the way of control of the civil service.

The second model may be called *entrepreneurial* and was much associated with the literature on development administration that came out of American schools of public administration. The notion here was that a new type of administrative service was needed because of the unique challenges of development. As Victor Thompson (1964, p. 91) argued:

> Administrative practice and principles of the West have derived from preoccupation with control and therefore have little value for development administration in underdeveloped countries where the need is for an adaptive administration, one that can incorporate change.

Edward Weidner (1963) devoted his attention to reforming technical assistance so that it would be more in tune with a change-orientated administration. Many of the ideas that influenced the proponents of the entrepreneurial model came from organization theory; for example, the distinction made between Theory X and Theory Y (McGregor 1960) and 'mechanistic' and 'organic' forms of management (Burns and Stalker 1962). Little empirical work was done to test this model, but one that did so concluded that civil servants in new states enjoy an unusual degree of freedom and flexibility because of the high degree of structural fragmentation and low level of role institutionalization (Dresang 1973 p. 82).

The third model was based on the assumption that a civil service functions best if it is *instrumental* in its relation to policy-makers. This was the least radical, in the sense that it accepted the conventional perception of what a civil service is. Proponents of this approach, such as Riggs (1964), Pye (1966), Abernethy (1971) and Selassie (1974), with reference both to Africa and Asia, argued that the relative weakness of policy-making institutions gives bureaucrats an opportunity to appropriate the political function. This, in their view, was the foremost weakness of many developing countries. Remedial measures, therefore, were needed more in the political than in the administrative realm. It was political rather than administrative development that was crucial for developing countries. Arguing from a somewhat different perspective, but endorsing the same view of the role of the civil service in developing countries, Leonard (1977, pp. 217–23) maintained that the conventional 'mechanistic' form of administration is as valid there as it is in developed countries. Well-designed procedures, careful definitions of tasks and other ways of formalizing operations that come with the instrumental perception of the role of bureaucracy are important not only for control but also development.

## Cases

The problem with much of the academic debate on this topic in the 1960s was that it bore little relationship to the political realities in many of the new states. Academic analysts assumed that there would be enough political space for adopting logical and empirical considerations in public policy-making. To them, the state, as an organization, was viewed as the embodiment of some supreme rationality that could not be found in the nation – the political community. Both socio-economic development and national political integration, therefore, could only be achieved through the state. As our two case studies of Kenya and Tanzania illustrate, however, the policy-making process proved to be something very different.

## Tanzania

When the political leadership soon after independence decided that it wanted to make quick strides forward, it ran up against two stumbling-blocks. The first was the backward nature of its economy and the poor physical infrastructure that allowed smallholder peasants to be only marginally integrated into the cash economy. The second was that transition to political independence had been rather peaceful and there were no evident class enemies that people could identify as targets of social struggle. In short, members of the public had little incentive to change their behaviour. Bringing about an accelerated change, therefore, had to be induced from above. For this purpose, Tanzania's political leadership developed a mode of policy-making which elsewhere (Hyden 1984) I have labelled 'we-must-run-while-others-walk', borrowing a phrase that President Nyerere often used to describe what he and his colleagues were engaged in.

It has four main features. The first is the strong urge to do everything and do it at once. The ambition is to maximize as many social values as possible through policies that serve to mobilize new resources for the achievement of these values. This was manifested in the 1960s and 1970s in the various ways in which programmes and policies were presented as 'frontal attacks' (for example, various measures aimed at socializing private property), 'operations' (the forced movement of peasants into villages), and 'matters of life and death' (efforts to raise agricultural production). Because the social values pursued were rarely operationalized in advance, the aspiration to maximize was carried out with an implicit acceptance that it may be necessary to settle for something less than the official target.

The second feature is that policy-makers often decide matters without first having obtained full and detailed knowledge of the possible consequences of their decisions. Feasibility considerations are deliberately ignored. Policy-makers start 'running' and take the consequences as they occur. In this respect, they come close to what Hirschman (1975), drawing on his Latin American experience, calls the 'motivation-outruns-understanding' style of policy-making.

The third feature is the unwillingness of policy-makers to use the past as a source of guidance for the future. Being associated with colonial rule, from which the leadership sought to break, the past was, by and large, irrelevant. Dror (1968) has identified this inclination as a main feature of policy-making in all new states. Policy-makers, therefore, constantly have to make moves into the unknown, hoping that the solution to their problem is not always where there is light but that it is hidden somewhere in the dark.

The fourth feature is that civil servants are compelled to work in a context where public expectations constantly exceed what is likely to be accomplished. The assumption is that the anxiety or insecurity that follows from this is beneficial because it makes the officers clamour for more security through improved performance. It is in line with an argument made by A. Gunder Frank (1964, pp. 238–42) that 'overdefined' roles, that is, where role expectations cannot actually be satisfied by incumbents, often produce positive results.

The implications of this mode of policy-making for the administrators were at best ambiguous. In several instances the genuine team-work that developed between politicians and civil servants no doubt propelled action, but because the latter were being judged more on their loyalty than their expertise, many programme activities ended in failure because not enough attention had been paid to technical or administrative considerations. As unsuccessful outcomes became more frequent, many civil servants became demoralized and, instead of 'lifting themselves by their bootstraps', adopted a position whereby they would only do the minimum required to stay in office. This pattern was exacerbated after 1977 when the ruling party constitutionally became supreme and civil servants had little choice but to become members. At least one senior Tanzanian civil servant, William Shellukindo (1992, pp. 42–3), has testified to how viable policy options were discarded in Cabinet and other political contexts on the pretext that they involved the discussion of some aspects of the political setting.

Tanzania, then, adopted a highly politicized model of bureaucracy, where it was expected that civil servants would not question decicions made by party leaders but would implement them fully. Technical and administrative feasibility considerations were ignored or short-changed; the bureaucrats always left at the receiving end. Lofchie (1988) has argued that it was Tanzania's socialist policies that were at the bottom of its dire economic predicament in the 1980s. I would add that as important was the way these policies were made.

**Kenya**

In Kenya, political aspirations were never as high-flying, and political orientations always more pragmatic. Politics there has always been more like a tug-of-war. People have organized along ethnic lines and have attempted to pre-empt each others' opportunities. While this rivalry has generated many local self-help activities, it has also created a context of instability in the political system and uncertainty in the policy-making process. The mode by which policies are typically made in Kenya may best be called 'we-must-pull-while-others-pause'.

It also has four main features. The first is to redefine the public realm into separate fiefs controlled by whatever groups happen to be pulling the hardest. Loyalty to the state – such a sacrosanct principle in most other countries – is being undermined by pressures from ethnic peers who want access to specific public resources, even if it is at the expense of official policy.

The second feature is that the performance of the civil servant is not measured so much in terms of his contribution to the goals of an abstract entity called the state as in terms of how well he is able to deliver resources to his home community. Unlike Tanzania, where the pressure on the civil servant was to prove loyalty to the official ideology of the ruling party, in Kenya the social pressures on him come from the grass roots, especially his own ethnic group.

The third feature is the readiness of ethnic groups to capture fiefs where one of theirs is well placed and capable of exercising influence. Here agencies are being captured, much as they are in the United States, by special interests who wish to see resources channelled only in their direction.

The fourth feature is the extensive grass-roots organization that takes place in order to maximize the gains for one's own ethnic group. The self-help principle is very much institutionalized in Kenya and serves to strengthen the involvement of people with politicians and administrators. The latter are expected as much as the politicians to make monetary contributions to various self-help projects in their home community. These communities often organize projects so as to put pressure on government to come up with matching funds, an approach that Holmquist (1970, pp. 222–3) calls 'the strategy of pre-emptive development'.

The implications of this mode of policy-making for the civil service have been that the pulls of ethnic communities on individual public servants leave them with little autonomy or ability to be fair and even-handed. As a result, official policies have been derailed and resources allocated in ways that are contrary to budgetary commitments. Although the empirical evidence on how 'tribalism' works in order to secure benefits, such as promotion and salary increases within the civil service, is ambiguous (Leonard 1991, pp. 303–5), there is more than anecdotal evidence that, when it comes to allocating public resources, politicians and administrators give priority to their home communities. In this respect, the state is weak because it is not making policies in its own long-term interest (Lofchie 1988). Although the pull of ethnic communities was quite strong during both the Kenyatta era (1963–78) and that of his successor, Daniel arap Moi (1978–), it was compensated by the ability of the President to stand above these pressures and regulate them through a strong Provincial Administration. Both Leonard (1991) and Barkan (1992) argue, however, that in recent years, President Moi has gradually lost this ability. Thus, the 'we-must-pull-while-others-pause' mode has contributed to greater friction between ethnic groups in the country. It is reasonable to conclude, therefore, that it works in a constructive way only if there is an umpire capable of standing above the contenders who ensure that actors conceive the game as fair.

**Comparison**

Evidence from other countries indicates that the problems of politicization of the civil service along lines suggested by either of the two case studies above have a more general validity. Particularly important here are the reports of the Ford Foundation-funded annual Inter-African Public Administration Seminars that took place between 1962 and 1972. They represent the views of a wide spectrum of senior public servants from all over anglophone Africa. The papers were compiled for publication on behalf of the African Association of Public Administration and Management (AAPAM) by Rweyemamu and Hyden (1975). Together with the views of participants in these seminars, they document the widespread disillusionment with the new political leadership that emerged quite early among these senior civil servants. There are specific comments about the politicization of the Public Service Commissions, the appointment authority that was supposed to stay free of politics (Wamalwa 1975, pp. 51–62), a point that has also been independently corroborated by Adu (1969, p. 136) and Mutahaba (1989, pp. 115–17). In the 1970 Seminar, Chief Oputa Udoji, one of Nigeria's most distinguished public servants, vented his frustration with the way in which politicians in Africa were trying to control the public service. He makes the distinction between the civil service being responsive to political policies and the civil service being politicized. It is the latter that he finds in most African countries and this turns the civil servant into a sycophant and time-server, and not the kind of person that helps improve policy-making (see Rweyemamu and Hyden 1975, p. 4). While the colonial administration had often emphasized organizational efficiency over its public authority *vis-à-vis* society (Fleming 1966, pp. 386–411), the new governments were so concerned with establishing the latter that making good use of the civil service became only a secondary priority.

There were differences, however, in the degree to which the politicians were able to turn the civil service into a discretionary device. It seems, at least in part, to have been determined by how long Africans had been allowed to serve in senior positions. The racial barriers to the promotion of Africans into the senior ranks of the civil service were removed in West Africa in 1946, in East Africa in 1954, and in Southern Africa only in 1960 (Adu 1969, p. 21). Thus, it is no coincidence that the most vocal critique of the politicization of the civil service has come from Ghana and Nigeria. Even so, the public service in those countries has lacked the kind of stability that characterizes the civil service in India (Bhambhri 1972).

## PRINCIPAL CHANGES IN THE PUBLIC SERVICE

### Context

Because of its limited involvement in affairs other than law and order, the colonial civil service was structurally a rather rudimentary organization. There were no ministries. Every activity was conducted out of the Governor's Office, which also served as the apex of the government, supervising the field political administration and its service departments. Moreover, since there was no legislative branch in the territory, the civil service was the state. This pattern only began to change on the eve of independence, when a ministerial structure of government and a Cabinet system were introduced (Adu 1969, p. 33). A local government system, seen as a way of preparing Africans for democratic governance, was also established in this last phase of colonial rule.

Developments after independence in African countries can be divided into three phases. The first involved a rapid expansion of government activities to cater for the needs and aspirations generated in the struggle for independence. This growth of government took place at the same time as the vast majority of colonial civil servants departed. Thus, the emphasis had to be placed on a rapid Africanization of the civil service. This involved upgrading those with long experience but with no opportunity in the past to rise to senior positions, and providing crash programmes to train incumbents as well as others in the intricate tasks of running the service. As in India and Pakistan in the 1950s, a large number of training institutions were created in Africa in the 1960s. The former British colonies typically established 'institutes of public administration', for instance three in Nigeria, and 'staff colleges', such as the East African Staff College, a peripatetic institution serving the three East African countries. The former French colonies invariably followed the model of the *Ecole Nationale d'Administration* (ENA) in Paris. Donors, such as the United Nations, USAID and the

Ford Foundation, usually played an important role in shaping the public administration curricula of these new institutes, drawing on those of North America or Western Europe. Because of the hurry with which training needs had to be met and the rivalry that often existed among donors, institutionalizing administrative training in these countries became a highly controversial matter, as a case study of the *Ecole Nationale de Droit et d'Administration* (ENDA) in Zaire illustrates (Rimlinger 1976, pp. 364–82).

Because of the urgency to fill senior positions in the service, little attention was paid in the 1960s to the adequacy of existing structures and modes of running them. This, however, became the priorities in the second phase, which began around 1970, as it became clear that the new governments were not very effective in getting policies implemented. The assumption throughout this second period was that the answer to these shortcomings was administrative reform. This, then, became the 'golden era' of administrative reform in Africa. Such reforms were pursued along two lines. The first was structural and involved decentralizing authority from headquarters to field levels. The second was behavioural and focused on the task of professionalizing the civil service. It was recognized that the crash programmes of the earlier decade were not enough and that much of what had happened in the 1960s in the field of organization studies, such as the introduction of Management by Objectives (MBO) and Planning–Programming–Budgeting Systems (PPBS), could not be ignored. Together with foreign consultants, AAPAM played a leading role in pushing for these innovations (Ankomah 1988). For example, Chief Udoji, then Secretary-General of the Association, became the chairperson of the most extensive administrative review commission in Nigeria in 1975.

The third phase began around 1980, when it had become increasingly evident that reforming the public services was not the answer to Africa's development problems. In fact, more and more observers, especially in the donor community (see, for example, World Bank 1981), argued that the state, including the public service, was becoming an albatross around the necks of these countries. Instead of contributing to development, it was halting it. More responsibility had to be given to the market for allocating resources and to private and voluntary agencies for managing development activities. These 'structural adjustment' programmes focused on changes in macroeconomic policies but included such demands as privatization of commerce and service delivery as well as trimming the size of the public service (Grindle and Thomas 1991).

**Cases**

**Tanzania**
In a country with as many poor districts as Tanzania has, the rapid expansion of governmental activities after independence began to take its toll quite early, especially among local governments that were responsible for managing primary

education, primary health care and other local development programmes. They simply did not have the funds to run these activities, nor did they, in many cases, have the personnel to do it (Dryden 1968). The bankruptcy and poor management of these local councils became a reason for the central government to take over all their services in 1969. This, however, only further clogged the machinery of government and forced the political leadership to introduce a major decentralization reform in 1972.

This was not aimed at restoring autonomous local government entities but rather at deconcentrating authority from Dar es Salaam, the capital, to the field, administratively divided into some twenty regions and about a hundred districts. Each region would be politically on a par with a ministry and have its own budget, which then would be shared among the districts within that region. In addition to the political head – the Regional Commissioner – the regional secretariat would consist of a development director, his immediate planning, finance and personnel officers, as well as the whole range of service departments, whose heads would now report not to their ministerial headquarters but to the development director. Worked out with the help of McKinsey & Co., the multinational consultancy firm, the idea behind this reform was to strengthen development management and bring government closer to the people (Mutahaba 1989, pp. 82–94).

A preliminary study of this reform in 1976, in which I participated but which was never published, indicated that while it did lead to accelerated implementation of policies, the quality of this work declined, largely because of the lack of professional oversight from the ministerial headquarters. The main problem with this decentralization effort, however, was that it became very management-intensive and increased staff expenditure levels at a time when government revenue in the late 1970s began to decline. In the early 1980s, it was not unusual for regions to spend 90 per cent of recurrent expenditure on personnel emoluments alone. Little was left for all other items, such as building and vehicle maintenance, telephones and other inputs to keep the offices going. The result was that government in the field was coming to a standstill, with officers sitting behind their desks having nothing to do but to chat. Although 10 per cent of the unskilled employees were laid off and the government made a half-hearted attempt to restore elected local government councils in 1982 – financed through an unpopular 'development levy' charged on every adult person over 18 years of age – the public service continued to deteriorate in the 1980s. This trend was exacerbated after 1986, when the government entered into an agreement with the International Monetary Fund and had to accept a creeping, but rapid, devaluation of the local currency. This forced up the cost of living very drastically and forced public servants to seek secondary sources of income, either through bribes or private projects, that took time away from public duty. As documented by Tripp (1990), these phenomena became very widespread and institutionalized in the public service. Initiatives taken with the help of the World Bank to reduce the size of the public service in recent years have yet to be implemented.

Finally, it should be added that, compared to other anglophone countries in Africa, professionalization of the public service has been of less concern, the main reason being that, for the nationalist leadership, political loyalty and commitment were deemed much more important than professional skills. To be sure, a fair amount of effort was devoted by the McKinsey consultants to imparting new management ideas into the heads of public servants running the decentralized system of government, but there is little evidence that it resulted in greater effectiveness or efficiency.

**Kenya**

Trends in Kenya after independence bear a lot of resemblance to what happened in Tanzania. The local government system soon found itself overloaded with an inadequate revenue base, and therefore greater dependence on central government grants-in-aid. This caused the same kind of transfer of basic services to central government in 1969 as happened in Tanzania that year (Mulusa 1970). Subsequent deconcentration, however, was much slower in coming in Kenya. There are probably three reasons for this. The first is that the demographic concentration in the southern third of the country made contact between central government and local communities easier. The second was that with the prevalence of strong ethnic competition in policy-making, it was necessary to retain central control to ensure that the process would not go out of control. The third is that the Kenya government never saw itself involved in a revolutionary transformation of society; hence there was not the same need as in Tanzania to strengthen the 'machinery'. Yet, in the mid-1980s, President Moi introduced his own version of deconcentrated administration called 'District Focus'. This was less radical than what was attempted in Tanzania (and the lessons from there may have influenced the Kenyan officials) in that it involved only partial financial autonomy. Furthermore, although development planning was now going to be carried out at the district headquarters, the final approval of these plans lay with the national ministry of planning (Makokha 1985). In Kenya, the reform was focused on the district as opposed to the superior provincial level, which was rendered much less powerful than it had been before. Like the initiative in Tanzania, 'District Focus' was being sold politically as enhancing popular participation in policy-making. In both instances, however, the most important outcome seems to have been that the central government strengthened its grip over local communities.

The issues of professionalization of the public service occupied more prominence in Kenya than in Tanzania and were the subject of two public review commissions: the Ndegwa Commission of 1969 and the Waruhiu Commission of 1980. The former recommended (and the government subsequently adopted) the notion that civil servants should be allowed to own private business side by side with their public office. Unlike Tanzania (and Zambia) where private sources of income had to be abandoned through the adoption of a special 'leadership code', applicable both to party and government functionaries, Kenya encouraged it as part of indigenizing capitalism. Both commissions offered valuable suggestions as to how government work could be rationalized, but the only issue that was actively implemented by government were proposed salary increases (Oyugi 1990, p. 69). The result was that the public service was becoming increasingly costly and a burden on society. The only difference between the two countries is that Kenya could more easily afford to carry this burden, because its overall economic performance was so much better. In the 1990s, however, even Kenya has reached the limit, in the sense that the World Bank is insisting on tighter control of public expenditure, including reduction in the size of the public service.

## Comparison

Both the extensive training and decentralization programmes introduced in Africa and Asia have been the subject of comparative evaluations. Schaffer (1974) conducted a major survey to see what impact training had had on administrative development on the two continents. Although the record was mixed, the Asian countries had, by and large, made better use of training than had the African. One reason is obviously that there was so much more stability in the Asian services, especially in India. Another was that innovations brought about by training were often treated as threatening by newly promoted but insecure African senior civil servants. Although individuals benefited from the professional training they received, there is less evidence that the organizations they served did also. In short, training became, at least in African countries, a private more than a public good.

In the late 1970s, the relative failure of so much of the investment in training and organization development led to a debate about whether Western theories of administration and management that had been peddled across Africa by expatriate consultants really were appropriate to the conditions in Africa. Particularly influential in arguing against the transferability of such theories was Jon Moris (1977) who suggested that administrative techniques cannot be seen in isolation from their cultural context. The cultural underpinnings of rational-legal administration (or any derivation thereof) simply do not exist in Africa, Moris maintained. In a personalized system of rule, as in Africa, rationality is not defined in terms of 'getting the job done as efficiently or fairly as possible' but rather in terms of the implications of decisions on relations among officials. For example, it becomes 'rational' in one situation to demonstrate who is the boss, but in another how consensus can be maintained. Moris does not propose an alternative system of administration for Africa, nor has anyone else done so. The conclusion that everybody seems to have drawn is that rational and legal considerations are better generated and sustained in non-governmental organizations where politicization of decision-making is less likely.

Decentralization, finally, has been reviewed in the 1980s in several documents. Particularly influential has been the work of Dennis Rondinelli. The main conclusion he arrives at in explaining the disappointing results of decentralization in many countries is that in order to function well, it requires supporting institutions and effective linkages both to the centre and to non-governmental organizations tied to local communities. Furthermore, these linkages must be mutually beneficial to both parties (Rondinelli 1981; Rondinelli *et al.*, 1989). Because of the problems of arriving at such 'positive-sum' solutions in contexts where governments are authoritarian and insist on central control, it is not surprising that decentralization in recent years has come to focus on delegating greater responsibilities to the market, including private and voluntary agencies. As Gerald Caiden (1991, p. 313) concludes in a recent review of administrative reform efforts throughout the world: at the beginning of the 1990s administrative reform had become only part of much wider and more sweeping institutional reforms in response to attempts by governments to regain national purpose and direction.

## THE PUBLIC SERVICE AND CIVIL SOCIETY

### Context

Relations between state and civil society in countries emerging from colonialism were bound to be different from those of others because the state was a foreign entity imposed on territories and peoples. The result was that these relations tended to be both arbitrary and artificial. Public officials were accountable not to the colonized society but to the Colonial Office back home. Only where the colonial presence was lengthy, as in India, did it result in some degree of integration of state institutions with civil society. Relations of accountability had time to come about, at least in an incipient fashion. This is one of the reasons why it became possible to institutionalize a democratic form of government there without questioning the relevance of the 'Westminster Model'. In Africa, however, where colonialism lasted little more than 60 years, people were never given a chance until the eve of independence to experience what political democracy entails. Whatever they learnt from this brief exposure they used principally to reject colonialism and, with it, the forms of governance that the Europeans had brought to their continent. Thus, while the relations between state and civil society in other countries were the product of long battles to define their nature, in Africa such a process of maturation never occurred. Two aspects of this particular legacy became especially important in the post-colonial period.

The first was the tendency to retain the notion of the state as primarily an instrument of control rather than development. To be sure, the political rhetoric in the days after independence emphasized 'development', but political practice was different. The new governments kept all those features of the colonial state that gave it its distinct power: laws permitting political detention without trial; an extensive political field administration; and the tendency to legislate by decree, to mention only some of the more obvious. Some efforts were being made in the name of 'development' to integrate the state with society. The adoption of a community development approach, borrowed from the Indian experience of the 1950s (Bhambhri 1972, p. 11), is a case in point. In Africa, as in India, however, these policies were very much top-down in character. Community development did not imply associational autonomy, and thus the existence of a civil society, but a centrally directed effort in which communities resembled more the extended arm of the state.

This emphasis on power and control is not surprising, given the sense of uncertainty that prevailed in the minds of most nationalists as they turned into governors and policy-makers. The spate of military coups that started in the mid-1960s only exacerbated such feelings. In order to keep themselves in power and hold their new nations together, most leaders resorted to an insistence on ideological uniformity as a prerequisite for national unity. Opposition parties were prohibited and the ruling party used to infuse the state with conformist ideas that pre-empted any debate about alternative policy options. Such was the trend in Africa until the late 1980s (Wunsch and Olowu 1990).

The second aspect of the colonial state legacy was the limited appreciation in African circles of state institutions forming part of a civic public realm that rested on the assumption of an ethical distinction between things private and public. As Ekeh (1975) emphasized in his influential article on this topic, the moral loyalty of most Africans lay with their home community – the 'primordial' public realm. The civil and military institutions making up the state were only there to be tapped for their resources. In short, the right thing to do was to milk the state to serve one's own community. In these countries, where ethnicity rather than social class divides society, the most important concern for people was not whether the election of leaders is competitive but whether their particular group is represented politically and thus has access to public resources (Chabal 1992, pp. 206–9). This is the foundation on which Africa's clientelist politics rests. As several studies of African politics (for example, Callaghy 1984 and Joseph 1987) have confirmed, its principal feature is not policy-making, as we know it in Western democracies, but patronage distribution. This form of government tends to be private in the sense that government offices are treated as private property and that patronage must be managed in a discreet and clandestine fashion (Jackson 1977, p. 44). Patronage is not publicly announced but privately bestowed. It is not publicly reviewed because, if it is, the risk of controversial exposure is high. Furthermore, patronage is dispensed, not with a view to the future, as policy is, but with an eye to rewarding past services. Patronage government engages in distributive politics, but one that is based on expediency rather than on reasoned arguments deliberated in public.

**Cases**

**Tanzania**
The rich variety of voluntary associations, mutual-aid societies and self-help groups that had served the population so well in the colonial days lost much of their public prominence after independence, as the state was being viewed by people as the principal resource and agency for development. Some were banned outright, but others were co-opted into mainstream politics and turned into support organizations for the ruling party, the Tanganyika African National Union (TANU). This was the case with the co-operative movement and the women's organizations. Community-based organizations continued to exist but had little life without the resources that were being secured by prominent political patrons (Tripp 1992, pp. 228–31). In this context, the scope for autonomous group representation and a civil society in which policy options evolve independently of the ruling party was deliberately discouraged. As Samoff (1974, p. 69) wrote:

> In Tanzania, party policy frowns on the formation of interest groups in general, and economic interest groups in particular ... It is assumed that the political functions performed by interest groups in other polities – especially interest aggregation, articulation and communication – are performed by TANU and its auxiliaries and that interest groups, which could be used to form competing centers of power, are both unnecessary and dangerous.

This system was further reinforced in 1977 when a new constitution was adopted that confirmed party supremacy in all public settings. Every initiative had to be channelled through a party branch. It served as a *pater familias* with the right to examine everything that citizens undertook.

Because this system turned politics into a private affair controlled by a small number of elected officials and appointed functionaries, and because no real public discourse was allowed on political issues, the state became increasingly parochialized and personalized. The leadership code that had been introduced in the late 1960s was blatantly violated with increasing frequency; the discrepancy between socialist rhetoric and political practice growing greater and greater. With a strangled civil society, there was no internal corrective mechanism. The Permanent Commission of Enquiry – Tanzania's own ombudsman – which had been established in the 1960s, made no effort to represent public interest. It is not surprising, therefore, that the Tanzanian authorities had to be forced to abandon their mode of making policies by intervention from outside, beginning with the economic adjustment policies in the 1980s and continuing with demands for political liberalization in the 1990s.

As a result of these pressures, Tanzania has changed dramatically in recent years. Socialism is gone, as is the notion of party supremacy. Opposition parties are allowed, a growing number of independent newspapers have been established, new voluntary associations are being formed and the market rather than the bureaucracy seems to reign. For the first time since independence, Tanzanians have a chance to participate in politics in their own right. The possibility of civil society exercising pressure on the direction of public policy and the public service is now a reality.

**Kenya**

Kenya became independent with an even more impressive array of voluntary associations, many of which had been playing their part in the struggle to get rid of colonialism. The self-help tradition was rooted in the rural communities and the new Kenyatta government encouraged it to continue after independence. Its developmental significance has been recorded in several studies (such as Winans and Haugerud 1977; Thomas 1985). In politics, self-help activities have been viewed as a defensive measure by the peasantry to carve out a measure of political space *vis-à-vis* central political authority (Holmquist 1980; Barkan 1992).

The Kenyan state during the reign of President Kenyatta never strove for the same degree of omnipotence as President Nyerere did in Tanzania. The Kenyan President emphasized control and made effective use of the provincial field administration to arrest tendencies towards political division. Yet most institutions in society retained a good measure of autonomy from the state. Within the state itself, politicization of appointments was never complete as in Tanzania and spheres of autonomy for institutions such as the judiciary and the Public Service Commission did exist.

This trend changed when President Moi, after his 'honeymoon period' was over in the early 1980s, began to crack down on autonomous political action which in turn led to the attempted coup by the air force in 1982. Particularly after that event, his way of running the country became much more closed and confined to a small clique of advisers drawn primarily from his own Kalenjin group of people. This tendency to silence civil society continued throughout the 1980s. Non-governmental organizations had to keep a low profile in order to be able to continue their development work. The most stubborn opponents to the Moi government were Christian clerics and professional lawyers. In particular, a number of prominent bishops argued for restoration of civil and political rights and lamented the brutal way in which the government was dealing with its opponents. One of these bishops was killed in a road accident that most Kenyans believe was arranged by the security services of the government. Even one of the most prominent members of Moi's cabinet, Robert Ouko, the country's foreign minister, was assassinated under suspicious circumstances after what appears, according to the local media, to have been a quarrel with another close confidant of Moi, Nicholas Biwott, over the government's political stand on human rights and related issues. Although these incidents lost the government much of its credibility in the country and the opposition was rapidly growing in strength in the early 1990s, it took a firm stand by the donor community in November 1991 to force Moi's government to change its attitude. Faced with the decision to freeze foreign aid to Kenya unless the government changed its human rights policy and adopted political pluralism, Moi agreed a few weeks later to introduce multi-party politics. Three major opposition parties were formed to challenge the rule of the Kenya African National Union (KANU), Moi's party, but because of their internal dissension and the ability of KANU to get away with sabotage of the nomination procedures, they could not dislodge it in the general elections that were held in December 1992. Thus, while the policy process had become increasingly strangulated in the 1980s, a new opening, similar to that in Tanzania, now exists for civil society to shape both public policy and the orientation of the country's public service.

## Comparison

The fear of civil society by political leaders in Africa has been highlighted in other studies (for example, Vengroff *et al.* 1991). The now-common explanation of Africa's economic and social woes as being self-inflicted through political malgovernance cannot be easily dismissed. By turning against civil society and creating a political monster of the state, African leaders created conditions under which their own rule could not be sustained. As public resources were consumed with increasingly little regard for economic and technical feasibility considerations, the state reproduced itself in ways that further marginalized African countries in the global economy. Declining commodity prices and other such changes in the world market only precipitated this trend.

In the situation that was allowed to develop in the years after independence, it is not surprising that the state failed to really grab hold of public issues and solve them in constructive ways (Wunsch and Olowu 1990). Nor should anybody be astonished that all those administrative reforms that were attempted, particularly in the 1970s, were never really implemented. Although administrative reforms always tend to fall short of expectations (Wilenski 1981; Caiden 1991), the stories told by students of such reforms in Africa (such as Mutahaba 1989; Ayubi 1990) indicate that the politicians' disregard for the needs of administrative institutions is in a class by itself. Preoccupied with their own patronage politics, which feeds on principles that run contrary to those that typically guide a public service, politicians in Africa have ensured that the prospects for administrative reform giving rise to better state performance have been particularly remote there. To be sure, there are differences among countries. Leonard (1991, p. 298) maintains that the enclaves of professionalism that continued to exist in the Kenyan public service made a difference, and explains many of the country's policy successes in rural development. So, according to the same source, does the fact that the political leadership, or the ruling class, had compatible interests with the peasantry in promoting agriculture, because they were farmers themselves.

Much has been made of recent trends toward democratization in various parts of the world. Little, however, has yet been said about the influence these may have on the future of public administration. To the extent that both economic and political liberalization is going to become real in developing countries, it is going to redefine relations between state and civil society, and thus the role of the public service in development. The problem to date has been that the state has been too dominant and unwilling to respond to initiatives from independent sources in civil society. There is a danger that as interest shifts toward private and voluntary sector organizations, the pendulum will be allowed to swing so far that concern about the quality of the public service will become secondary. At least one analyst (Argyriades 1991) argues that what the world is witnessing now is a more fundamental disenchantment with hierarchical authority models. This process of 'debureaucratization' questions old administrative legacies, but in doing so it also confronts us with a more direct choice between disorganization – including ungovernability, lawlessness, alienation and passivity – on the one hand, and a more democratic, open but also self-directed society, on the other.

## CONCLUSIONS

This latter observation is relevant to the conclusion of this chapter. The world has changed a lot since the 1960s when comparative public administration was first attempted. Those were the days when it was right to accept the leading role of the state in development; when an exclusive focus on how to improve the public services was justified. Three decades later, the public sector is increasingly viewed as only one actor, side by side with the private and voluntary sectors. From the perspective of developing countries, therefore, the state must be analysed in its relation to civil society. This external dimension of the public service becomes particularly crucial. The aspirations of the new democratization efforts in these countries emphasize that the best guarantee for an improved public service is not internal administrative reforms but a stronger and more vibrant civil society that can hold public officials accountable. The problem in developing countries is no longer shortage of trained and skilled personnel but rather the institutional imbalances that were allowed to grow in the era of authoritarian patronage politics.

The research proposition that grows out of this argument is that public services will work best when they are held in check by an active civil society. Only then will the internal components of such a service fall into place and begin to function with better results. This proposition, which incidentally was one that also guided the first generation of administrative comparativists, seems as fruitful as any for today's students of comparative public administration to adopt for future investigation, not least because it speaks to conditions that exist in many regions of the world. The difference between now and then is that we have the benefit of three decades of experience in investigating this and related issues. The possibilities of a renaissance for comparative analysis in public administration are certainly there in ways that we have not seen for three decades.

# REFERENCES

Abernethy, D. (1971), 'Bureaucracy and Economic Development in Africa', *African Review*, 1, 93–114.

Adu, A. L. (1969), *The Civil Service in Commonwealth Africa* (London: Allen & Unwin).

Ankomah, K. (1988), 'Professionalising Public Administration in Africa', *Indian Journal of Public Administration*, 31, 1020–44.

Argyriades, D. (1991), 'Bureaucracy and Debureaucratization', in A. Farazmand (ed.), *Handbook of Comparative and Development Public Administration* (New York: Marcel Dekker), pp. 567–86.

Ayubi, N. N. (1990), 'Policy Development and Administrative Changes in the Arab World', in O. P. Dwivedi and K. M. Henderson (eds), *Public Administration in World Perspective* (Ames, Iowa: Iowa State University Press), pp. 23–53.

Barkan, J. (1992), 'The Rise and Fall of a Governance Realm in Kenya', in G. Hyden and M. Bratton (eds), *Governance and Politics in Africa* (Boulder, Col.: Lynne Rienner).

Bhambhri, C. P. (1972), *Administrators in a Changing Society* (New Delhi: National Publishing House).

Burns, T. and G. M. Stalker (1962), *The Management of Innovations* (London: Tavistock Publications).

Caiden, G. E. (1991), *Administrative Reform Comes of Age* (New York: de Gruyter).

Caiden, G. E. and N. Caiden (1990), 'Towards the Future of Comparative Public Administration', in O. P. Dwivedi and K. M. Henderson (eds), *Public Administration in World Perspective* (Ames, Iowa: Iowa State University Press), pp. 363–99.

Callaghy, T. (1984), *The State–Society Struggle: Zaire in Comparative Perspective* (New York: Columbia University Press).

Chabal, P. (1992), *Power in Africa* (London: Macmillan).

Dresang, D. (1973), 'Entrepreneurialism and Development Administration', *Administrative Science Quarterly*, 18, 76–85.

Dror, Y. (1968), *Public Policy-making Re-examined* (San Francisco, Cal.: Chandler).

Dryden, S. (1968), *Local Administration in Tanzania* (Nairobi: East African Publishing House).

Dwivedi, O. P. and K. M. Henderson (eds) (1990), *Public Administration in World Perspective* (Ames, Iowa: Iowa State University Press).

Ekeh, P. (1975), 'Colonialism and the Two Publics: a Theoretical Statement', *Comparative Studies in History and Society*, 17, 91–112.

Esman, M. J. (1991), *Management Dimensions of Development: Perspectives and Strategies* (West Hartford, Conn.: Kumarian Press).

Fleming, W. G. (1966), 'Authority, Efficiency, and Role Stress: Problems in the Development of East African Bureaucracies', *Administrative Science Quarterly*, 12, 386–404.

Frank, A. G. (1964), 'Administrative Role Definition and Social Change', *Human Organization*, 22, 238–42.

Grindle, M. and J. W. Thomas (1991), *Public Choices and Policy Change: The Political Economy of Reform in Developing Countries* (Baltimore, Md.: Johns Hopkins University Press).

Hirschman, A. O. (1975), *Journeys Towards Progress* (New York: Doubleday).

Holmquist, F. (1970), 'Implementing Rural Development Projects', in G. Hyden, R. H. Jackson and J. J. Okumu (eds), *Development Administration: The Kenyan Experience* (Nairobi: Oxford University Press), pp. 201–32.

Holmquist, F. (1980), 'Defending Peasant Political Space in Independent Africa', *Canadian Journal of African Studies*, 14, 157–67.

Hyden, G. (1984), 'Administration and Public Policy', in J. Barkan with J. J. Okumu (eds), *Politics and Public Policy in Kenya and Tanzania* (New York: Praeger), pp. 93–113.

Jackson, R. H. (1977), *Plural Societies and New States: A Conceptual Analysis* (Berkeley, Cal.: Institute of International Studies, University of California).

Joseph, R. (1987), *Democracy and Prebendal Politics in Nigeria* (New York: Cambridge University Press).

Leonard, D. K. (1977), *Reaching the Peasant Farmer: Organization Theory and Practice in Kenya* (Chicago, Ill.: University of Chicago Press).

Leonard, D. K. (1987), 'The Political Realities of African Management', *World Development*, 15, 899–910.

Leonard, D. K. (1991), *African Successes: Four Public Managers of Kenyan Rural Development* (Berkeley, Cal.: University of California Press).

Lindenberg, M. and B. Crosby (eds) (1981), *Managing Development: The Political Dimension* (West Hartford, Conn.: Kumarian Press).

Lofchie, M. (1988), *The Policy Factor: Agricultural Performance in Kenya and Tanzania* (Boulder, Col.: Lynne Rienner).

Makohka, J. (1985), *The District Focus* (Nairobi: Africa Press Research Bureau).

McGregor, D. (1960), *The Human Side of Enterprise* (New York: McGraw-Hill).

Moris, J. (1977), 'The Transferability of Western Management Concepts and Programs: an East African Perspective', in *Education and Training for Public Sector Management in Developing Countries – A Special Report from the Rockefeller Foundation* (New York: Rockefeller Foundation), pp. 73–83.

Mulusa, T. (1970), 'Central Government and Local Authorities', in G. Hyden, R. H. Jackson and J. J. Okumu (eds), *Development Administration: The Kenyan Experience* (Nairobi: Oxford University Press), pp. 233–51.

Mutahaba, G. (1989), *Reforming Public Administration for Development: Experiences from Eastern Africa* (West Hartford, Conn.: Kumarian Press).

Mutahaba, G. and J. Balogun (eds) (1992), *Enhancing Policy Management Capacity in Africa* (West Hartford, Conn.: Kumarian Press).

Oyugi, W. (1990), 'Civil Bureaucracy in East Africa: a Critical Analysis of Role Performance since Independence', in O. P. Dwivedi and K. M. Henderson (eds), *Public Administration in World Perspective* (Ames, Iowa: Iowa State University Press), pp. 54–72.

Pye, L. W. (1966), *Aspects of Political Development* (Boston, Mass.: Little, Brown).

Riggs, F. (1964), *Public Administration in Developing Countries: The Theory of Prismatic Society* (Boston, Mass.: Houghton Mifflin).

Rimlinger, G. (1976), 'Administrative Training and Modernisation in Zaire', *Journal of Development Studies*, 12, 364–82.

Rondinelli, D. (1981), 'Government Decentralization in Comparative Perspective', *International Review of Administrative Sciences*, 47, 133–45.

Rondinelli, D., J. McCullough and R. Johnson (1989), 'Analysing Decentralization Policies in Developing Countries: a Political Economy Framework', *Development and Change*, 20, 57–88.

Rweyemamu, A. H. and G. Hyden (eds) (1975), *A Decade of Public Administration in Africa* (Nairobi: East African Literature Bureau).

Samoff, J. (1974), *Tanzania: Local Politics and the Structure of Power* (Madison, Wis.: University of Wisconsin Press).

Savage, P. (1976), 'Optimism and Pessimism in Comparative Administration', *Public Administration Review*, 36, 415–23.

Schaffer, B. (ed.) (1974), *Administrative Training and Development: A Comparative Study of Zambia, Kenya, Pakistan, India and U.K.* (New York: Praeger).

Selassie, B. H. (1974), *The Executive in African Governments* (London: Heinemann).

Shellukindo, W. H. (1992), 'A Strategic and Analytical Approach to Policy Management', in G. Mutahaba and M. J. Balogun (eds), *Enhancing Policy Management Capacity in Africa* (West Hartford, Conn.: Kumarian Press), pp. 39–54.

Thomas, B. P. (1985), *Politics, Participation, and Poverty: Development Through Self-help in Kenya* (Boulder, Col.: Westview Press).

Thompson, V. (1964), 'Administrative Objectives for Development Administration', *Administrative Science Quarterly*, 9, 91–108.

Tripp, A. M. (1990), 'The Urban Informal Economy and the State in Tanzania', Ph.D. dissertation, Northwestern University.

Tripp, A. M. (1992), 'Local Organizations, Participation, and the state in Urban Tanzania', in G. Hyden and M. Bratton (eds), *Governance and Politics in Africa* (Boulder, Col.: Lynne Riennel Publishers), pp. 221–42.

Van Wart, M. and N. J. Cayer (1990), 'Comparative Public Administration: Defunct, Dispersed, or Redefined?', *Public Administration Review*, 50, 238–48.

Vengroff, R., M. Belhaj and M. Ndiaye (1991), 'The Nature of Managerial Work in the Public Sector: an African Perspective', *World Development*, 11, 95–110.

Wamalwa, W. N. (1975), 'The Role of Public Service Commissions in New African States', in G. Hyden and A. H. Rweyemamu (eds), *A Decade of Public Administration in Africa* (Nairobi: East African Literature Bureau), pp. 51–62.

Weidner, E. W. (1963), *Technical Assistance in Public Administration Overseas: The Case for Development Administration* (Chicago, Ill.: Public Administration Service).

Wilenski, P. (1981), 'Administrative Reform Commissions and Administrative Reform: the Australian Experience', in N. Scott (ed.), *International Perspectives on Administration,* Proceedings of the IASA Roundtable (Canberra, Australia: Canberra College of Advanced Education), pp. 90–123.

Winans, E. V. and A. Haugerud (1977), 'Rural Self-help in Kenya: the Harambee Movement', *Human Organization*, 36, 334–51.

World Bank (1981), *Accelerated Development in Sub-Saharan Africa* (Washington, D.C.: World Bank).

Wunsch, J. and D. Olowu (eds) (1990), *The Failure of the Centralized State: Institutions and Self-governance in Africa* (Boulder, Col.: Westview Press).

# 9. The Europeanization of the national bureaucracies?
## Edward C. Page and Linda Wouters

## INTRODUCTION: THE MECHANISMS OF EUROPEANIZATION[1]

Bureaucracies in member states of the European Communities now share the administration of a large and expanding range of public affairs with a supranational level. This raises the question of the degree to which national administrative systems can remain the same. Certainly we know that national policy-making processes in many areas have been fundamentally transformed through the development of the European Community (Wallace *et al.* 1983).

Such changes in the process of decision-making have been taken to mean that there must be some reform of national administrative structures too. Toonen, for example, talks of a 'Europeanization' process involving a 'destabilization of existing national administrative systems and patterns' which, he claims, has 'already triggered debates on the fundamental nature of existing state structures and the possible need for constitutional reform' (Toonen 1992, pp. 110–11).

The scope of EC activities has grown considerably over the years. The Europeanization of policies, of course, has had a profound influence on the functioning of national administrations. The number of areas where they are the sole regulating instances has been reduced sharply. However, the relationship between the European and national levels of administration is not one of a strict hierarchy. National administrations are closely involved in most phases of the European policy cycle (through common working parties, experts on secondment to the EC, through the national permanent representations in Brussels). In administrative terms, there exists a relationship of mutual dependency. This leads Wessels to observe an important trend to '*Verflechtung*' between the administrative levels (Wessels 1983, p. 230). However, whether this will have consequences for the structure and the organization of the national civil services remains to be seen.

Almost all discussions of administrative change in Europe in the wake of the development of closer European integration are couched in terms of a potential.

EC institutions are now in their fifth decade and the examples of any direct impact of EC membership upon national institutional structures are very slight.

Even in cases where one would expect a clear and direct influence, such as in the extension of the principle of 'free movement' to the public sector, the outcomes are half-hearted. The EC's cautious request that member states should consider changing nationality requirements for public servants met with highly diverse responses: the Dutch opened all posts to any nationality; the French maintained with some exceptions the French nationality requirement; and the nationality requirement will not be dropped in Belgium for posts which involve 'participation in the exercise of public authority' (Kessler 1992, p. 305).

In what way we might expect changes in national administration in the wake of the European Community is rather unclear. An important change in one aspect of administration does not necessarily mean wider change throughout the whole. National administrative institutions might be fundamentally transformed by closer European integration, yet there are no *a priori* reasons to assume that they will. Administrative diversity can easily coexist with close political union.

A good example of this can be found in the United States federal system. States have vastly differing administrative systems despite being part of the same polity, with (to name but a few) a nationwide set of social security, economic development, education and public health programmes on top of those things to which many in Europe still aspire: a single currency, a federal bank and a common defence and foreign policy. State constitutions give vastly differing powers and structures to legislatures and executives, some have powerful governors and some have weak governors and a fragmented executive. In administrative terms even 'merit systems' in appointments and promotions have spread in a very uneven pattern since the turn of the century.[2]

None of this is to say that the process of European integration will leave European administration unchanged. However, the huge significance of the administrative effects of European integration under Charlemagne and Napoleon could only be adequately assessed with the benefit of great hindsight. Any contemporary assessment of the impact of EC integration must therefore be highly tentative. Yet such an exercise is important for two reasons. First, because the expectation that change is imminent is quite widely held among academics, although discussion seldom gets beyond a rather diffuse 'need' for change. An explicit discussion of the form and mechanisms of change therefore goes some way to filling a gap in the literature of public administration. Secondly, there is a practical purpose behind this. As we know from the experience of national as well as local government, the *Zeitgeist* exercises a powerful influence over institutional reform. Just as the 'planning mood' in the 1960s shaped reforms of national ministerial organization as well as local government, the 1980s and 1990s have been heavily influenced by concepts of markets, competition and consumer choice (Drewry and Butcher 1988, ch. 10). If the impetus to closer

European co-operation and convergence survives the early 1990s, it is quite possible that the *Zeitgeist* of integration, the 'Europeanization' of which Toonen speaks, will assume a prominent role in future debates about administrative reforms in nation states. A critical look at the issue of administrative change suggested by closer integration might help to give the *Zeitgeist* its proper weight in evaluating the requirements of future administrative reform.

The potential for EC influence on national administrations is huge: the EC bureaucracy has different ways of doing things, ranging from the structure of its internal organization to the way it appoints and rewards senior officials. Furthermore, this potential influence is variable since some EC practices conform closely to those of some member states while they contrast strongly with those found in others. How, then, given such a huge range and diversity of potential impact can one begin to discuss the influence of EC membership on the reform of national bureaucracies?

One way to identify the areas of national administration most likely to experience major administrative change is by first thinking about the mechanisms by which EC influence may be exerted. The first basic distinction is between types of influence which are direct and indirect. Direct influence covers legal and quasi-legal methods of effecting change by a directive, a regulation, a European court decision or some other form of legal or quasi-legal communication.

So far, direct influences have had the strongest impact upon the civil services of member states, above all through court decisions concerning the rights of employees. The lifting of restrictions on employment mobility under the Single European Act, for example, requires that countries such as Germany somehow reform their civil service laws to exempt applicants for posts such as teachers and train drivers from any nationality requirement.

However, such direct influences have not so far been specifically directed at the core ministerial civil service. Because there is no evidence that the EC is likely to exert direct influences in order to produce major changes in the ministerial civil services of member states, we must look to other forms of influence.

Indirect influences are those where there is no formal requirement for member states to conform. These might be exerted through a variety of methods. First, they might result from the demands of national civil servants themselves. National civil servants may put pressure on their governments to bring things closer into line with EC administration. This is most likely to occur in the field of pay and conditions of service.

Secondly, the 'aerodynamics' of EC institutions and policies might influence national institutions to adapt to those with which they interact in Brussels. This is most likely to be found in the structure of government institutions. Adaptation might be expected in the organization of the civil service as national ministries increasingly interact with Commission Directorates General (DGs) or in sub-national government if EC policy instruments such as regional development programmes tend to favour some structures over others.

The third mechanism is that of what may be termed contagion. It is a well-documented feature of public organizations that they tend to adopt the values of those with whom they most frequently deal. Through exposure to counterparts in Brussels the culture of national civil servants might be expected to change in subtle ways. As Coombes wrote in 1968 (p. 61):

> increasing contact with other European civil servants ... could produce what might be called a feedback into the British civil service from the procedures and customs of other European countries.

A fourth possible form of influence is a demonstration effect, where some administrative practices to which national administrations are exposed more intimately than previously might be adopted as good or superior practice. This could occur in any area of EC experience where there are substantial differences between a single nation and the administration of the EC.

From a British perspective there are two prominent areas in which EC experience is important. These two have featured in discussions of the civil service since at least the 1960s, and are among the most frequent of subjects for which foreign experience is cited as an example of 'good practice': the process of recruitment and the institutional structure for the relationship between officials and politicians.

A possible fifth form of influence is a redundancy effect. As functions are taken on by the EC the nation state bureaucracies will no longer need to exist. At the current level of development of Europe there is little prospect of EC administration actually replacing national administration. Even in those areas where EC policy is most developed, such as agriculture, competition and environmental policy, implementation of EC legislation by national agencies ensures their continued existence. Consequently this possible impact will not be explored in this paper.

Of course, it is impossible to predict in advance how powerful the combination of these mechanisms will prove to be. One can, however, begin to assess the potential for change by examining whether there are distinctive European patterns which contrast with national practices and can thus be emulated or can find their way through some other means into national practice. How different and distinctive is the EC in relation to the national bureaucracies of member states?

## PAY AND CONDITIONS OF SERVICE

A position in the European civil service has been termed a 'bureaucrat's paradise' partly because of the alleged power of bureaucrats. The EC is relatively small. This implies that even junior officials are faced with considerable responsibilities and are dealing with large budgets. The relative independence of DGs from Commissioners' instructions can offer EC civil servants additional freedom of action, which might be less common in national administrations. Yet the most striking difference from the national civil services is financial: the pay level of the EC civil service is considerably higher than that of the member states.

The philosophy behind the EC recruitment policy explains much of this. The EC administration aims to recruit highly qualified people, capable of speaking at least one other Community language, while simultaneously 'officials shall be recruited on the broadest possible geographical basis from among nationals of Member States of the Communities' (Article 27 of the Staff Regulations). To ensure the representation of people from all over the Community, wages have to be high enough to attract people of different specialities as well as from those countries where rewards are highest. This implies of course that the marginal surplus will be different for every member state.

Pay is directly determined by a pay matrix which lists the basic pay for every category of officials (A/LA, B, C, D) and every grade (a different number of grades in every category: A has eight, D only four, and within each category and grade there is a series of steps). Everyone with the same category, grade and step receives the same basic pay. Once a year the matrix is adjusted to the changing cost of living. Furthermore, there exists a system of weightings to establish an equivalence in purchasing power for all EC officials, regardless of their place of actual employment.

Next to basic pay, officials receive a number of additional financial benefits. Every official with a family receives a household allowance of 5 per cent of his or her basic pay. Officials also get a dependent-child allowance, plus an additional education allowance for children in full-time education. Most importantly, EC officials working in a country other than their country of origin, receive a 16 per cent expatriation allowance. The amount of money each official receives at the end of the month will vary according to his or her personal circumstances. Apart from this, there are a number of other benefits that EC officials enjoy (Page and Wouters, 1994).

Contrary to popular belief, EC officials do pay taxes. They are exempt from national income taxes, but remain liable for every other national tax. EC civil servants pay a progressive Community income tax, although the level of taxation (after a number of possible deductions) is on the whole lower than what would be due in any member state. This differential tax regime might be considered as another of the privileges that EC officials enjoy. However, it could just as well be interpreted as a measure to prevent double taxation in countries of origin. Furthermore, the EC officials pay an additional tax, a 'temporary levy', which is established at 5.83 per cent of basic pay (after deductions). They must also pay social security and pension scheme contributions.

The advantageous pay level of EC officials might create envy among the ranks of national civil servants, as it does among the inhabitants of regions where many EC officials reside. It cannot be denied that the pay level is very attractive indeed. It should not be forgotten, however, that living abroad does entail a number of extra costs. Also, if the wages are high compared to those of national civil servants, they are not so high when compared to diplomats' salaries (*Courrier du personnel,* no 8, March 1993, p. 2).

The material benefits EC officials enjoy might induce national civil servants to demand similar remuneration for their work. It is unlikely, however, that the member states will be inclined to give in to any pressure of this sort. Budgetary austerity has placed member states very much *en garde* when dealing with the financial demands of EC officials. Financial constraints in all member states are likely to prevent any demands in this direction from rising, and certainly from being fulfilled.

Were civil service pay levels to rise in member states this would have a direct impact on EC levels of pay since domestic civil service salaries are included in the annual calculations for upgrading European civil service pay. Moreover, the philosophy that has produced high EC wages would not tolerate national pay levels reaching that of EC pay. The EC pay level is doomed to remain higher if the Community wishes to continue recruiting people from all member states, while not deviating from the principle of 'same pay for same work' irrespective of nationality, or without ignoring the hierarchical structure.

## THE AERODYNAMICS OF EC ORGANIZATION

Writing of the US executive system, Harold Seidman argued that 'one could as well ignore the laws of aerodynamics in designing an aircraft as ignore the laws of congressional dynamics in designing executive branch structure' (Seidman 1980, p. 40). The power of Congress in the US federal system is such that executive organization mirrors congressional organization. It is quite possible that the European bureaucracy will, in time, have a similar sort of effect. In contrast to Congress's ability to define some organizational structures, the European bureaucracy has no direct powers to shape the executive organization of nation states. Nevertheless, the exigencies of being heard within Brussels might make it more attractive and rewarding for national governments to reorganize along the lines of the European Community. Are there any equivalent laws of aerodynamics in the European system that make national reforms likely or even attractive?

Jean Monnet had very clear ideas in mind about the conception of the European administration, based on his experiences in the League of Nations and the French post-war Planning Commissariat. He discovered there that if 'you take people from different backgrounds, put them in front of the same problem, and ask them to solve it, they're no longer there to defend their separate interests, and so they automatically take a common view' (Monnet 1978, p. 248). He was weary of mastodon secretariats; a small and lean body which would act as the nerve centre of the organization was to be preferred. The European administration was supposed to resemble a traditional administration as little as possible. The European administration would occupy itself with planning and motivation. If technical expertise was needed, this could be provided by national experts.

According to Monnet, the focus of European administration was to be a few dynamic officials energizing the governments and bureaucracies of member states. He stated: 'if one day there will be more than two hundred of us, we shall have failed' (Monnet 1978, p. 405). He realized that this centre of European decision-making would inevitably grow as the number of tasks to perform increased, but this central conception of the core of European administration should be kept intact. This conception was criticized from the beginning by those who feared the construction of a supranational centre of technocrat decision-making. Some member states also preferred a system based more on regular interchanges between the national and European civil services (Henig 1980, p. 47).

The vision of the European administration as a nerve centre proved to be untenable. Compared with 4883 permanent posts in 1968, there are currently 13,797 permanent posts in the EC administration.[3] On average, since 1968 the EC civil service has grown about 4 per cent per year. Over the past five years, however, the growth rate has been limited to about 2 per cent because of budgetary austerity.[4] The requirement of national representation in the European civil service – or geographical representation, as it is usually termed – exerts pressures on the size of the EC administration. Every enlargement of the EC brought with it the need to incorporate nationals from the new member states in the EC administration. Enlargement has never resulted in a proportional growth of the administration, although in the years in which enlargement took place, the growth rate was always above the average 4 per cent: over 17 per cent in 1973, 4.7 per cent in 1981 and almost 6 per cent in 1986. The expanding scope of EC responsibilities is the other decisive factor: more tasks to be fulfilled require more people to do them. A task force that screened the EC administration in 1991 reported that the EC was actually understaffed.[5] The multicultural environment also poses demands: of the 13,797 EC civil servants in 1993, 1614 (over 11 per cent) are translators and interpreters (grade LA).[6]

Relative to the tasks to be performed and relative to the national administrations, the EC certainly has a small administration, but it is certainly larger than Monnet envisaged and too large to constitute the cohesive, energizing nerve centre he hoped it would be. Instead, it is an organization with a level of complexity similar to that found within many national ministries.

The European Commission bureaucracy consists of 22 Directorates General, numbered from DG I to DG XXIII.[7] This number is similar to the number of separate ministries found in member states.[8] The number of DGs has remained very much the same since 1972 when there were 20 Directorates General. Of the DGs, 16 are identical to those existing in 1972, although there have been a number of reshuffles of competences and services between the DGs. For example, DG VI (Agriculture) lost fisheries in 1977; DG X for a while in the 1970s had incorporated within it the Spokesman's Group, which before and after was a commission organization outside any DG; and DG III (Internal Market and Industrial Affairs) in 1977 gained the functions of a disbanded DG XI (Internal Market).

The DGs without direct counterparts in 1972 reflect expanded areas of EC activity, either through effectively developing new policy areas (environment and nuclear safety in DG XI; customs and indirect taxation in DG XXI; enterprise policy, distributive trades, tourism and co-operatives in DG XXIII; telecommunication, information industries and innovation in DG XIII) or through giving prominence to activities that had been subsumed under those of other DGs (DG XIV for fisheries and DG XV for financial institutions and company law).

Whereas before there was a trend towards 'parcelization' of DGs and the creation of separate task forces and services, there now is a trend to create larger DGs. An example of this are the recent developments in DG I (External Relations). This DG now comprises most competences dealing with foreign affairs. It has been broken up in two separate parts: DG I-A for external political relations and DG I-B for External economic relations (each under a different Commissioner). The Commission also wants to incorporate all communication matters within DG X.

Given that the EC has fewer functional responsibilities than national governments of member states, Directorates General are somewhat more specialized than most ministries. For example, the Directorates General of Agriculture (DG VI) and Fisheries (DG XIV) have functions that are usually carried out by single ministries in European nation states; and most of the functions carried out by DG III (Internal Market and Industrial Affairs) and DG IV (Competition), DG XV (Financial Institutions and Company Law), DG XVIII (Credit and Investments), DG XIX (Budgets), DG XX (Financial Control) and DG XXI (Customs and Indirect Taxation) would be carried out by only a two or three ministries within nation states. The organization is less specialized where the reponsibilities of the EC are fewer, such as DG V (Employment, Industrial Relations and Social Affairs). And, of course, some traditional ministries of member states, such as interior, defence, health, social security and education, have as their closest counterparts within the EC a mere division or directorate within a DG.

Like most national government ministries, the real action in policy-making takes place not at the level of the DG as a whole, but much lower down within the organization. Like national bureaucracies, the organization of DGs is highly fragmented: relative to the number of employees, many are divided into a large number of directorates (146) and units (708) (see Table 9.1). Whether or not the directorate or the unit is the most important entity is difficult to determine on the basis of current research. The answer is likely to depend upon the Directorate General concerned. For example, research has shown that within DG XV (Financial Institutions and Company Law) the division into two parts – financial institutions (Directorate A) and company law, company and capital movements taxation (Directorate B) – defines two bodies each with its own *esprit de corps*. Yet many units within a directorate have quite different tasks, such as units concerned with tourism and charities within Directorate A of DG XXIII.

The organizational structure of the Commission, like that of the administration in most nation states results from a mixture of, among other things, historical inheritance, past and present internal political conflicts, individual pieces of legislation as well as fashions in organizational thinking. It displays no overall principles of construction, whether those set out by Monnet or those that can be detected by looking at the contemporary administrative structure, which are likely to be adopted by member states because of their intrinsic soundness. The fact that the organization does not appear to have a logic that makes it intrinsically attractive and worth copying does not preclude it from being copied. It is quite possible that Commission organization will be imitated or at least reflected in national government organization as the European level of government increases in importance and as national civil servants increasingly have to deal with it.

There is no evidence, however of any such process. If the aerodynamics of the Commission, or those of any other institutions within the EC for that matter, were such that nation states would be inclined to adapt their institutions to correspond to them, we should expect some degree of convergence within EC institutions themselves to be already apparent. The institutions that interact most closely at present with the Commission – the Committee of Permanent Representatives (COREPER), the national delegations and the European Parliament committees – all have highly diverse forms of organization and divisions of responsibility. Few of them have any more exact relationship to Commission structures than to ministerial structures of nation states.

Table 9.2 presents some of the features of the permanent representations of the member states in Brussels. The number of listed divisions, usually headed by a counsellor, in each national delegation varies from one (Luxembourg) to fifteen (Greece) and has an average of eleven. The way in which these divisions are grouped in functional terms is highly diverse. The only fairly common factor was a separate division for foreign affairs (nine out of twelve delegations had

Table 9.1  Organizational divisions of the European Commission 1991

| Organization | Employees | Directorates | Units | Staff per Directorate | Staff per Unit |
|---|---|---|---|---|---|
| DG IX: Personnel and Administration | 2,536 | 4 | 33 | 634 | 77 |
| DG XII: Science, Research and Development | 2,486 | 18 | 82 | 138 | 30 |
| Central Translation Service | 1,678 | 8 | 71 | 210 | 24 |
| DG VI: Agriculture | 826 | 10 | 41 | 83 | 20 |
| DG VIII: Development | 766 | 6 | 37 | 128 | 21 |
| DG I: External Relations | 613 | 12 | 37 | 51 | 17 |
| Central Joint Interpreting and Conference Service | 506 | 2 | 18 | 253 | 28 |
| DG XIII: Telecommunications, Information Industries and Innovation | 492 | 6 | 40 | 82 | 12 |
| DG III: Internal Market and Industrial Affairs | 430 | 6 | 30 | 72 | 14 |
| DG XVII: Energy | 409 | 7 | 20 | 58 | 20 |
| DG X: Audiovisual, Information, Communication and Culture | 369 | 3 | 24 | 123 | 15 |
| Central Statistical Office | 352 | 6 | 27 | 59 | 13 |
| Central Secretariat General | 335 | 8 | 24 | 42 | 14 |
| DG IV: Competition | 309 | 5 | 26 | 62 | 12 |
| DG V: Employment, Industrial Relations and Social Affairs | 295 | 5 | 24 | 59 | 12 |
| DG XIX: Budgets | 260 | 3 | 17 | 87 | 15 |
| DG II: Economic and Financial Affairs | 231 | 6 | 22 | 39 | 11 |
| DG XXI: Customs and Indirect Taxation | 229 | 3 | 17 | 76 | 13 |
| DG XVI: Regional Policy | 196 | 5 | 16 | 39 | 12 |
| Central Legal Service | 170 | 0 | 0 | na | na |
| DG XIV: Fisheries | 164 | 4 | 15 | 41 | 11 |
| DG XX: Financial Control | 164 | 3 | 15 | 55 | 11 |

| Organization | Employees | Directorates | Units | Staff per Directorate | Staff per Unit |
|---|---|---|---|---|---|
| DG XI: Environment, Nuclear Safety and Civil Protection | 119 | 3 | 17 | 40 | 7 |
| DG XVIII: Credit and Investments | 101 | 2 | 9 | 51 | 11 |
| DG XV: Financial Institutions and Company Law | 82 | 2 | 7 | 41 | 12 |
| DG XXII: Co-ordination of Structural Policies | 60 | 1 | 5 | 60 | 12 |
| DG XXIII: Enterprise Policy, Distributive Trades, Tourism and Co-operatives | 56 | 2 | 7 | 28 | 8 |
| Central Task Force, Human Resources, Education, Training and Youth | 55 | 1 | 5 | 55 | 11 |
| Central Security Office | 55 | 0 | 0 | na | na |
| Central Spokesman's Service | 52 | 0 | 0 | na | na |
| Central Consumer Policy Service | 40 | 1 | 4 | 40 | 10 |
| Central Euratom Supply Agency | 23 | 0 | 2 | na | 21 |
| Total | 14,586 | 146 | 708 | 100 | 21 |

one; see Table 9.2). One way of showing the diversity of functional groupings within national representations in the European Community is to look at two important groups of functions: finance, taxation and economic affairs, on the one hand, and agriculture, fisheries and food, on the other. Table 9.2 shows that in economic affairs some countries, such as France with its division for Economic Affairs, Finance and the Budget, have just one division; others, such as Italy, have three: Finance, Treasury and Bank of Italy. In a similar way organizational divisions within other EC institutions have little relationship to those found in the Commission or even to each other. In the European Parliament the committee structure allocates functions to the eighteen committees which cut across the structure of DGs in the Commission.

*Table 9.2  Stated organizational divisions of permanent representations*

|  | No. of divisions | Foreign Affairs | Economic Affairs | Agriculture and Food |
|---|---|---|---|---|
| Belgium | 6 | No | 2 | 1 |
| Denmark | 16 | Yes | 3 | 2 |
| France | 10 | Yes | 1 | 1 |
| Germany | 9 | Yes | 2 | 1 |
| Greece | 15 | Yes | 2 | 1 |
| Ireland | 14 | Yes | 2 | 2 |
| Italy | 13 | Yes | 3 | 1 |
| Luxembourg | 1 | No | 1 | 0 |
| Netherlands | 9 | Yes | 2 | 1 |
| Portugal | 15 | No | 1 | 2 |
| Spain | 14 | Yes | 3 | 1 |
| United Kingdom | 10 | Yes | 1 | 1 |
| Mean | 11.00 |  | 1.92 | 1.33 |

All this might mean that the institutional structure of the EC in terms of the grouping of functions reveals no particular aerodynamic structure that is likely to find its way into the structure of national ministerial organizations. In fact, in many ways the decision-making structure within the EC is highly fluid, with many important decisions shaped by *ad hoc* groups with no official status, such as working parties of the European Parliament or unofficial task forces under the auspices of COREPER.

In the United States, although power within Congress is dispersed among a variety of committees and sub-committees, Congress serves as a major locus of authority and thus as focus for the political system. It is thus not surprising that Congress has a pervasive effect upon the organizational structure of the executive branch. In the European Community power is dispersed within each institution, through the directorates within the Commission, the individual national ministers within the Council of Ministers and the variety of often *ad hoc* and informal groups formed of permanent representatives and seconded national civil servants in the permanent representations. In addition, power is dispersed among these institutions, with no single institution having the dominance that Congress has in the United States system.

While the Council has a veto over legislation, legislative initiatives originate and develop in a complex process of bargaining between actors in institutions of shifting composition and importance. Of course, within nation states similar degrees of flexibility and fluidity in the process of decision-making can be detected. Moreover, the EC seems to function perfectly well without the imposition of a common grid or matrix of organizational structures throughout its major institutions. For the purposes of this chapter this flexibility and fluidity in the European Community's institutions is significant since it suggests that if there is no pressure towards organizational convergence within the EC, then the necessity for convergence among nation states is likely to be very weak indeed.

## SOCIALIZATION AND THE 'CULTURE' OF NATIONAL CIVIL SERVICES

The 'contagion' effect of the EC on national civil services refers to the influence exerted on the national administration above all by those who return from a limited period of secondment to the EC or who regularly deal with EC civil servants as part of their national civil service duties. Certainly, the scope for such influence has increased with apparently more national civil servants having direct experience of working life in Brussels. The number of national civil servants officially recorded as temporarily in EC service rose from a mere trickle of 17 in 1982 to 600 in 1991.

Some civil servants are likely to find the environment of the higher levels of the European service more of a contrast to their national experiences than others. Law and social science qualifications far outnumber all other types of university degree held by European officials (Rotacher and Colling 1987, p. 16). In terms of background, the arts- or humanities-trained civil servant with a degree from Oxford or Cambridge is less likely to be used to dealing with trained lawyers or social scientists in equivalent or senior positions than are German or Belgian officials. But is there a European style or culture of administration which is likely to spread through interaction with the temporary visitor from the bureaucracies of individual member states?

It is well known that different parts of any civil service, whether this be corps or departments, have their own distinctive 'cultures'. For example, officials within ministries responsible for law and order tend to have a very different outlook from those responsible for social services. We know that this applies to at least some parts of the European civil service: some DGs seem to have developed a distinctive style of operation (Wilks 1992). At a service-wide level discussions of culture tend to focus upon codes and patterns of interpersonal relations among the administrative elite, such as found in Heclo and Wildavsky's (1981) study of the Treasury's interaction with other ministries, Anton's (1976) study of Swedish bureaucracy and Suleiman's (1974) study of France. We simply do not know, to use Coombes's (1968, p. 5) question of 30 years ago, 'how far the Eurocrats have adopted a truly "European" style of administration which is distinct from styles of administration current in the member countries. Do these officials belong to a distinct professional corps with its own standards of conduct?'

Two British anthropologists have suggested that there is 'something of an embryonic European culture ... emerging within Community institutions' due to the fact that its staff 'share a similar set of experiences and lifestyles, certain distinctive patterns of behaviour and a common (bureaucratic) language' (Shore and Black 1992, p. 11). However, the culture to which they refer is primarily concerned with an identification with a European ideal rather than a European Community service-wide ethos. We can, however, see whether conditions are, at least at face value, favourable to the development of such a service-wide culture.

One reason that we might not expect a service-wide culture based on some identity with a coherent group lies in the fact that nationality remains an important factor affecting career prospects within the EC service. It is well known that senior posts within the Commission, from the commissioners down through most of the top A grades, reflect nationality. The larger nations (France, Germany, Spain, Italy and Britain) have two Commissioners, the smaller nations, one. Among Directors General there is some broad proportionality, with smaller nations (Greece, Portugal, Luxembourg) having only one DG and larger nations, such as Germany and Italy, having two. Moreover, in cabinet posts, there is a marked tendency for Commissioners to surround themselves with advisers from their home country.

This tendency does not produce a direct proportionality, however. The degree of disproportionality is generally least in the top ranks of A and LA (Table 9.3), yet throughout the senior levels the smaller nations tend to be over-represented and the larger nations under-represented. Among senior grade (A) staff, Italy, Germany, France, Spain and Britain have only between two-thirds and four-fifths as many staff as population size would lead one to expect, while Luxembourg has over twelve times as many, Belgium four times as many, Denmark, the Republic of Ireland and Greece around twice as many and Portugal and the Netherlands are somewhat less significantly over-represented. At the more junior levels the very large over-representation of Luxembourgeois and Belgians is understandable in view of the location of EC institutions.

Table 9.3 *Index of proportionality at different grades in the EC, 1989[a]*

| Grade | L | B | EIR | DK | GR | NL | P | F | I | D | E | UK |
|---|---|---|---|---|---|---|---|---|---|---|---|---|
| A | 1253 | 414 | 271 | 153 | 139 | 121 | 114 | 92 | 86 | 85 | 69 | 66 |
| LA | 376 | 371 | 92 | 552 | 277 | 127 | 223 | 44 | 69 | 72 | 91 | 73 |
| B | 2474 | 842 | 209 | 120 | 86 | 156 | 76 | 70 | 95 | 68 | 59 | 35 |
| C | 3919 | 1097 | 193 | 169 | 90 | 70 | 79 | 48 | 120 | 51 | 38 | 27 |
| D | 6990 | 1138 | 11 | 46 | 102 | 24 | 61 | 40 | 213 | 10 | 14 | 7 |

*Note:* [a] 100 = officials in category directly proportionate to population 1989. Higher scores indicate more officials than expected on the basis of population; lower scores fewer than expected.

Nevertheless, despite these disparities the nationality of the candidate is an extremely important consideration when considering who should fill a vacant post, especially at the senior levels. As Hay writes, 'the political need' to secure national balance at these levels 'is seen as affecting the careers of some officials and can produce some frustration' (Hay 1991, p. 27). Moreover, he goes on to suggest that the multinational character of the bureaucracy has not so far generated any common EC administrative culture since a multilingual bureaucracy undoubtedly makes it more difficult to communicate. Language is the expression of a culture; national thought processes are not identical. So meetings take longer, and more effort is required to understand, and to cope with, situations in which misunderstandings come to light.

In addition, cultural differences affect management styles. Many officials feel some inhibition about exercising management in as direct a way as they would do in a single-culture situation because they are not certain that their colleagues of different nationalities share an identical approach to questions of authority, discipline and so forth (Hay 1991, p. 27). As Hofstede (1984, p. 273) has suggested, there exist differences in patterns of thought and action that vary by nation since these ' "mental programs" are developed in the family in early childhood and reinforced in schools and organizations, and ... contain a component of national culture. They are most clearly expressed in the different values that predominate among people from different countries.' In these circumstances, he continues, 'creating the organization's own subculture' is one of the most important tasks.

Another factor likely to retard the development of a service-wide identity among senior officials within the Community is that many of the very senior positions, from Director upwards, can be considered as outside appointments. Of the Directors General or Deputy Directors General under one-third joined the Commission at a position below that of section head and five of the ten non-parachuted DG/DDGs were outside the mainstream DG structure, being employed by the translation, interpreting and legal services, the Joint Research Centre or Euratom. There are also some fast tracks to promotion within the European civil service, notably through service in a *cabinet* of one of the commissioners (de la Guérivière 1992).

Many of the senior positions, then, are similar to those of political appointees. Moreover, many senior officials come from backgrounds more typical of senior officials within national civil services than of a developing one. This is part of a wider distinction between the very senior A1 and A2 officials and much of the remainder of the European civil service; they are more likely to enter the European civil service later in life, frequently having achieved prominence in their home civil service or in politics or international organizations than are lower level officials. Rotacher and Colling (1987, p. 25) point to the persisting national orientation of top officials when they conclude that

[I]n meeting the Euro-elite we encounter a meritocracy of diverse national and regional backgrounds, well-educated, and particularly in its top bracket, with entry into Community institutions often furthered by good political ties to the national capital ... What may be good for the Community institutions (namely to keep good political and personal ties to the national capitals in offering promising career opportunities and to maintain a healthy diversified administrative elite) may not always be beneficial or motivating to the able and dynamic junior and middle level European officials, who increasingly may see themselves deprived of the chance of joining the European meritocracy through truly European service.

The unfavourable age pyramid among EC staff, with too many people qualified for too few senior positions, further reduces the chances for promotion.

Of course, it is not unusual to see senior officials and those on faster-track career paths with different backgrounds to those in less-elevated ranks in national civil services. However, one of the key factors that gives the higher civil service of, for example, Britain or France its distinctive character is that people in top posts share features in common, above all in these cases a distinctive form of education. In the European Community there is little evidence so far that the senior officials share much more in common in this respect than their seniority and their general commitment to making European institutions work.

## THE POLITICIAN–ADMINISTRATOR INTERFACE

The form of interaction between politicians and bureaucrats in the EC is one that is not found in any single member state. Outwardly it appears close to those countries such as France, Spain, Belgium and Portugal which have a *cabinet* system. According to this system each minister surrounds him or herself with a group of officials who not only advise, but also act as the eyes and ears and sometimes even the hands of the minister of the department.

This contrasts with the simple ministerial structure of countries such as Germany and Britain where ministers, although they have advisers and junior ministers, have no formalized body of appointees to advise them. In the EC each Commissioner, a political appointee who generally has some experience of national ministerial as well as elective office, has a *cabinet* of around half a dozen people who are responsible for advising the Commissioner, liaising with the officials in his DGs, conducting relationships with other DGs and also, through the meetings of different *chefs de cabinet*, 'pre-digesting' many of the decisions taken collectively in the name of the Commission.

In practice the members of the *cabinets*, or at least the most senior of them, tend to be officials from the native land of the commissioner. It was possible to find detailed biographies of 38 of the 49 *chefs de cabinet* since 1989. With only two exceptions out of the 38, Commissioners appointed fellow-countrymen as senior cabinet members. Of these, 19 had career backgrounds in the national civil service and 24 had been EC civil servants. Another six had backgrounds in national and the European civil services, which means that a total of 37 out of the 38 were career bureaucrats. Only one senior adviser, Martin Bangemann's *chef de cabinet*, had a party political rather than a bureaucratic background. Christine Scrivener's *chef de cabinet* also had party political experience, having served as a UDF councillor in Dijon, but had also served in the national civil service and, like most of the senior cabinet members, had an education characteristic of senior civil servants of his home country: study at the IEP in Paris and at the École Nationale d'Administration. As such, this reinforces the impression of similarity between national cabinet systems and that operating in the EC.

Yet the politician–administrator interface in the EC is far more complex than this because of the multicephalous nature of EC institutions. The Commission and the Commissioners must share power not only with the Parliament, from which it is largely separate (with the exception of Parliament's power to dismiss en bloc), but also with the Council of Ministers and those who represent members states through the Committee of Permanent Representatives and other less formal groupings of officials that surround it.

The role of the Commissioner as politician is thus very different from that of the national minister. Unlike most national ministers the Commissioner has neither direct electoral legitimacy nor can he call upon direct support within an elected chamber. Also a Commissioner cannot be held responsible or accountable for what is done in the DGs under his authority since he is routinely subject to the authority of a higher political body, the Council of Ministers, in which he does not directly participate. In fact, the position of Commissioner is probably closer to that of a bureaucrat than a politician since, as Max Weber argues, ultimate subservience is one of the main distinguishing characteristics of the bureaucrat while public responsibility for one's actions is that of the politician.

The form of the cabinet system may well come to countries such as Britain over time. There it has been mooted for many years, even before Britain joined the EC, and it even appeared as firm Labour Party policy in 1982. When some form of cabinet system was introduced in the 1970s in the British Ministry of Defence it conflicted with the more powerful norms of non-partisanship and non-zealotry in British administration. EC membership could give debates about cabinet systems a filip, yet the impact of EC membership in this sphere is likely to be small. One reason for this is that relatively few Commissioners, who could thus act as evangelists for this institutional arrangement, actually resume ministerial political careers after Commission mandate. Another explanation is that the position of Commissioner is sufficiently different from that of a minister to make the lessons to be drawn from EC experience far less compelling than those to be drawn from nation states with ministerial cabinets.

## CONCLUSIONS

There are two main reasons to cast doubt upon the idea that membership of the European Community will lead rapidly to major reforms in the structure of national government bureaucracies. First, the Treaty of Rome has been in force for 35 years, and so far European Community membership has had only limited impact upon the domestic administrative structures of even its oldest members. Secondly, and this has formed the bulk of this chapter, there is no clear 'EC model', distinctive and relevant to the national bureaucracies of nation states, that is likely to find its way through contagion, emulation, the demonstration effect or the natural process of adaptation to an important source of political power.

This conclusion is reinforced by recent experiences of administrative reform in the member states of the EC. In Britain the most important reforms of the 1980s were substantively ideological in origin, in the sense that they reflected a belief that the public sector should emulate private-sector practices. Hence the introduction of audit-style scrutinies of govenment organizations under Rayner, the introduction of performance indicators, the decentralization and apparent hiving-off of agencies under the Next Steps initiative and the introduction of private-sector-style competitition through market testing. In none of these cases could EC membership be identified as a major cause of change. To underline this, the ideological basis of reforms of the French civil service were the opposite. As the Communist minister who is attributed with setting the reforms in motion said, 'on ne sert pas l'État comme on sert IBM [you don't serve the state like you serve IBM]' (Bernard-Steindecker 1990, p. 235).

The intention behind the reforms was to bring full civil service status to many public servants who did not enjoy the privilges of titularization. Again, domestic political forces rather than any impetus from the EC were at the heart of these reforms. In Germany, it is possible that the abandoning of nationality requirements might be a catalyst for wider changes in the status of civil servants, but dissatisfaction with the costs of a nineteenth-century system of privileges in the late twentieth century have been expressed at least as far back as the early 1970s when the federal government initiated major and wide-ranging inquiry into the civil service (*Der Spiegel*, 5 August 1991).

The EC is a relatively young bureaucracy. It has not so far developed a distinctive style of organization or culture likely to be emulated or spread through those who come into contact with it. Features of the EC bureaucracy which appear more likely than others to find their way into national practice – the cabinet system and better salaries – are hardly distinctive aspects of the Community bureaucracy. In short, national administrations are becoming 'Europeanized' in the sense that the decisions of the EC, as well as the people who make them, are increasingly becoming part of national decision-making processes, but there is no strong reason to believe that this 'Europeanization' necessarily brings with it any substantial change in the national administrative structure of member states.

## NOTES

1. The research on which this paper is based was supported by a British Economic and Social Research Council grant no. R0002333768.
2. See US Advisory Commission on Intergovernmental Relations, *The Question of State Government Capability*, A-98 (Washington, D.C.: US Advisory Commission on Intergovernmental Relations, 1985).
3. Budget appropriations for 1968 and 1993.
4. The growth percentage from 1992 to 1993 is somewhat higher (6.8 per cent) because of the incorporation of some staff not included before.
5. Report Task Force, 1991, p. 38. About 1800 extra staff members were needed, of which about 400 could be provided through internal restructuring and redeployment.
6. The LA corps comprises 1614 posts compared to the 4112 A posts (1993 budget appropriations). Hay (1991) argues that these figures certainly underestimate the amount of manpower that is used up in language and language-related tasks.
7. DG XXII (Co-ordination of Structural Policies) has recently disappeared. One of the reasons was the increasing overlap between DG XXII and DG XVI (Regional Policy). The staff of DG XXII will be redistributed over the Secretariat General, which is to co-ordinate the Cohesion Fund, over DG II (Economic and Financial Affairs), DG XVI and DG XVII dealing with Transport (*European Report*, nr. 1833, 6 February 1993).
8. Defined as government departments with ministers of cabinet rank.

## REFERENCES

Anton, T. (1976), *Administered Politics* (The Hague: Martinus Nijhof).
Bernard-Steindecker, C. (1990), 'Le demi-échec de la réforme des agents non-titulaires de la fonction publique en France (1982–1986)', *Revue française de la science politique*, 40, 230–49.
Coombes, D. (1968), *Towards a European Civil Service* (London: Chatham House, PEP).
Drewry, G. and T. Butcher (1988), *The Civil Service Today* (Oxford: Basil Blackwell).
Guérivière, Jean de la (1992), *Voyage à l'intérieur de l'eurocrate* (Paris: Éditions le monde).
Hay, R. (1991), *The European Commission and the Administration of the Community* (Brussels: Commission of the European Communities).
Heclo, H. and A. Wildavsky (1981), *The Private Government of Public Money* (London: Macmillan).
Henig, S. (1980), *Power and Decision in Europe* (London: Europotential Press).
Hofstede, G. (1984), *Culture's Consequences: International Differences in Work-related Values* (Beverly Hills, Cal., and London: Sage).
Kessler, M. C. (1992), 'La fonction publique française et l'Europe', paper delivered at a conference of the European Group of Public Administration, Pisa, September.
Monnet, J. (1978), *Memoirs* (Glasgow: Collins).

Page, E. C. and L. Wouters (1994), 'Paying the Top People in Europe', in C. C. Hood and B. G. Peters (eds), *The Rewards of High Public Office* (Newbury Park, Cal., and London: Sage).

Rotacher, A. and M. Colling (1987), 'The Community's Top Management: a Meritocracy in the Making', *Staff Courier* no. 489, October, 10–25.

Seidman, H. (1980), *Politics, Position and Power,* 2nd edn (New York: Oxford University Press).

Shore, C. and Black, A. (1992), 'The European Communities and the Construction of Europe', *Anthropology Today*, 8, 11–12.

Suleiman, E. N. (1974), *Politics, Power and Bureaucracy in France* (Princeton, N.J.: Princeton University Press).

Toonen, T. A. J. (1992), 'Europe of the Administrations: the Challenges of 1992 (and Beyond)', *Public Administration Review*, 52, 108–15.

Wallace, H., W. Wallace and C. Webb (eds) (1983), *Policy Making in the European Community,* 2nd edn (London: John Wiley).

Wessels, W. (1983), 'Administrative interaction', in H. Wallace, *et al.* (eds), *Policy Making in the European Community,* 2nd edn (London: John Wiley).

Wilks, S. (1992), 'Models of European Administration: DG IV and the Administration of Competition Policy', paper delivered at a conference of the European Group of Public Administration, Pisa, September.

# 10. Conclusions: a framework of comparative public administration
## Jon Pierre

### UNDERSTANDING PUBLIC ADMINISTRATION CHANGE

The framework employed in this book portrays public administration as the administrative interface between the state and civil society. The three clusters of variables in our framework – the relationship between policy-makers and the bureaucracy; the organizational dynamics of the public administration; and the relationship between the public administration and civil society – are closely related to each other in a set of fairly complex relationships. Each one influences, and is influenced by, the other two.

Policy-makers have the *formal* power necessary to control both the formal nature of their relationship to the public administration as well as the exchange between public administration and civil society. They can regulate the former interaction by making constitutional changes or by simply changing the organization of the public bureaucracy. However, the relationship between policy-makers and the bureaucracy – as are all the relationships in the model – is a two-way street. We have a large number of studies, not least those reported here, which substantiate the bureaucratic influence on policy-making. Therefore, if organizational changes initiated by policy-makers aim at making the public administration more available for control and evaluation by the political echelons of government, we are likely to see some degree of resistance from the public bureaucracy. We would probably also, following Moe (1989), see organized interests opposing such changes, because such changes would threaten to reduce their influence over the bureaucracy.

As regards policy-makers' capabilities to alter the relationship between the public administration and civil society, we can see that they can do so only in a formal, legal sense. Here, they have two options, which are by no means mutually exclusive. First, they can redesign public administration in order to make it more accessible to civil society. Policy-makers can also introduce new measures of bureaucratic efficiency, for example, in terms of customer satisfaction, which is a key part of the customer-driven process of public-service delivery. The second policy option is to revise the legal framework in order to strengthen the position of the citizen *vis-à-vis* the bureaucracy.

As we have seen in this volume, most countries have implemented reforms along both of these strategies. With regard to various institutional reforms to increase communication between public administration and civil society we have seen such reforms being conducted in Germany, Sweden, the UK and, to a lesser extent, also in France and the US. Furthermore, a large number of countries have revised the legal framework pertaining to these issues. Cases in point are the Citizens Charter in Britain, the new Public Administration Act in Sweden, and the Charter of Rights and Freedoms in Canada. There is no doubt that there is a strong desire among policy-makers in most advanced democracies to open up the public bureaucracy to civil society actors.

Let us now turn to the variables associated with the organizational dynamics of public administration. It seems clear that these variables are highly important in explaining the nature of the bureaucracy's relationship with policy-makers. Bureaucratic organizations' dynamics can make the bureaucracy less susceptible to political pressures in different ways. By modifying their organizational design, the bureaucracy can try to reduce its contacts with policy-makers, or to ensure that such contact only occurs at the apex of the political and bureaucratic organizations. Moreover, bureaucracies insulated from political control can develop a high degree of professionalism and thus introduce a system of steering signals, which are likely to differ from political signals, such as higher emphasis on quality, less attention to costs, and so on (Slayton and Trebilcock 1978).

The organizational dynamics of the bureaucracy are also significant in explaining the exchange between public administration and civil society. Policy-makers in several of the countries studied here have realized just that, and have consequently conducted extensive organizational reform in order to open up public bureaucracy towards civil society actors. However, to what extent such reforms achieve their aims depends only in part on the administrative reform itself; equally important is how the new administrative organization interconnects with organizations in civil society. As Hall (1986, p. 17) argues, '[T]he capacities of the state to implement a program tend to depend as much on the configuration of society as of the state.'

Finally, with regard to civil society actors we have seen that they have two different objectives in creating networks with the public administration. In some cases, this is because the public bureaucracy – by virtue of its autonomy – is an important allocator of goods which are of interest to a particular organized interest. These networks are typically sectorial in nature. In other cases, it seems as if organized interests try to penetrate public administration because they see it as a gateway to influencing policy-makers. Thus, we can make a distinction between organized interests either influencing the bureaucracy or influencing *through* the bureaucracy.

Let us now look closer at these three sets of variables in a comparative perspective.

# THE POLITICS–ADMINISTRATION DICHOTOMY REVISITED

Scholars of public administration have long debated whether political decision-making and the administration should be seen as two different realms of government or as *de facto* integrated processes. Advocates of the first standpoint argue that such a clear division is necessary not least from a normative point of view, if only because this is the essence of the *Rechtsstaat* model of public bureaucracy. Also, it has been argued that politics and administration operate according to very different logics and dynamics and hence cannot – and should not – be perceived as parts of the same system. And given the (formal) separation of politics and administration in the real world, scholars should not merge them into one phenomenon.

Those who advance the opposite standpoint – that politics and administration are inseparable and intertwined processes and steering systems – often sustain their argument by looking at what seems to be a far-reaching (actual) fusion of politics and administration in most countries. Elected political officials are less-permanent features and less knowledgeable in the mechanics of government than the bureaucrats, hence the latter tend to accumulate influence over public policy and the implementation of political programmes. This is the essence of what is often referred to as 'the administrative state': a political system to a significant extent governed by the bureaucracy but with elected officials politically accountable ultimately for public policy (Aberbach and Rockman 1985; Morstein Marx 1957; Peters 1987; Redford 1969; Waldo 1948).

Today, very few would maintain that politics and administration are separate spheres of government. Instead, it seems as if the 'administrative state' model offers the most accurate description of the ways in which most current systems of government operate in these respects. The country reports presented in this volume corroborate to a large extent the assumptions of the administrative state model. What they bring out very clearly is the many different ways in which politics penetrates what should be a strictly administrative process, void of any partisan division or political presence in the public administration.

In all the countries covered in this volume – albeit to a slightly different extent – the ideal model of bureaucratic 'neutral competence' has been replaced by a politico-administrative relationship characterized by more-complex patterns of interaction and interdependence. This 'realistic' model, which is strongly influenced by the administrative state model – portrays political–administrative interaction essentially as a two-way street phenomenon. On the one hand, there is politicization of the bureaucracy; policy-makers have increasingly come to realize that the public administration is a source of tremendous executive powers and capabilities which require strong political control to ensure that they serve the objectives formulated by the policy-makers. On the other hand, there is what could be called a 'bureaucratization of politics'; due to its higher degree of continuity and specialized expertise, the civil service has become politically more assertive, more engaged in creating networks and linkages to other (public and private) organizations, and more inclined to use its discretion to pursue its own interests and ideals.

There are two factors which seem to be of importance in explaining the nature of the relationship between the civil service and elected officials. The first factor relates to the organizational structure and cohesion of the civil service. In most countries, line administrative and vertically integrated bureaucratic systems have gradually been replaced by more decentralized and horizontally integrated (for example, cross-sectorial) organizations of public administration.

The second factor is personnel and the degree to which political and administrative careers are intertwined or separated in practice and culture. In countries where senior civil servants frequently embark on political careers, or, conversely, politicians – for shorter or more extended periods of time – hold administrative offices, the chances of creating stable networks between the policy-making and administrative spheres of government increase significantly. Such networks may have positive effects on the co-ordination of government. The downside to this arrangement is a weaker civil service *esprit de corps* and a lower degree of administrative professionalization. However, personal networks alone cannot warrant co-ordination of a highly fragmented political and administrative machinery; the effect of such informal contacts is probably marginal.

Figure 10.1 offers a very general categorization of the countries studied in this volume with regard to the organizational stability and the relationship between political and administrative careers.

*Figure 10.1   Organizational structures and different types of political and administrative career patterns*

|  |  | Career patterns | |
|---|---|---|---|
|  |  | *Integrated* | *Separated* |
| Organizational structure | *Integrated* | Japan | Germany<br>Britain |
|  | *Fragmented* | France | Sweden<br>United States |

It hardly needs to be emphasized that the figure presents a very rough categorization indeed. The two dimensions describe different instruments of civil service organization and recruitment employed to increase bureaucratic co-ordination and effectiveness. Together they help to explain the overall capabilities of the public administration. Thus, where the organizational structure and the career paths are both integrated, as in Japan, this may be an important explanation of the concerted behaviour of the Japanese civil service and the fairly smooth politico-bureaucratic interaction. That said, as Ellis Krauss argues in Chapter 6, in policy areas other than industrial policy the Japanese bureaucracy may very well be significantly politicized. In Sweden, political and bureaucratic careers normally do not coincide. Together with the significant organizational and political division between ministries and agencies, the Swedish system finds itself lacking some of the co-ordinating features which seem to hold together the political and administrative systems in most other countries.

In Germany, administrative and political careers are also distinctly separate. Although Germany is a federal political system with extensive regional and local autonomy, the federal politico-administrative system remains highly integrated. Unlike the fragmented system of government in the US, Germany is a party government; policy co-ordination between the legislative and executive branches of government occurs largely through the political parties. Thus, where the German system may lack some co-ordinating mechanisms in terms of personal networks, the political parties can compensate to some extent for this loss.

The developing countries display a couple of features which must be observed in the current discussion and which suggest that they should not be included in Figure 10.1. The relationship between the civil service and the political elite, and also the state–society relationship are of a highly specific nature in these countries. Following independence, these countries embarked on a rapid process of 'Africanization', including the training of civil servants with no connections to the former colonial state. Despite this ambition, however, much of the bureaucratic culture conveyed in this training was inspired by that of the former colonial power (cf. Hyden, Chapter 8 in this volume). Moreover, the role of the civil service differed significantly from that of the developing countries. For these countries, economic development became the overarching objective of policy-makers and the public administration and the task for which the civil service was primarily designed. In some countries, such as Tanzania, the public administration became strongly politicized. Kenya, on the other hand, seemed to follow a different strategy and attempted to develop a less-politicized civil service. However, in both cases, as Hyden shows in his chapter, there soon emerged widespread frustration among senior civil servants with the political leadership of the country. Furthermore, in both cases the state was weakened; in Tanzania because of the politicization of the civil service and in Kenya because of the significance of the ethnic dimension which led to a biased allocation of public goods. As Hyden shows, the public institutions of these countries are weak and fragmented. While the civil service career appears to be separated from the political career, the problems of the weak state has caused several observers to see the civil service not as a vehice for economic development but rather as an impediment to progress.

Figure 10.1 suggests that the general characteristics of the system of government is of minor importance when it comes to explaining the fragmentation of the organizational structure or whether political and administrative careers are integrated or separated. The federal systems of Germany and the United States display very different features in this analysis. To the differences between the two systems described in the figure should be added the significance of the political parties in Germany, as mentioned earlier.

Furthermore, France and Britain – countries which are traditionally perceived as 'strong states' – differ diametrically with respect to organizational structure and the relationship between political and administrative career paths. Thus, the system of government – parliamentary vs. federal; strong vs. weak party governments; extensive vs. limited regional and local autonomy – does not explain very well which informal or institutionalized forms the interaction between policy-makers and the civil service will develop into over time. To understand these processes better, we should look more closely at factors such as the significance of *Rechtstaat* traditions, civil service elite recruitment and training patterns, turnover rates among elected politicians, civil service tenure systems, and so on.

Put differently, the formal structure of the system of government *per se* is of limited significance in explaining what practices and procedures will develop over time within any given system. To be sure, in most countries formal constitutional design says very little indeed about the role of politics, political parties, different career patterns and similar variables, which seem to be important in the present context.

A different problem, which the figure does not take into account, is the nature and role of 'politics' in the civil service. As the chapters in this volume suggest, politics and politicization of bureaucracies refers to more than merely the exercise of political power over bureaucrats or public administrators moving closer to the locus of policy-making. Public administration, it must be remembered, is *the* executive arm of government, and hence bureaucracies work for elected politicians. In this perspective, politicization of bureaucracies can fulfil a number of functions other than ensuring that policy is implemented according to the plans laid down by policy-makers.

The presence of politics in the public bureaucracy has different meanings and plays different roles in different countries. In some developing countries, such as Tanzania, the civil service was highly politicized as a means of mobilizing it for the huge tasks related to facilitating economic development. In the relative absence of formal, powerful means of controlling the public bureaucracy, the political elite attempted to employ partisan sentiments to steer the civil service. Interestingly, this strategy is remarkably similar to that of the Social Democrats in Sweden to gain control over the public bureaucracy in the early years of their rule.

In Germany, there is what Derlien calls a 'functional party politicization'; partisan conflicts run parallel with functional divisions within the bureaucratic system. In France, this type of politicization does not seem to be of any major importance; instead, we see politics emerging as an instrument of co-ordination, as the glue which holds the bureaucratic system together. Conversely, it may very well be that the very lack of such a political presence in the Swedish system helps to explain why agencies have become closely associated with organized interests, something which has led to exacerbated sectorization and fragmentation. In Japan, finally, where politics and administration is highly integrated vertically and horizontally, 'turf battles' over ministries' jurisdiction quickly become politically charged. Here, politics plays the role of mediator between different elements of the bureaucracy.

These examples suggest that while politicization of the civil service is normally implemented in order to open up a new channel of policy-makers' control over public bureaucracy, 'politics' at large may fulfil many other functions as well. Of these functions, policy co-ordination appears to be the most important.

Next to these observations, we have also seen that the nature of the relationship between policy-makers and the civil service to a large extent depends on contextual factors. This comes out very clearly in instances of policy change. Such processes easily generate friction between elected politicians and bureaucrats, not so much because of the traditional bureaucratic enigma and inertia but rather because policy change alters the political game and thus undercuts the power-base of bureaucratic coalition-building efforts.

Some cases of policy change are met with downright bureaucratic resistance. The case of Mrs Thatcher's endeavours to 'deprivilege' the civil service in Britain is the most obvious – and predictable – example of such resistance. However, there are several other examples of this phenomenon; for instance, the advent of new labour-market and school policies in Sweden.

Thus, while there are a number of systemic factors which strongly influence the nature of the relationship between politicians and bureaucrats – the constitutional autonomy of the civil service; patterns of recruitment of administrative personnel; and bureaucratic discretion on budgetary matters, to mention just a few – it must also be remembered that the nature of specific political issues is equally important in explaining the nature of politico-administrative interaction.

## THE ORGANIZATIONAL DYNAMICS OF PUBLIC ADMINISTRATION

The introductory chapter argued that for the past ten to fifteen years, the public bureaucracies of most countries have faced a number of challenges which together have triggered processes of change, both within the public bureaucracy but also in its relationship to policy-makers and civil society. In the country-by-country chapters we have seen several examples of successful bureaucractic adaptation to these external changes and challenges.

Much of what has happened in these respects have been attempts to increase the points of contact between public administration and civil society. Alongside this type of change there are those which are enforced in order to make the bureaucracy more efficient. These latter types of change are particularly complicated for public bureaucracies. While there certainly exist a number of measures which can be introduced to enhance the efficiency of the public administration judged by its own logic, it is much more difficult to do so if efficiency is to be judged by the same standards as in private organizations. The reason for this is very simple: public bureaucracies were never constructed or designed in order to be efficient in the market sense of the concept. Similarly, as Goran Hyden shows in Chapter 8, a civil service is probably not the ideal organizational vehicle for implementing programmes to generate rapid economic growth. Instead, most civil services were given an organizational design which would enable them to safeguard the administrative process and also be constrained and controlled by it. Clearly, this objective relates to an organizational purpose almost completely opposite to private sector efficiency. The near future will tell us what the consequences for public administration are of this slight confusion between public- and private-sector definitions of efficiency, organizational design and management, and criteria for measuring service quality.

Keeping in mind the limited number of cases on which we have reports, as well as the complexity of these issues, we dare make the assumption that the amount of administrative organizational dynamics in any public administrative system is inversely related to the degree of political control of the bureaucracy. In those systems where political control over public bureaucracy is extensive and continuous, there is little leeway for intra-organizational initiatives. On the other hand, in systems with a high degree of bureaucratic autonomy we expect more opportunity for such initiatives, which may range from changes in the structure and process of the organization to new concepts in public-service delivery. Political control over public administration cannot very easily order the bureaucrats to behave in a spontaneous fashion and come up with new and original ideas on how to best deliver public services. Instead, what policy-makers can do is to create the administrative discretion necessary for such innovative processes to occur. That said, we have also seen that autonomous public bureaucracies cause significant problems in terms of governance, control and accountability. Sooner or later, policy-makers will have to balance one objective against the other.

## PUBLIC BUREAUCRACY, THE STATE AND CIVIL SOCIETY

Most countries have experienced extensive political and administrative reform aiming at reducing the distance between citizens and the public administration. In France, the customer-driven model of public-service delivery has had significant internal effects on the public bureaucracy. In the US, following the Grace Commission during the 1980s and the Gore Commission's report (the 'National Performance Review') in 1993, we are likely to see major changes in the federal bureaucracy. This process has been fuelled by the ideas formulated by Osborne and Gaebler (1993) which seem to have become the fad of the politics of public administration in many countries during the 1990s. In Sweden, customer-driven processes of service delivery are still a fairly recent phenomenon and it is too early to assess its long-term significance. Similarly, in Germany the concept of *'Bürgernähe'* (closeness to citizens) has become the shorthand expression for reducing the geographical, political and administrative distance between citizens and the authorities.

No doubt, many of these efforts will have no significant long-term effects on the interaction between public administration and civil society. What appears to be more probable is that these projects indicate the general direction of administrative reform in Western democracies. The overall policy objectives are remarkably similar in the developed countries covered in this volume. Therefore, while specific projects may turn out to be not very conducive to reaching these goals, it seems clear that the overall policy objective of bridging the gap between citizens and the state – in the shape of the public administration – will remain important.

There are several reasons for this. First, in many countries the public administration has been struggling to reaffirm its legitimacy in civil society. Secondly, the heyday of massive spending by the public bureaucracy is gone; we are not likely to relive the days of the 1950s and 1960s when steady economic growth facilitated a continuous expansion of public institutions and public service programmes. Instead, what appears to be a more likely scenario is the continued adaptation of public administration both to new budgetary levels and to new administrative roles and purposes.

The chapters in this volume show that much of the exchange between the state and civil society occurs at the local level. While this observation may appear trivial it has some profound implications on how we conceive of public administration change. If we assume, as the contributors to this volume do, that such change to a larger or smaller extent is triggered by changes in civil society which manifest themselves primarily at the local level, then we must ask ourselves how the effects of these changes are channelled upwards in the administrative system. Since most communication routines in public administrative systems are typically top-down, not bottom-up, it quickly becomes a difficult matter (Wilensky 1967).

This raises the issue of the politics of public-sector organization, particularly its structural design and the mechanisms sustaining vertical integration of the bureaucracy. The structure of public administration is sometimes – and predominantly in the US context – seen as a metaphor for the power relations between different branches of government and special interest groups (Moe 1989, p. 282):

> Bureaucratic structure emerges as a jerry-built fusion of congressional and presidential forms, their relative roles and particular features determined by the powers, priorities, and strategies of the various designers. The result is that each agency cannot help but begin life as a unique structural reflection of its own politics.

This approach to bureaucratic structure may offer some insights into the power game surrounding the design of public bureaucracy. It may also be of some help when we wish to understand the relationship between public administration and civil society in a broader context than just special-interest groups. However, Moe's analysis leaves out two important aspects of the politics of public administration organization. First, bureaucratic structure is not merely a reflection of the power struggle between different branches of government and organized interest at the national level. Of equal importance is the extent to which existing bureaucratic structures enable societal actors to penetrate the bureaucracy and, conversely, to what extent they increase the bureaucracy's capabilities to penetrate civil society. There is a very clear political dimension to these issues; different institutional arrangements create different relationships between public bureaucracy and civil society, and this feeds back into the politics of bureaucratic structure.

This leads us to our second general observation. Moe's theory of the politics of bureaucratic structure, highlighting different power dimensions between branches of the government and peak-interest organizations, is typically horizontal in perspective and approach. However, there is also a vertical dimension to the politics of bureaucratic structure. The degree of decentralization has consequences for the geographical distribution of wealth; for the promotion of local and regional economic growth; for the responsiveness of public services to local and regional needs; and, most importantly, for the ways in which public institutions can penetrate civil society and *vice versa*. Thus, other societal forces than those engaged in the politics of bureaucratic structure come into play as soon as the vertical integration of the public sector is altered.

To take this argument one step further, what comes out quite clearly in this comparative analysis is the significant challenge to public administration from civil society. Put into a longer historical perspective, this tendency represents a major novelty for the civil service. Previously, public administration in most countries had to struggle with other types of problems: creating some amount of discretion in relationship to the political echelons of government and mobilizing resources (not just in the Niskanen sense of maximizing the bureau's budget but also because professional considerations, objectives and perspectives create new concepts and strategies for public-service programmes). In the new situation facing public bureaucracies, the game plan becomes very different. Instead of struggling hard to maintain some kind of arms-length distance from policy-makers, many bureaux will find that policy-makers are just as anxious as the bureaucrats to accomplish this.

For the developing countries, the main problem does not seem to be to open up new channels for interaction between the state and civil society, but rather the opposite: that is to create institutions which are sufficiently autonomous and insulated from a variety of different societal pressures to be able to implement public policy efficiently. In some countries, the strong politicization of the civil service has prevented the development of such institutions. In other countries, parochial and ethnic influence over the civil service has distorted and biased the allocation of scarce public resources. The common denominator behind these problems is related to the awkward relationship between the state and society in many of these countries. The states emerged in many instances not as the political system of a territory sharing some ethnic, political or social commonalities but rather as the institutional arrangement which would best cater for the economic and administrative interests of the colonial power. After independence, this inconsistency between state and society has often been the cause of domestic conflict and political instability. Therefore, in many developing countries a key political issue is how to reconcile the tensions between state and society.

In most of the countries studied here, there is an interesting parallelism between administrative growth and expansion, on the one hand, and political ambitions to control the public bureaucracy, on the other. Growth and control appear to go hand in hand, as cutbacks seem to be associated with a relaxation of political guidance, for example, decentralization and deregulation. To some extent, this is because policy-makers want to displace conflicts generated by the down-sizing of public services from the policy-making level to the bureaucratic level of the state.

But there is probably more to this problem than just clever political strategy. Cutback programmes can have detrimental effects on the public legitimacy of the bureaucracy. This development appears to be particularly the case in those countries where the state has assumed responsibility for the well-being of its citizens in all phases of life, from the cradle to the grave. In these countries, cutting back on public services may generate nothing short of a paradigmatic shift in attitudes towards the public sector. In order to smooth this process and also to enhance the legitimacy of the public sector, various measures are taken to invite civil society actors – voluntary associations, sports clubs, organized interests, citizens, and so on – into the process of public-service delivery. This process in turn presupposes increased bureaucratic autonomy from policy-makers. The public bureaucracy, metaphorically speaking, cannot serve two masters at the same time, and so for it to be able to become more responsive to civil society it must be accorded more autonomy from policy-making institutions.

In this perspective, decentralization – leaving aside the slippery political rhetoric surrounding this concept – and other measures that reduce political control over the bureaucracy help to make the public bureaucracy more apt to respond to changes in civil society and increase the points of contact between public bureaucracy and civil society. Put differently, decentralization is both a cause and an effect of the changing relationship between public bureaucracy and civil society.

This may be one of the major changes we shall see taking place in the Western democracies during the 1990s. The only thing certain is that the public administrations of the early twenty-first century will look different, behave differently and perform differently from those of the mid-twentieth century. Since the public bureaucracies of most countries have demonstrated considerable adaptive capacity during the 1980s and 1990s, we should expect them to be just as vital and dynamic in the future. But since we do not know very much about what type of society we shall see, it is (at least) equally hard to predict what type of public bureaucracy we shall see, except that there will be one.

With this paraphrase of the Caidens' statement about the future of comparative public administration (Caiden and Caiden 1990, p. 384), which also was the epigraph to the first chapter of this volume, we can conclude by saying that the need and potential for future comparative analyses of public administration appears to be tremendous. What is needed is not so much studies of comparative bureaucratic structures or systems, but instead, what is apparently becoming increasingly important is to develop a deeper understanding of the role of public administration for state–society interaction at large and under what conditions public administration operates as an interface between elected officials and civil society. Furthermore, we need to know more about the internal bureaucratic consequences of this new emerging relationship with civil society actors.

Finally, on a more general level, we need analyses of public-sector organisational adaptation to the new types of tasks which are being put upon it. First, while customer-driven processes of public-service design and delivery appear very appealing in many ways, they have internal organizational impacts which we have not yet begun to assess. We see similar organizational challenges coming out of the process of inviting civil society actors into the process of public-service delivery.

The key problem here is simply that public bureaucracy was not constructed for playing these roles or to operate in these types of processes. Instead, the typical public administrative decision-making process was designed to achieve other objectives, such as legal security and – albeit to a lesser extent – bureaucratic efficiency. Similarly, the internal resource-allocation process resulted from planning based on demographic data and political directives, not on customer choice. These changes – most of which are probably just beginning to emerge – will have profound effects on the public bureaucracy as well as on public institutions at all levels of the political system. Here, as well as in the other fields mentioned earlier, should be very good potential for further comparative analysis of public administration.

# REFERENCES

Aberbach, J. D. and B. A. Rockman (1985), *The Administrative State in Industrialized Democracies* (Washington, D.C.: American Political Science Association).

Aberbach, J. D., E. S. Krauss, M. Muramatsu and B. A. Rockman (1990), 'Comparing Japanese and American Administrative Elites', *British Journal of Political Science*, 20, 461–88.

Caiden, G. and N. Caiden (1990), 'Towards the Future of Comparative Public Administration', in O. P. Dwivedi and K. M. Henderson (eds), *Public Administration in World Perspective* (Ames, Iowa: Iowa State University Press), pp. 363–99.

Hall, P. (1986), *Governing the Economy* (New York and Oxford: Oxford University Press).

Moe, T. M. (1989), 'The Politics of Bureaucratic Structure', in J. E. Chubb and P. E. Peterson (eds), *Can the Government Govern?* (Washington, D.C.: Brookings Institution), pp. 267–329.

Morstein Marx, F. (1957), *The Administrative State* (Chicago, Ill.: University of Chicago Press).

Osborne, D. and T. Gaebler (1993), *Reinventing Government* (New York: Plume Books/ Penguin).

Peters, B. G. (1984), *The Politics of Bureaucracy* (New York: Longman).

Peters, B. G. (1987), 'Politicians and Bureaucrats in the Politics of Policy-making', in J. -E. Lane (ed.), *Bureaucracy and Public Choice,* Sage Modern Politics Series, vol. 15 (Beverly Hills, Cal., and London: Sage Publications), pp. 256–82.

Pierre, J. (forthcoming), 'Public Administration, the State and Society: Towards a Comparative Framework', *International Journal of Public Administration*.

Przeworski, A. (1987), 'Methods of Cross-national Research, 1970–83: an Overview', in M. Dierkes *et al.* (eds), *Comparative Policy Research: Learning from Experience* (Aldershot: Gower), pp. 31–49.

Redford, E. S. (1969), *Democracy in the Administrative State* (New York: Oxford University Press).

Rothstein, B. (1986), *Den Socialdemokratiska Staten* [The Social Democratic State] (Lund: Arkiv Förlag).

Rothstein, B. (ed.) (1991), *Politik som Organisation* [Politics as Organization] (Stockholm: SNS Förlag).

Skocpol, T. (1985), 'Bringing the State Back In: Strategies for Analysis in Current Research', in P. B. Evans, D. Rueschmeyer and T. Skocpol (eds), *Bringing the State Back In* (Cambridge and New York: Cambridge University Press), pp. 3–37.

Slayton, P. and M. J. Trebilcock (eds) (1978), *The Professions and Public Policy* (Toronto and London: University of Toronto Press).

Waldo, D. (1948), *The Administrative State* (New York: Ronald Press).

Wilensky, H. (1967), *Organizational Intelligence* (New York: Basic Books).

# Index

Aberbach, J. D. 5, 8, 10, 18, 30, 77, 81, 125, 126, 147, 207
Abernethy, D. 165
Abromeit, H. 67
administration *see* public administration
Adu, A. L. 164, 169, 170
African Association of Public Administration and Management (AAPAM) 169, 171
Ahrland, K. 150
Allard, C. K. 32
Almond, G. 132
American Society for Public Administration 5
Anderson, S. 126
Anheier, H. K. 88
Ankomah, K. 171
Anton, T. 197
Appleby, P. H. 29
Argyriades, D. 180
Ayubi, N. N. 179

Balogh, T. 92
Ban, C. 24
Barkan, J. 169, 178
Barker, R. 112
Belgium 186, 198
Benn, Tony 92
Bernard-Steindecker, C. 202
Bhambhri, C. P. 170, 176
Birnbaum, P. 40
Biwott, Nicholas 179
Black, A. 198
Bodiguel, J.-L. 41, 49, 53, 54
Böhret, C. 81
Brandt, Willy 82
Britain *see* United Kingdom
bureaucracy *see* public administration
Burns, T. 165
Bush, George 2, 34
Butcher, T. 105, 186

Caiden, G. E. 5, 34, 175, 179, 216
Caiden, N. 5, 216
Calder, K. 126
Callaghy, T. 176
Campbell, Colin 71
Campbell, J. C. 126, 129
career patterns
 in Germany 69–70, 75
 in Japan 128–9
 in USA 22–4
Castle, Barbara 92
Chabal, P. 176
Chevallier, J. 57
Chirac, Jacques 55
civil society/citizens, relationship of public administration with 1, 12–13, 206
 in developing countries 175–80
 in France 56–60, 213
 in Germany 84–8, 213
 in Japan 131–6
 in Sweden 154–5, 213
 in USA 19, 30, 32–3, 213
Clinton, Bill 35
Colling, M. 197, 199–200
communist administration 70–71, 85
Comparative Administration Group 5, 161
comparative public administration, 4–13, 205–17
Coombes, D. 188, 197
corporatism *see* interest groups
Cox, G. W. 18
Craig, A. 129
Cresson, Edith 43
Crosby, B. 165
Crossman, R. H. S. 92
Crozier, M. 61

Daly, M. 100
Daneke, G. A. 1, 57

*219*

220  *Bureaucracy in the modern state*

D'Arcy, F. 43
De Baecque, F. 40
decentralization 1, 216
　in developing countries 172, 173, 175
　in France 42–3, 46
delivery of services 13
Denmark 198
Denoueix, J.-M. 52
Derlien, H.-U. 5, 7, 8, 69, 76, 77, 78, 82, 83
developing countries 5, 9, 161, 162–4
　public administration in 180–81
　　organization of 170–75
　　reform programmes of 171, 172–5
　　relationship with civil society of 175–80
　　relationship with political authorities of 164–70, 209–10, 211
Doig, J. W. 31
Donnelly, M. 135
Dresang, D. 165
Drewry, G. 105, 186
Dreyfus, F. 43
Dror, Y. 167
Dryden, S. 172
Dunleavy, P. J. 98, 110
Dunsire, A. 96, 97, 98, 102, 108
Dwivedi, O. P. 5, 6, 161

education and training
　in developing countries 170–71, 174
　in Germany 69
　in Japan 128
Ehn, P. 149
Ekeh, P. 176
Ellwein, T. 72
employment in public administration
　in EC 191
　in France 41–2, 52–3
　in Germany 65, 71
　in Japan 121
　in Sweden 142
　in UK 96–7, 108
　in USA 22–4, 27–8
equal opportunities: in USA 27–8
Esman, Milton 161, 165
ethnic minorities: in USA 23, 24, 27–8
European Community (EC), public administration in 185–8, 202–3
　organization of 190–97
　relationship with political authorities of 200–202
　reward system of 188–90
　socialization and national cultures in 197–200
Europeanization 2, 58
　mechanisms of 185–8
examinations: in Japan 120, 127–8

Farazmand, A. 6
Fiorina, M. P. 18, 30
Flanagan, S. C. 124, 132
Fleming, W. G. 169
Ford Foundation 5
Foster, C. D. 96
France
　EC and 58, 198
　public administration in 60–62, 186
　　modernization and 39–40, 51, 54–5
　　organization of 39–47, 51–5
　　political problems of 41–2
　　reform programmes of 50–51, 54–5, 202
　　relationship with civil society of, 56–60, 213
　　relationship with political authorities of 43, 47–51, 211
Frank, A. G. 167
Freedman, J. O. 31
Freeman, R. B. 27
Friedman, Milton 96
Fry, G. 111
functionalism 5

Gaebler, T. 1, 13, 151, 213
Gates, M. J. 30
George, A. 100
Germany
　EC and 198
　public administration in 64–5, 88–9, 202
　　civil service 69–71
　　functioning of 80–84
　　reform programmes of 72–3, 89, 202
　　relationship with civil society of, 84–8, 213
　　relationship with political authorities of 73–84, 89, 209, 211

size of 71–3
structure of 65–9, 78–80
Gillio, C. 57
Gilmour, R. 20
Giscard d'Estaing, Valéry 48
Goodsell, C. T. 34
Gore, Al 35
Gormley, W. T. 18, 19
government
in Germany 73–5
in Japan 119–20
in USA 18–19
*see also* policy-makers
Grace, J. Peter 33–4
Great Britain *see* United Kingdom
Greece 193, 198
Grindle, M. 171
Guérivière, Jean de la 199
Gustafsson, L. 154

Haley, J. O. 133
Hall, P. 206
Hancock, M. D. 140, 141
Hargrove, E. C. 31
Hartman, R. W. 25
Haugerud, A. 178
Hay, R. 199
Hayward, J. E. S. 48
Heady, F. 5, 7
Heclo, H. 29, 140, 141, 145, 197
Henderson, K. M. 5, 6, 161
Henig, S. 191
Hennessy, P. 92, 96, 105, 107
Herlitz, N. 155
Hirschman, A. O. 167
Hodder-Williams, R. 18
Hofstede, G. 199
Holmquist, F. 168, 178
Hood, C. 8, 96, 97, 98, 102, 108
Horner, C. 24
Hoskyns, John 92
Hula, R. C. 2
Huntford, R. 141
Hyden, G. 166, 169
Hyman, R. 97

Ichniowski, C. 27
Ilchman, W. 5
Ingraham, P. W. 24

interest groups
in France 58
in Germany 87–8
in Japan 134–6
in Sweden 154–5
in USA 32–3
International Monetary Fund 2, 172
internationalization 1–2
*see also* Europeanization
Ireland 198
Italy 198

Jacobsson, B. 1, 2, 147
Japan, public administration in 118–19, 136–7
organization and functioning of 119–23, 127–31
reform programmes of 122, 130–31, 135
relationship with civil society of 131–6
relationship with political authorities of 123–7, 209, 211
Jeannot, G. 57
Jessop, B. 9
job security: in UK 105–6, 109–10
Johannes, J. 30
Johnson, C. 124, 125, 129, 130, 132, 133
Jones, C. O. 29
Joseph, Keith 92
Joseph, R. 176

Kaiser, R. 83
Katzenstein, P. J. 140
Kaufman, H. 29
Keeler, J. T. 58
Kelman, S. 34
Kenya 162–4
civil society in 178–9
development of public administration in 173–4
policy-making in 168–9, 209–10
Kenyatta, Jomo 163, 169, 178
Kernell, S. 18
Kesler, J.-F. 50
Kessler, M. C. 186
King, D. S. 25, 92, 103
Kleeman, R. S. 19
Koh, B. C. 119, 120, 121, 127, 128

Kohl, Helmut 78
König, K. 72
Krasner, S. D. 9
Krauss, E. S. 123, 125, 126, 127, 134, 135, 144
Kritz, M. 35

Larsson, T. 143, 144, 154
legal system
  in Germany 88
  in Japan 124
  in USA 31
Lehmbruch, G. 72, 88
Lemak, D. J. 1, 57
Leonard, D. K. 161, 166, 169, 180
Levin, Bert 150
Levine, C. H. 19
Lindenberg, M. 165
Lipsky, M. 32
lobbying *see* interest groups
local government
  in developing countries 171–2
  in France 42–3, 45–6
  in Germany 68–9, 86
  in Japan 120, 122
  in Sweden 141, 153, 154
Lochak, D. 57
Lofchie, M. 168, 169
Lowi, T. J. 20
Lundquist, L. 5, 8, 13
Luxembourg 193, 198

McGregor, D. 165
McKinsey & Co. 172, 173
Madsen, H. 140, 141
Makokha, J. 173
market ideologies 2
  in USA 33–4
Mauroy, Pierre 43
Mayntz, R. 73, 76, 77, 78, 80
Mellbourn, A. 148–9, 152, 153
Metcalfe, L. 3
Mills, C. W. 5, 97
Mitterrand, François 48
modernization policy: in France 39–40, 51, 54–5
Moe, T. M. 11, 205, 214
Moi, Daniel arap 169, 173, 178–9
Molin, B. 146
Monnet, Jean 190–91
Montin, S. 153

Moore, M. H. 30
Moris, J. 174
Morstein Marx, F. 207
Mosher, F. 21
Mulusa, T. 173
Muramatsu, M. 123, 125, 126, 127, 129, 130, 135
Mutahaba, G. 164, 169, 172, 179

Nakamura, K. 132
Nakasone, Yasuhiro 130, 131
Netherlands 186, 198
Nioche, Jean-Pierre 59
Noble, G. W. 133
Nordlinger, E. 9
Nyerere, Julius 163, 166

Okimoto, D. I. 134
Olowu, D. 176, 179
ombudsmen
  in Japan 132
  in Sweden 155
organization and functioning of public administration 11–12, 206
  in developing countries 170–75
  in EC 190–97
  in France 39–47, 51–5
  in Germany 65–9, 78–84
  in Japan 119–23, 127–31
  in Sweden 142–7, 152–3
  in USA 19–28
Osborne, D. 1, 13, 151, 213
Ouko, Robert 179
Oyugi, W. 174

Page, E. C. 5, 8, 189
Palmer, J. L. 2
pay *see* reward systems
Pempel, T. J. 120, 121, 125, 126, 130, 135
pensions: in UK 107
Perry, J. L. 23
Petermann, T. 74
Peters, B. G. 2, 5, 6, 7, 8, 10, 19, 25, 47, 147, 155, 207
Petersson, O. 141, 142, 144, 146, 152
Pfeffer, J. 11
Pierre, J. 5, 7, 127, 134, 144, 155
policy-makers/politicians, relationship of public administration with 3, 10–11, 205, 207–11

in developing countries 164–70, 209–10, 211
in EC 200–202
in France 43, 47–51, 211
in Germany 73–84, 89, 209, 211
in Japan 123–7, 209, 211
in Sweden 147–52, 209, 211
in USA 28–32
political activity
in Germany 76–7
in USA 27
political appointments
in France 49–51
in Germany 76, 89
in Japan 124
in Sweden 143
in USA 22–3, 26–7, 31
Pollitt, C. 110
Pompidou, Georges 43
Portugal 198
pressure groups *see* interest groups
private sector 1, 13
in Germany 72
in Japan 135–6
in UK 111
in USA 33–4
Przeworski, A. 8
public access: in Sweden 155
public administration
challenges to 1–4
comparative analysis of 4–13, 205–17
*see also individual countries and topics*
public interest model 8, 20
Pye, L. W. 165

Quermonne, J.-L. 40, 47, 49

Ranson, S. 13
Reagan, Ronald 2, 25
*Rechtstaat* concept 8, 70, 84–5
Redford, E. S. 207
reform programmes 3, 206
in developing countries 171, 172–5
in France 50–51, 54–5, 202
in Germany 72–3, 89, 202
in Japan 122, 130–31, 135
in Sweden 152–3, 154
in UK 2–3, 92–112, 202
in USA 2, 19, 33–5

regional government: in Germany 66, 67–8
reward systems
in EC 188–90
in France 51–2
in UK 95, 103–7, 108–9, 111
in USA 25–6
Richardson, B. M. 124, 132
Riggs, F. 5, 165
Rimlinger, G. 171
Rist, R. 21
Robinson, G. O. 31
Rocard, Michel 54
Rockman, B. A. 9, 10, 18, 147, 207
Rondinelli, D. 175
Rose, Richard 18
Rosenbloom, D. 29
Rotacher, A. 197, 199–200
Rothstein, B. 11, 150
Rouban, L. 3, 41, 49, 53, 54, 55, 61
Rowat, D. C. 6
Rückwardt, B. 79
Rudzio, W. 75
Ruin, A. 144
Rweyemamu, A. H. 169

Sadran, P. 43
Samoff, J. 177
Samuels, R. J. 133, 134
Sawhill, I. V. 2
Sayre, W. 29
Sbragia, A. 2
Schaffer, B. 174
Scharpf, F. W. 66, 67, 80, 83
Schmidt, Helmut 82
Schoppa, L. J. 126
Seibel, W. 88
Seidman, H. 20, 190
Selassie, B. H. 165
Shellukindo, W. H. 167
Shore, C. 198
Shostak, A. B. 27
Shuppert, G. F. 8
Sisson, C. H. 107
Sjöland, M. 94
Slayton, P. 206
social class: in UK 111
social mobility: in France 40, 52
socialist administration 70–71, 85
Söderlind, D. 141, 142, 144, 152

Spain 198
Stacey, F. 8
staff *see* employment in public administration
Ståhlberg, K. 8
Stalker, G. M. 165
state
  nature of 9–10
  *see also* civil society; government; policy-makers
Steiner, K. 120, 122
Stewart, J. 13
Stoker, R. P. 22
Strömberg, L. 153
Suleiman, E. N. 40, 47, 197
Sweden
  public administration in 155–7
    reform programmes of 152–3, 154
    relationship with civil society of 154–5, 213
    relationship with political authorities of 147–52, 209, 211
    structure and organization of, 142–7, 152–3
  welfare state in 140–42

Tanzania 162–4
  civil society in 177–8
  development of public administration in 171–3
  policy-making in 166–8, 209–10, 211
taxation
  in EC 189
  in Japan 121–2
  in Sweden 141
Thatcher, Margaret 92, 112, 211
Theakston, K. 111
Third World *see* developing countries
Thoenig, J.-C. 45
Thomas, B. P. 178
Thomas, J. W. 171
Thompson, Victor 165
Toonen, T. A. J. 185
trade unions
  in France 53, 58
  in Japan 121
  in UK 105
  in USA 27
training *see* education and training

Trebilcock, M. J. 206
Tripp, A. M. 172, 177
Tsunekawa, K. 135

Udoji, Oputa 169, 171
unions *see* trade unions
United Kingdom
  EC and 198, 201
  public administration reform in 2–3, 92–6, 112, 202, 211
    cost reductions 98–102
    impact on departments 95, 102–3
    impact on senior staff 95, 107–12
    reward systems 95, 103–7, 108–9, 111
    staff reductions 96–7
United States of America
  government of 18–19
  public administration in 186
    characteristics of 19–28
    reforms of 2, 19, 33–5
    relationship with civil society of 19, 30, 32–3, 213
    relationship with political authorities of 28–32

Vedung, E. 142, 155
Vengroff, R. 179
Verba, S. 132

Wagener, F. 79
Waldo, D. 207
Walker, J. L. 29
Wallace, H. 185
Wamalwa, W. N. 169
Weaver, R. K. 140, 147, 152
Weber, Max 75, 84, 201
Weidner, Edward 165
welfare state: in Sweden 140–42
Wessels, W. 185
Wildavsky, A. 197
Wilenski, P. 179, 214
Wilks, S. 197
Winans, E. V. 178
Wollmann, H. 82
women employees: in USA 27, 28
World Bank 2, 173
Wouters, L. 189
Wright, V. 43, 48
Wunsch, J. 176, 179